To Harass Our People

THE IRS AND GOVERNMENT ABUSE OF POWER

by
Congressman
George
Hansen

POSITIVE
PUBLICATIONS

... To Harass Our People ...

, . . is an incredible story of brute force, harassment, lies and cover-up—a true tale which is so extraordinary that it approaches the implausible. I must admit that I remained skeptical of the evidence at first. Like most Americans, I respect our system of government and searched for any reasonable explanation for the misconduct of this agency. But looking harder and digging deeper into the activities of the IRS only convinced me that my worst suspicions were more than justified.

—Congressman George Hansen

A Positive Publications Book
Box 23560
Washington, D.C. 20024

Based on material from previous books by Congressman George Hansen: . . . *To Harass Our People . . .*, © 1980, . . . *How the IRS Seizes Your Dollars and How to Fight Back . . .*, © 1981.

Notice from the Author and the Publisher

This book is designed to provide the author's findings and opinions based on research and analysis of the subject matter covered. This information is not provided for purposes of rendering legal, accounting, or other professional services, which can be provided only by a trained professional.

The author and publisher disclaim any responsibility for any liability or loss incurred as a consequence of the use and application, either directly or indirectly, of any advice or information presented herein.

America is a land richly blessed with liberty, opportunity, and abundance. Harassment and coercion have no place in our Constitutional self-government.
This book is dedicated to those fine citizens of courage and integrity who as taxpayers, professional counselors, and government employees, have stepped forward to help expose the shocking and dangerous practices of the Internal Revenue Service.

Congressman George Hansen

EVERY TAXPAYER MUST READ IT. Internal Revenue agents are supposed to be employees of the people. In this book, Congressman George Hansen documents in a serious way how they have been misbehaving.

—JACK ANDERSON
Nationally Syndicated Columnist

AUTHOR'S SPECIAL THANKS

- **To my wife Connie**—a strong leader in the struggle for freedom and good government—who has shared the tough days of combat with great courage, and whose hard work and fighting spirit make success possible.

- **To Jim McKenna** for his strong contributions to this writing and for his sterling legal counsel and straight-to-the-point analysis of IRS practices and government abuse of power.

- **To Larrey Anderson, Jr.,** for his outstanding efforts in the research and writing of material drawn from earlier editions of this book.

- **To Alice Tate and Jack Gerard** who provided considerable time and expertise to typing, organizing and editing the manuscript.

Contents

Foreword

The story of the Internal Revenue Service is a history of a tax collection agency drunk with power, ruthlessly smashing dissent among its own personnel and brazenly roughing up taxpayers at will. The IRS defies and intimidates its Congressional creators to go virtually unchallenged in its blatant illegal exercise of awesome powers against the American public.

The IRS story told in this book is drawn from several large file drawers of documents and testimony collected from frustrated government employees and indignant citizens. It was so imperative that this shocking material be shared with the public, that the book has practically written itself.

In reading this book, it should be remembered that our American system of constitutional free enterprise is the envy of the people of the world. We love our country and its traditions, but such love carries a responsibility to protect the integrity of the system from the excessive use of power and abuse of civil rights.

Recent developments show the mechanics of our system to be dangerously "out of sync"; our oversized bureaucracy is sick, bloated with the confiscated fruits of the labor and the property of the people. The federal establishment is slipping alarmingly close to totalitarianism.

The violations of the rights of American people today by their own government are ironically parallel to the injustices suffered by the Colonists in the years preceding the Revolutionary War. **The Declaration of Independence** states that the British King "has erected a multitude of new offices, and sent hither swarms of officers **to harass our people,** and eat out their substance."

The IRS is so independently arrogant and arbitrary in its abuse of power that it is legally and politically dangerous to challenge or oppose—no matter how legitimate your case may be. A good case in point is that my effort as a congressman to question the conduct and activities of the IRS resulted in a vicious retaliation by that agency. A division of the IRS from another state illegally fed distorted and inaccurate figures regarding my tax returns to political opponents in my state in the closing days of a general election. This was a blatant attempt to rig that election by creating embarrassment in the press, and to justify opening an investigation, not of the illegal leaks of the IRS, but of the Congressman.

Although this IRS venture into politics failed, such underhanded and conspiratorial practices are not unusual and frequently succeed, as this book will demonstrate, which makes reform of the IRS a most difficult task.

Nevertheless, we believe that this situation can be changed. It is interesting to note that my charges did at least force an IRS Commissioner to disclose information relating to personnel and practices—something almost unheard of, as top IRS officials point out. The system with proper legislation and administration can serve the people appropriately and without intimidation.

It is good to remember that in most other countries of the world this book could not have even been written.

GEORGE HANSEN

Washington, D.C.

INTRODUCTION

The Secret Police

The Germans called it *Kristallnacht*—the night of glass—the night that Hitler's secret police smashed the windows of the homes and businesses of the Jewish community. This was the time in which the German people learned to say "yes" to totalitarianism. But the harassment and coercion did not go away with the fall of the Third Reich. It exists today in the psychiatric wards of Soviet Russia and on the slave labor farms of Communist China. It is even present here in the United States in the heavy hand of bureaucracy, particularly in the Internal Revenue Service.

This book reveals armed searches, hit lists, and numerous other abuses of civil rights which demonstrate beyond a shadow of a doubt that the Internal Revenue Service has turned its back on its legal charter as a tax collector in a *voluntary* compliance program for the United States government. The IRS has deserted its role as servant to the people. As is shown in this book—with numerous and heretofore restricted IRS documents, and through the previously untold story of its victims—many officers, agents, and officials of this power-mad bureaucracy currently vie for rank and position even as they grind hard-working American citizens under the heels of their boots.

The IRS has created for itself a new charter of nit-picking and captious regulations. It has taken upon itself the role of master and intimidator of the public. A former IRS agent once expressed it to me this way:

"I was talking to a lady in an accountant's office Tuesday. She was from Germany and she said to me, 'You know, the IRS is getting just like the Gestapo was in Germany. When it first came out, nobody thought too much about it, but within two or three years when you'd hear the name *Gestapo*, you'd really get a chill.' She said, 'That's the way it is now with IRS.' I'm not sure she wasn't absolutely right. I think people are afraid."

The people of this country *are afraid;* they are frightened by this runaway arm of government which has powers that no business or no other government agency would dare claim or use.

- Only the IRS can attach 100 percent of a tax debtor's wages and/or property.
- Only the IRS can invade the privacy of a citizen without court process of any kind.
- Only the IRS can seize property without a court order.
- Only the IRS can force a citizen to try his case in a special court governed by the IRS.
- Only the IRS can compel production of documents, records, and other materials without a court case being in existence.
- Only the IRS can with impunity publish a citizen's debt to the IRS.

• Only the IRS can legally, without a court order, subject citizens to electronic surveillance.
• Only the IRS can force waiver of Statute of Limitation and other citizen rights through power of arbitrary assessment.
• Only the IRS uses extralegal coercion. Threats to witnesses to examine their taxes regularly produces whatever evidence the IRS dictates.
• Only the IRS is free to violate a written agreement with a citizen.
• Only the IRS uses reprisals against citizens and public officials alike.
• Only the IRS can take property on the basis of conjecture.
• Only the IRS is free to maintain lists of citizens guilty of no crime for the purpose of harassing and monitoring them.
• Only the IRS envelops all citizens.
• Only the IRS publicly admits that its purpose is to instill fear into the citizenry as a technique of performing its function.

The citizens of the United States are *angry*, because their constitutional and civil rights are being ignored for the mere convenience of the tax collector. They are outraged by an agency of government which tramples on the Constitution in order to provide smooth sailing for the functionaries—for the henchmen—of the IRS.

It has not always been this way. There was no income tax in the United States until after the passage of the Sixteenth Amendment in 1916. For the next twenty-six years (until 1943), income taxes in our country were limited to the wealthy and upper-middle classes. For example, in 1920 only 12 percent of the adult population paid income taxes. By 1940 this percentage had doubled, but even so, less than one quarter of U.S. citizens were on the tax rolls. During these years income taxes were not withheld from wages but were paid at the end of each tax year (then March 15) on income earned the previous calendar year. The citizen figured his own tax, which rarely exceeded 10 percent of his gross income, and made out a check to the government. The system was simple and for all practical purposes voluntary.

The Social Security Act, passed in 1935, provided the first truly mandatory levy on U.S. citizens' incomes. Even though this was not, strictly speaking, an "income tax," it paved the way for the increasingly Draconian laws which would follow.

In 1943 Congress passed the Current Tax Payment Act, which brought into being the "Withholding Tax" (income taxes which are withheld by the taxpayer's employer) and the "Estimated Tax" (a tax paid quarterly on all income which is not wages). Both of these taxes were mandatory, and the law stipulated severe penalties for failure to comply. America's "voluntary" tax program was no more. As a result of the application of these laws, approximately 57 percent of the adults in the United States paid income taxes in 1950, and by 1960 the figure reached 67 percent. Best estimates indicate that 75 to 80 percent of America's citizens presently pay income taxes. Furthermore, U.S. citizens now render approximately 25 percent of total earnings to the Internal Revenue Service. In fact, taxes in all forms eat up about 34 percent of America's paychecks.

As the percentage of taxpayers and the percentage of income taken from those taxpayers mushroomed, so did the powers of the agency charged with tax collection. For instance, in 1955 the IRS used 50,000 employees and spent $278 million to collect what amounts to an average of $400 from each man, woman, and child in the United States. By 1979 the IRS had over 87,000 employees and expended well over $2 billion to collect an average $2,083 from every single person in America! Even more shocking, in 1979 over 60 percent (some $1.25 billion) of IRS appropriations was budgeted to programs whose purposes are to enforce collection procedures, to audit, investigate, and prosecute—in other words, to harass and intimidate U.S. taxpayers! Little wonder, then, that Americans are fed up with this runaway bureaucracy. (These figures are taken from the *Annual Report of the Commissioner of Internal Revenue* for the fiscal year 1979. Department of the Treasury, Internal Revenue Service, Publication 55. This document is for sale by the Superintendent of Documents, U.S. Government Printing Office, Washington, D.C. Stock Number 048-000-00333-8.)

The first thirteen chapters of this book discuss the structure and procedures of the IRS and detail a number of specific crimes committed by the IRS against the citizens of this country. These are incredible stories of brute force, harassment, lies, and cover-up—true tales so extraordinary that they approach the incredible. These chapters expose the increasing power and presence of the IRS, a presence which is expanding into the otherwise "separated" realms of education, the family, and religion. These institutions, vital to our spiritual and physical well-being, have fallen prey to the escalating power-grab of the IRS. Certainly we can expect that the continuation of the encroachment will eventually cause severe and extensive damage to the social and economic foundations of our culture.

The IRS is an extraordinary example of the end justifying the means. The *means* of this agency is *growth*. Like a fungus the IRS lives by growing, by consuming, by expanding. And what it grows on is us. It is interesting that the revenue officers within the IRS refer to taxpayers as "inventory."

There is only one justification or explanation for this incredible expansion of the IRS into areas far removed from its legitimate duty as tax collector. The IRS embodies the political realities of the selfish human desire to dominate others. Thus, the *end* of this gigantic pretense of officialdom is *power*—pure and simple. The meek may inherit the earth, but they will never receive a promotion in an agency where efficiency is measured by the number of seizures of taxpayers' property and by the number of citizens and businesses driven into bankruptcy.

There are resolutions to this predicament; there are things that the average citizen can do to protect himself from the strong arm of the IRS; there are ways for the taxpayer to fight back; and there are avenues open to us to return the IRS to its legitimate role. These are found in the last two chapters of this book.

We can reduce the Internal Revenue Service to its proper role as a servant of the people. We can master our destiny and preserve our freedoms. But we must move quickly—even as this book goes to press the IRS has called on the Congress to exempt the agency from certain portions of the Fair Debt Collections Practices Act. Buried in the appendix of President Carter's 1981 budget is a provision which would allow the Internal Revenue Service to arbitrarily collect funds any way it can, blithely disregarding any laws passed by the Congress to prohibit abusive practices in the collection of debts.

On page 775 of the appendix to the budget, the President proposed that the general provisions governing Treasury Department appropriations be altered to delete the requirements that IRS personnel comply with certain provisions of the Fair Debt Collection Practices Act.

The effect of this proposed deletion would be to license the practices forbidden by the act, which include "the use of threat or use of violence or other criminal means to harm the physical person, reputation or property of any person," and other abusive activities.

In other words, the IRS is demanding that the Congress expand the presumed right of that agency to intimidate U.S. taxpayers. We must act to see that the IRS collects only the taxes, not the scalps, of the American taxpayer.

The events and the statements in this book have been thoroughly researched. Some of the important documents are reproduced in their entirety in these pages. I believe that the reader will find them extremely enlightening. This evidence has been gathered from IRS officials and agents on both local and national levels. It has also been collected from citizens across the nation.

I have taken extra care to protect the identities of those who have willingly turned this information over to me. Thus, the particulars of some of the pieces of information have been disguised to prevent the IRS from recognizing or identifying those involved. No tax information of particular individuals which is not already public knowledge has been disclosed in this book. The need for such caution will become clear during the course of the book.

I have utilized a small fraction of the vast array of material in my possession. In other words, this book contains only a few representative samples of the countless atrocities committed by the IRS against American citizens.

I must admit that I remained skeptical of the evidence presented here at first. Like most Americans, I respect our system of government, and I searched for any reasonable explanation for the gross misconduct of this agency. But looking harder and digging deeper into the activities of the IRS has only convinced me that my worst suspicions were more than justified.

I believe in our limited form of government; therefore, I can see the need for a well-defined and restricted tax-collecting organization. We should all pay our fair share of the national rent, but there should be proper gathering of these taxes according to law. There is no need, there is no excuse, for the intimidations, the harassments, and the abuses of the IRS. It is time to get tough; it is time for a change.

1

Acts of
Terror

The "secret police" arm of the IRS is very real and growing in power and ruthlessness. Three recent, and widely reported, stories showing how the IRS brutally, sometimes fatally, strikes out at U.S. citizens are told in this chapter.

Even though they occurred in widely separated areas— Alaska, Minnesota, and Maryland—the cases have much in common. The taxpayers involved in all three cases had legitimate questions regarding the original IRS assessment against them. All of these taxpayers tried to obtain reasonable explanations from the IRS for the tax levied upon them. In each instance, the IRS refused to respond. Litigation by the taxpayer against the IRS was ongoing in at least two of the three cases discussed. In other words, the IRS's attacks on these citizens came, in every example, without due process of law— a sure sign of the emergence of a police state. All of the taxpayers discussed were stunned to find themselves under siege. Only one had advance warning or notification that his property was to be seized. Finally, in only one of the three examples was the IRS able to procure a search warrant prior to its act of terror. (Even this search warrant was granted on questionable grounds, because the case was still in litigation in federal court.) Nevertheless, the IRS claims that in every example it acted according to the law. If this is so, these laws must be changed—and soon.

Stephen and Mona Oliver

In 1977, Mona and Stephen Oliver of Fairbanks, Alaska, received notification from the Internal Revenue Service Regional Office in Ogden, Utah, that they owed the IRS $3,300. No explanation of how this sum was determined accompanied the bill. The Olivers, while examining the IRS bill, discovered an error in arithmetic, so they wrote to the IRS and pointed out the mistake.

IRS bureaucrats made no response at first, but several months later the IRS informed the Olivers that they now owed $4,700, again failing—or refusing—to state how this figure was selected. The Olivers, who have always filed their income tax returns, continued to write to various IRS officials but received no adequate explanation.

By February 1979, the IRS had grown tired of the "obstinate" Olivers who refused to comply with the manifestly arbitrary assessment of the IRS. During this time the IRS changed its mind again and decided that the correct amount of taxes owed was $4,200. Then the agency proceeded to place a levy on Stephen Oliver's wages, which reduced the Olivers' income below the poverty level.

On August 1, 1979, the Olivers were informed that they now owed $9,600 in back taxes. That same morning, Stephen and Mona Oliver drove to the Fairbanks federal building on business relating to the IRS. According to Mona Oliver, she and her husband were on the top floor of the federal building when "someone came up and said, 'They're towing away your car outside!' We were in such a hurry that we didn't even wait for the elevator . . . we ran down the stairs."

The Olivers found their car hitched to a tow truck. It had been towed off of the public street in front of the federal building and into the building's parking lot.

"I was upset, I was shaking. There must have been ten IRS agents around it [the car]. I said, 'Is it all right if we remove our personal belongings?' They said that was all right, so we started to take our things out of the car. I was so close to breaking into tears, but that was the last thing that I wanted to do in front of them," Mrs. Oliver said.

The Olivers claim that they were never notified by the IRS that their property was going to be seized. In any event it is unusual and perhaps even foolish to place a levy on a person's wages and then seize his only means of transportation to work.

As she was unloading her belongings, Mrs. Oliver thought to herself, "Where are they taking my car? If they're taking my car somewhere, I want to know where."

She said, "So then I just sat down on the seat, closed the door, and locked it."

Stephen Oliver quickly joined her in their small dilapidated Volkswagen. He sat in the driver's seat and locked his door too.

This defiance of the IRS infuriated the agents, who began yelling threats and warnings at the Olivers. IRS agents quickly summoned the city police to help them against the unarmed Olivers and from the rapidly gathering crowd of onlookers.

The operator of the truck towing the Olivers' Volkswagen was shaken when he learned that the IRS agents did not have a court order allowing them to seize the car. The driver uncoupled his truck from the Olivers' car and left. The IRS agents immediately surrounded the Volkswagen with vehicles of their own. Members of the large group of bystanders sympathetic to the Olivers' plight suggested that they might remove the IRS vehicles and set the Olivers free. Stephen Oliver vetoed the idea. Minutes later his car was chained to an IRS agent's jeep.

For seven hours the determined Olivers held their position inside their car until the IRS secured a search warrant from a magistrate brought in by the IRS specifically for that purpose. (It is difficult to imagine what the IRS was "searching" for in the Olivers' car.)

"With no warning at all, they began smashing the windows with billy clubs," Mona Oliver said. "I saw them start on the driver's side; my husband's arm was right up against the glass. I thought, 'If I put my hand up against the window they'll see it and won't break the glass.' But they smashed the window right into my hand," she said.

After the IRS agents had hurled Stephen from the car, they went after Mona. Several agents dragged her across the broken glass and shoved her onto the pavement, leaving her bruised and bleeding. Even under the authority of a search warrant, what these IRS ruffians did is tantamount to assault and battery. These agents seem to have knowingly committed the crime of assault by using excessive force against noncriminal, nonviolent citizens in a civil matter.

A government-owned tow truck soon whisked the car away. The next day the IRS informed the Olivers that they now owed "only" $4,010.

On August 23, 1979, the Olivers' Volkswagen was auctioned for $500. The crowd of protesters who had gathered outside the building where the auction took place was photographed by IRS agents. License-plate numbers of those at the rally were taken down.

Dwight and Hallie Snyder

Hallie Snyder was alone in her home in Oakland, Maryland—a suburb of Baltimore—with her five-year-old daughter on the morning of February 20, 1980. She had just sent her nine-year-old son off to school. Her husband, Dwight, was working in his small cabinet shop located next to their home.

At 9:00 A.M. someone knocked on the door of the Snyder residence. As Hallie Snyder walked across the living room toward the door, it was flung open by a man carrying a high-powered automatic rifle. Eight men, all heavily armed, burst into the room with weapons pointed and ready to fire.

Next door, James Dwight Snyder was busy at his saw cutting out a set of custom-made cabinets. He heard the door to his shop swing open and turned his head instinctively. "Freeze!" someone shouted. Snyder looked down at the floor in front of the entry to his shop. Several men carrying M16s and submachine guns lay in the prone position with their weapons aimed at Snyder.

Outside, in front of Snyder's shop, state policemen had blocked off the road. Federal marshals and IRS special agents armed with M16s had surrounded the Snyder property. More than thirty men had just captured the unarmed Snyder family.

James Dwight Snyder is no criminal. He has no criminal record and has never been accused of a crime, and neither has his wife. In fact, the IRS agents who attacked Snyder and his family knew this. The Internal Revenue Service had not come to arrest Snyder, but to seize his property for his alleged failure to pay income taxes in 1971 and 1972. (Whether or not Snyder actually owes the money claimed by the IRS has not yet been decided. At the time of this writing, Snyder has two cases pending in the Fourth Circuit Court of Appeals.) The Snyders had no idea that the IRS was going to grab their property.

About ten of the IRS agents immediately began tagging various household goods, equipment in Snyder's workshop, vehicles, a tractor, and numerous other items belonging to Snyder. (They even tagged Snyder's mother's pickup truck.) The twenty remaining storm troopers camped around the edge of the Snyder property keeping an eye on Snyder, his wife, and their daughter "preventing them from interfering in the seizure of federal property." Late that afternoon the IRS brought in a moving van and three wreckers and proceeded to haul their loot away.

All of this was done without a search warrant. Because Snyder had committed no crime—indeed, the IRS would not accuse him of a crime because this would have given Snyder the opportunity to a trial by jury—a search warrant could not be issued. The IRS, however, got around this obstacle by a technicality called a "writ of entry." This order of entry, along with Section 6331 of the IRS code, allows the IRS to seize, by force, a citizen's property without due process of the law. The IRS seized thousands of dollars' worth of property from the Snyders and sold some of it at public auction. (An injunction recently issued by a federal court has stopped the IRS from selling at least some of the seized property.)

The Snyder case dramatically demonstrates the police-state power and mentality of the IRS. An Internal Revenue Service official in Baltimore who was asked to explain why the IRS sent in more than thirty armed men stated, "When resistance is anticipated, steps are taken to assure the safety of the IRS officials . . . involved." What ever happened to the liberty, the safety, and the well-being of America's citizens?

Donald McGrath

Donald McGrath did not believe that he owed the IRS $39.65. He wrote to them and told them so. He asked to have an Internal Revenue Service official meet with him and explain to him why he owed thirty-nine dollars and change. The IRS never did respond.

According to McGrath, "Sensing that the IRS may try to implement a seizure on my account, I wrote to the bank and asked them not to honor any IRS demands other than by my consent or an order issued from a competent court. I then received a note from the bank stating that they . . . would honor an IRS levy. . . . Shortly I received another letter from the bank stating that they had turned my money over to Mr. Thoen of the IRS and sent me a canceled check they had forged on my account ($39.65)."

It was a small sum, but Mr. McGrath was furious. Donald McGrath, crop duster and farmer, acting as his own attorney, filed a claim against his bank in district court.

In the meantime, McGrath agreed to pay half of a $3,000 loan he had taken out with his bank to purchase a combine, but, because of displeasure with the bank over the IRS incident, he refused to pay the remainder until the courts made a decision on the levy made by the IRS. The battle in the local courts between McGrath and his bank and the IRS raged on for months until Tuesday, July 29, 1980, when an order to seize McGrath's combine was issued by a local court.

The Grand Forks, Minnesota, *Herald* carried the following account of the next fateful day:

> The incident occurred after Schroeder, Lt. Larry Bangle and Sheriff Deputy Robert Rost escorted an implement dealer's truck to a farm field where McGrath's combine was located. Officers had served notice on McGrath Tuesday warning him that they intended to seize the vehicle.
>
> Sheriff Taylor said the deputies arrived at the field about 11:30 A.M. and were told by someone on the site that McGrath had said not to move the combine because he was coming back with a gun. Taylor said the person was not a member of the McGrath family.

The combine was picked up and sheriff's vehicles escorted it toward Grand Forks on County Road 4 with one car heading the entourage and another behind.

Taylor said McGrath's car approached the group from the rear when they were less than two miles from Grand Forks and passed one car and the truck with the combine, cutting in front of the two vehicles.

McGrath, his wife and son were in the car. McGrath jumped out and words were exchanged, Taylor said. He said one sheriff's car pulled in front and blocked the road, warning McGrath on his loudspeaker that they were from the sheriff's department and that he was under arrest and should drop his weapon. The trucker towing the combine pulled into a ditch.

Taylor said McGrath got in his car, which drove straight toward the sheriff's car. His son was driving while McGrath leaned out of the passenger's side window with a pistol. A number of shots were exchanged between McGrath and Schroeder, Taylor said, and the flurry ended when McGrath was shot [in the head] through the windshield with a 12-gauge shotgun. Schroeder was the only one from the department to fire. [The police report admits that Schroeder may have fired first. McGrath was the only person injured in the foray.]

Taylor said that McGrath, 51, appeared to be the only one in the car who fired at officers. [It is far from clear that McGrath was actually firing at the officers since his bullets only hit the tire of the other car.]

The sheriff said McGrath apparently has no criminal record.

McGrath was taken to the hospital in critical condition.
His son, who had driven McGrath's car during the incident, was charged with attempted murder. Mrs. McGrath was charged with being an accomplice to attempted murder—even

though she was merely riding in the back seat of the car when her husband was shot.

A week later, Donald McGrath died from extensive brain damage he suffered as a result of "a shotgun wound to the head and massive loss of blood leading to shock from the time he was injured until he received medical care." As of this writing the charges against Mrs. McGrath and her son have not been dropped. All of this stemming from a disagreement over $39.65—arbitrarily assessed and arbitrarily collected.

The normal reaction is to say this McGrath must have been crazy to make a fuss over less than $40. But there is another consideration. McGrath was born and raised in this country. Throughout his life, he had been told by his schools, his newspapers, his government that he was a free man living in a free society. His Bill of Rights, he had been told ad nauseam, was the envy of the entire world.

Then he ran across the IRS. He assumed, as he had been trained to, that if someone claimed that he owed them money, he would get a fair hearing and a jury trial if he wanted one on the issue. So he told the bank not to give his money away without his consent or *a court order*. The bank, conditioned to fear the IRS, paid the IRS out of McGrath's money. Maybe McGrath is not the one who is out of step. Maybe we have all become so conditioned to fear the IRS that any resistance seems absurd.

Now consider the bank. From what other claimant would the bank have accepted a claim as absolute without a court order? The answer is simply no other agency or claimant. No government, no creditor, could come into a bank and demand a depositor's money solely on its own say-so and get it. The bank knew how McGrath viewed the matter. It knew that it was the focus of a battle between the IRS and an indignant citizen. Yet for $39.65, it played a major part in putting a man in the ground. The bank routinely spends more than that to advertise or in contributions to United Way or for office coffee.

Not only did it fail to compromise or give McGrath back his $39.65, but it spent substantially more to fight McGrath in court over the note on his combine. There are few lawyers in the world who will fight a $1,500 battle when a $39.65 compromise will solve it. But the bank fought out its battle and McGrath is forever dead.

Even after the bank achieved its triumph over a farmer who represented himself in court, it still isn't McGrath who looks crazy. The bank called in the sheriff to execute the judgment and repossess the combine. There are more than a few ways to collect the debt without ever forcing a confrontation with a man who they knew was fighting a matter of principle over $39.65. But the bank appeared to choose confrontation, and McGrath is forever dead. Was a lien against his real property too private? Did the IRS want the bank to make a public issue of the power of the tax collector to destroy people for a few pennies?

On the fateful morning, the sheriff apparently knew that he was provoking a confrontation. He sent three armed men with the implement truck. Was anyone in doubt about how McGrath viewed the whole matter? *Three armed deputies.* One can wonder which side prepared, provoked, and accomplished lethal violence. McGrath is forever dead. Even the local police believe the deputy fired first. He fired into a car in which there were three people, only one of whom could be considered dangerous.

In McGrath's case, all the normal rules for apprehending a *criminal* were seemingly abandoned—and at that point McGrath was a civil matter. It is normal law enforcement procedure for heroic attempts to be made to capture without killing even an armed felon. But not here. Where there are innocent people involved such as McGrath's wife and son, even more caution is exercised. But not here.

From whatever direction the McGrath killing is viewed, it fails to conform to the normal procedures of banks, sheriffs' and police departments, or even the courts.

Despite the deformities of the whole matter, McGrath looks more and more a victim and less and less a violent person. We have not even mentioned the single most telling piece of evidence that McGrath did not consider violence likely on that fatal morning. Put yourself in his place. On the sheriff's story, McGrath was likely to be violent. So, expecting violence, would you take your wife and son along? "Come along, Mom, and watch me shoot—or get shot by—the sheriff. Get in, son. There will be bullets flying around and I want you and Mom to have your chance to get shot." The presence of those two in McGrath's car almost proves that he did not really expect violence.

Then McGrath's son and wife were charged with attempted murder and accomplice to attempted murder. Why? Any smart cop can tell you why. If these two in the McGrath car were not felons, then the sheriff's deputy who opened fire on the car would be open to a charge of felonious assault or attempted murder. At minimum, if they were not criminals, the sheriff's department would be guilty of criminal negligence in handling the matter.

The worst part of the whole thing is that no creditor—not the federal government, not the state, no private citizen, no foreign government, literally no one—is empowered by law to take another's property without due process of law, *except the IRS.* It would take the declaration of martial law by the President to authorize any other federal agency to seize private property without a court order.

Based upon experience elsewhere, it is even conceivable that the IRS arranged the entire matter by provoking an incident to teach the locals a lesson that over even so little as $39.65, they can be destroyed. I do not suggest that they intended McGrath to end up dead, but he is dead and they cannot reverse that result.

And if you think the IRS overkill for $39.65 is a one-time occurrence that cannot be repeated, let me give you another unbelievable IRS overreaction for, in this instance, $35.

A prominent citizen reports that one day he found the IRS had seized $12,000 from his checking account. Most of that money was there to pay against checks that had already been written, and he didn't know that he owed the IRS anything. He had had no prior contact with an agent. As it finally turned out, he owed them $35 from a past return. The taxpayer explained he was shocked to learn that the agent had just arbitrarily selected $12,000 as the figure to assess—" 'To get your attention,' he said. He would have gotten my attention just as well with a phone call or a letter," he complained. The agent's reason for not notifying him was, "If we had notified you by telephone or letter, you might have removed the funds, and we would not have been able to secure our interest."

Such action is not unusual—it is within the power assumed by the IRS and granted to it by numerous court decisions. The IRS can go into your bank and obtain bank records without your knowledge or consent. And the IRS can seize your funds and hold them until they are satisfied or until they have been forced to release them. In this case, it was reported that over forty-five checks written on the taxpayer's business account bounced all over the United States. The principal supplier of the business he was conducting at the time cut off his credit; his reputation with the bank was damaged; the harm was almost irreparable. Even after it was determined that he owed them only $35, it was also reported that it took two weeks for the funds to be released.

Recently when he applied for credit to lease a car, he

found that the lien was still on his credit record because the IRS had neglected to record the release, which caused a lot of embarrassment and a great deal of explaining.

In no way can the IRS justify creating such disasters for private citizens over token amounts of unpaid taxes. It is situations such as these which may well have provoked the phrase "the power to tax is the power to destroy."

2

Education
at
Gunpoint

Maybe I haven't made the question clear enough," I said while looking across my desk at Warren Bates, the Assistant Commissioner for Inspection (Internal Security) of the IRS. "Did you or did you not plan and nearly execute an armed door-to-door raid on my constituents in eastern Idaho, specifically, I believe, in Fremont County, and do you keep violence hit lists containing the names of U.S. taxpayers?"

"Well, sir," Bates, a man with a meticulous but energetic air, began, "I think calling it a 'raid' is taking the matter a little bit too far. Besides, that particular project was canceled. We never really were able to get it off the ground."

"You admit that you were planning to go door-to-door?"

"Yes."

"With armed men?"

"Yes. It's what we call an RCP—Returns Compliance Project. We do them all the time, but generally speaking, special agents are not used. Here in Washington we consider the part of your Congressional district that you just mentioned to be a very volatile area. The IRS felt that a show of force would be a valuable educational instrument."

"In America . . ." I shuddered as I pictured the small, peaceful farming community of Fremont County. "In America you use armed agents to *educate* taxpayers?"

"Well, yes, sir. Some of these people understand nothing but force."

"And what about the lists?" I asked. Bates hesitated. He appeared to be confronted by a question he had never heard before.

"The lists?" he asked nervously.

"Yes. Files or catalogs of taxpayer's names. Citizens you seem to regard as somehow 'dangerous' to your people."

Bates thought for a few more seconds and then he slowly replied, "We need to protect our employees—we have to identify our enemies. So, we keep lists of people we know to be dangerous or a threat to IRS personnel. Where'd you hear about those lists, Congressman? How did you know?"

"I know," I said. "Believe me, I know, I have some of those lists." Warren Bates' cool, sophisticated composure had dissolved like a snowball in a pan of hot water.

After Bates left I took out a copy of the IRS "violence list" and studied it. I knew a good number of the twenty-five names included and could not believe any of them advocated violence against the government or anyone else. Since then I have accumulated several other lists with hundreds of names and have yet to find an identifiable violent person.

This is the cover letter for the list I had in my possession at the time that this conversation took place.

December 31, 1975
District Director, Boise
Regional Inspector, Western Region
Taxpayers Who May Advocate Violence Toward Western Region Personnel

We are transmitting a list of individuals in your District who may advocate violence toward government officials including Revenue employees.

The list was compiled from a system of records dealing with criminal law enforcement and was exempted from disclosure under 5 U.S.C. 522a(j)(2) by the Commissioner. You are not to make this list a part of your system of records or associate it with any individual's record which you have. Any requests for access to the list under the Freedom of Information Act or Privacy Act should be directed to the Inspection Service.

[NAMES OMITTED]

We are currently in the process of identifying other individuals in your District who may have a propensity toward violence. Additional information will be forwarded periodically. Specific inquiries should be forwarded to this office as the need arises for additional information concerning any of the individuals listed above.

(Signed) F. R. Rowe
F. R. Rowe
Regional Inspector

I drove home slowly that night, running the day's conversation with Bates over and over in my mind. Had I discovered the tip of an iceberg—an awesome superstructure of intimidation—or had I stumbled on to a freak accident?

I asked my wife, Connie, who was with me, "Do you remember when Arlen Larson tried to tell me about the problems he had discovered when he was with the IRS? It was in '67, ten years ago, remember?" I was thinking out loud.

"I sure do," she replied.

"He told me about the tactics being employed by the IRS. He said they were improper and even excessive. I didn't pay much attention—remember? At the time I just couldn't believe my government would do such things."

"I remember. He even came to see you here in Washington," she recalled.

"Right, he was here on vacation. Anyway, he complained to me, and then I started hearing more constituents complain, and now these complaints seem to be more numerous each year—as if the IRS were getting bigger and more powerful like the rest of the bureaucracy. Hasn't our casework on the IRS increased considerably since I've been in Congress?"

Connie, who manages our day-to-day office work, as my unpaid Administrative Assistant, thought for a minute then said, "Yes, now that I think about it, I'm almost sure that you're right. I'll ask Tom to check the files tomorrow."

As I reached a stoplight I turned to my wife and said, "Warren Bates admitted today that the IRS uses armed agents to go to taxpayers' homes and demand their tax returns. They have lists of people who they claim are violent. I've gone over one of those lists and even called several of the people on it. Most Americans aren't violent, Connie. Their names shouldn't be on a hit list. What in the world is the IRS trying to do? The implication from Bates was that this is becoming standard procedure for the IRS. Can you believe they almost conducted an armed raid on homes in Fremont County—in St. Anthony?"

The events of that day marked an important turning point for me. The admissions that armed shakedowns of innocent citizens have been and still are planned and executed by the IRS at the national level, and the fact that the agency maintains hit lists of citizens whom the IRS arbitrarily considers to be hostile to the state, lit the fuse.

Further research began to tell me what Bates meant when he said about Returns Compliance Projects, "We do them all the time." IRS agents even start "investigating" taxpayers before they owe anything, particularly if they might be facing financial hardship. Like vultures, the IRS seems determined to circle around its victims waiting to pick their bones—even before they are financially dead or known to have any taxes ·due.

The following is a typical RCP request. Notice that this particular project involves businesses. Private homes are also subject to these searches—the plan for such a search is the topic of the next chapter.

October 8, 1975

District Director
Boise District

Chief, CTS
Boise District

Initiation of Returns Compliance Project
To Determine Taxpayer Compliance
Reference: I.R.M.S. 5(12)G-25, Section 7

Purpose: To determine the degree of tax compliance in the business district of Bliss, Idaho.

Scope: The business district of Bliss, Idaho consists of approximately 17 businesses. These businesses are primarily restaurants, service stations and bars which cater to local travelers and tourists. As of June 1975, the Bliss business district was virtually by-passed by the opening of the new Interstate Highway 80.

Due to the substantial decrease in retail sales by Bliss merchants, it is anticipated that substantial delinquency may exist in the payment of payroll taxes for the periods ended June 30, 1975 and September 30, 1975.

Life of Project: The three Revenue Officers assigned to the Twin Falls P.O.D. and the RCP Coordinator will spend one day during the week of October 20-24 to conduct a complete returns compliance investigation for each business in Bliss, Idaho.

It is requested that a saturation canvass of businesses in Bliss, Idaho be authorized. Please indicate your approval of this project.

_____

Chief. CTS

_____

District Director   (Date)

Approval: (Yes)_____ (No) _____

These shocking revelations from a high-ranking IRS official compelled me into an exhaustive investigation of the procedures and policies of the Internal Revenue Service. What I discovered was an agency out of control. What I found was a gross violation, at least in spirit, of the Bill of Rights for American citizens in the Constitution.

It became apparent that the traditional view in this country, that justice is even-handed and the same for all, is attacked and undermined by the usually secret machinations of the IRS. For some, the issue is the right to free speech, free assembly, and free practice of religion as provided under the First Amendment. For others, it is the right to due process by law. And for yet others it is the right to be secure from illegal and unreasonable search and harassment.

The common theme that emerges is that the IRS considers itself above the law—so much so that certain IRS employees themselves were the most shocked and most helpful in exposing such abuses of authority. Without the volumes of documentation in my files, which they largely provided, I recognize the difficulty one might have in understanding where various pieces fit in the mosaic. This is especially true since flagrant actions and proposals are often disguised in innocent-sounding "governmentese"—the language of the bureaucrat which can call an armed search a Returns Compliance Project (RCP).

Over a period of time, I was able to piece together the plan for an armed raid on St. Anthony. As that story fell into place a greater and even more terrifying nightmare unfolded when the magnitude of IRS crimes against the rights of American citizens everywhere began to emerge.

3

Armed Raid
on
St. Anthony

On October 16, 1975, Howard Martin, District Director for the IRS in Idaho, authorized an armed assault on the unsuspecting residents of St. Anthony (population: 3,021). This is the letter requesting authority for a Fremont County Returns Compliance Project (RCP) which Martin approved. Note how the language of the bureaucrat can casually describe an armed search as a program "to determine the degree of voluntary compliance, to secure any delinquent returns and to educate the public about tax laws."

October 16, 1975

TO: District Director
    Boise District

FROM: Chief, Collection & Taxpayer Service Division
      Boise District

SUBJECT: Authority to Conduct RCP Program
        (M.S. 5(12)G-25, Sect. 4.045 & Sect. 7.01 & .02)

Purpose: To determine the degree of voluntary compliance, to secure any delinquent returns and to educate the public about tax laws.

Scope: The State of Idaho, Department of Law Enforcement will make available all driver license receipts in Fremont County for calendar years 1972, 1973 and 1974. These receipts provide name, address, social security number and date of birth. From these receipts those individuals which are male, ages 21 to 65, and who reside in the St. Anthony, Chester, Parker or Sugar communities will be selected for research on accounts registers to ascertain compliance with IMF filing requirements. Individuals with apparent delinquencies will be the subject of an RCP investigation.

Life of Project: An estimated 300 leads will result from the screening process. Sufficient staffpower from all divisions will be utilized to enable program completion in one work week during the month of November. The screening process will begin immediately upon receipt of authorization.

Please indicate your approval of this project.

C. L. Fuqua

Approval (yes)_____ (no)_____
Date 1-16-75

_____

District Director

This project was to generate enough alarm among IRS personnel concerned with their own safety that an in-house investigation was forced and then quickly swept under the rug. In this regard an Internal Security Drop-File (or "Top Secret") report written a few days after the project was terminated calls the affair a "planned armed, door-to-door search."

The report indicates that the state director, "excited about protesters," ordered an operation to "educate" the people of eastern Idaho—to instill in them a "respect" for the power and the authority of the IRS.

This is the set of questions used by Internal Security in its investigation of the armed raids. Notice that there is no date or name on this questionnaire. Most copies of the report were destroyed shortly after I requested a copy under the Freedom of Information Act. This document was given to me by an IRS source.

FREMONT COUNTY PROJECT

Speaking to your allegation regarding planned armed, door-to-door search.

Full report:
1. How did it get started?
2. Why was it started?
3. Who started it?
4. When did it get started?
5. How was the Fremont County Project identified?
6. What was the rationale?
7. Were any other geographical areas identified for compliance checks?
8. How was the methodology decided upon regarding the population in that area?
9. How was the screening accomplished?
10. What rationale was used in screening, from 800 and some, to the 175 involved with the compliance check?
11. How was the project terminated?
12. Who terminated the project?
13. Any follow through on it? If so, how handled?
14. Was there any correspondence with the 175 taxpayers, if so, what kind?

15. Results of the project?

Enclose any exhibits we can.

John Johnson indicated that Howard was quite excited about protesters.

Calvin Fuqua is a possible contact.

John Johnson indicated that ACTS gave the instruction to steer down on the project when it was called off.

Why was the project so unusual as to require special security, such as Special Agents and Internal Security?

Description of plan.

Number of people involved.

Arrange in chronological sequence and tie-in narrative with significant dates and events.

Contact person in Regional Office—Mick Lindsey.

Response needs to be in the hands of ACTS, Wednesday.

On the same day that Martin approved the program, RCP Coordinator Sherrill Ohman began a computerized comparison of driver's license receipts in Fremont County for the calendar years of 1972-74 with the IMF (Individual Master File, the computerized register of all taxpayers) to discover which of the citizens of the county had not filed income tax returns for any of the three previous years.

Working with a small staff, Ohman used 190 man-hours to reduce the 2,773 names from the license receipts to a list of 167 people. In theory, Ohman isolated the names of "males aged 21 to 65" who resided in Fremont County. Those whose names were arbitrarily selected were tagged "delinquent" and "may be dangerous." Because of nothing more than this statistical foolishness, the innocent people on the list were to be the victims of an armed search.

The paranoia of the IRS or a concern that they were provoking a confrontation is apparent from the brief letter to the regional security chief conveying the accumulated list of 167 names to be evaluated for any potential to violence.

October 30, 1975

B. DeBoer
Inspector in Charge

Sherrill Ohman
Revenue Officer, Boise District

Transmittal of Names and Addresses of Those Individuals Selected for Investigation in Fremont County, Idaho

Purpose: To enable screening by the Inspection Division: identification of those individual taxpayers which may be dangerous to contact.

If I can be of any further assistance, please contact.

Later scrutiny of the characteristics of persons on the list showed the gross inaccuracy of IRS methods. First, not all of those listed were male. Women with first names like Marion or Clare were mistaken for men and placed on the list. For example, a sixty-two-year-old lady, the local church organist, was scheduled for a visit from the IRS stormtroopers.

Second, many of the people on the list were not even legally obligated to file tax returns. Several of those whose names made the list were serving two-year missions for their church. These full-time missionaries working without remuneration were not legally required to file income tax returns. Another "dangerous delinquent" had been bedridden in a local hospital for the two previous years. This individual certainly posed a "threat" to the special agents of the Internal Revenue Service.

Third and fourth, many of the tax returns of those selected were not delinquent after all, and none of those on the list could be reasonably considered "violent."

After the names on the list were made public by my investigation, community leaders in Fremont County checked to determine whether or not any of the people whose names appeared on the list fit the IRS description. The results? Almost without exception, the people on the list were good citizens and respected members of the community. Church leaders, businessmen, bank officials, and farmers were on the list—not because their taxes were delinquent, but because they had made generous contributions to their churches and to other nonprofit organizations and therefore had been audited in the past by the IRS. The only "violent" person positively identified was a man who had once been involved in a barroom brawl.

The IRS, armed with an inaccurate and meaningless collection of names amassed by ridiculous methods, but with very deadly weapons, prepared to "educate" the citizens of Fremont County. On November 3, 1975, Howard Martin gave the final go-ahead for the Fremont County RCP by approving the following document detailing the requested staff power for the project.

November 3, 1975

TO: District Director
FROM: Chief, Collection & Taxpayer Service Division
SUBJECT: Fremont County RCP
         Staffpower Approval
    In order to accomplish the objectives of this RCP Program within a 5 day workspan, the following staff-power is needed to be detailed to such:

    Revenue Officers—15
    Revenue Agents—2
    Special Agents—5-6
    TSR's—1
    Revenue Representative—1

    All personnel will travel to Idaho Falls on Sunday, November 16, 1975, and return on Friday, November 21, 1975.

Please indicate your approval of detailing the necessary staff power to this program.

C. L. Fuqua

Approval (yes)_____ (no)_____
Date: 1-3-75

_____

Signature

What actually happened during the next ten days after his approval was not easy to reconstruct. Since it was difficult with my limited evidence to persuade Congress to hold hearings on these matters and force the IRS to explain this atrocity, I had to piece together the scenario by collecting evidence from various contacts inside the IRS.

Finally the picture emerged as the documents accumulated, including one seven-page plan of action, a checklist detailing fifty points to be covered from preparation of the hit list to the care and keeping of the IRS personnel involved to briefings on "assaults or threats" and "protection."

Martin first carefully selected twenty-five IRS agents from several states. (Interestingly, the total police force in St. Anthony, that hotbed of violence and lawlessness, was only five full-time officers.) The group was to meet in Idaho Falls (a city thirty-five miles from St. Anthony) on Sunday, November 16. Unbelievably, *two headquarters* were to be secretly established in St. Anthony. The revenue officers were to report to the Collection Headquarters while the Inspection and Intelligence personnel reported to a headquarters manned by the super-secretive Internal Security branch of the Investigative Division of the IRS. Members of the "strike teams" were to be carefully briefed on "assaults and threats." A complicated communications system was put into place in order to expedite "backup forces." The sleepy little town of St. Anthony lay like a nesting bird, unaware of the pending strike of these bureaucratic cobras.

Ostensibly, the specific task of the strike team was "to determine the degree of voluntary compliance, to secure any delinquent returns and to educate the public about tax laws." Apparently, the IRS believes that people learn more easily, volunteer more readily, and pay up more rapidly when they are staring down the barrel of a .38 Special. The operation ran smoothly at first. Lodging reservations were made at the Stardust Motor Lodge for twenty-three people. Travel arrangements were finalized. The stage was set; the witless troops of an asinine General Sherman prepared to march on defenseless St. Anthony.

But a few of the agents began to get nervous about the senseless scheme. Some of the local agents involved in the raid balked when they were "oriented" on the true nature of the project; apparently they felt that it would be an embarrassment for them to go to the door of a prominent citizen and demand a copy of his tax returns, which he legally is not required to maintain on his premises. Even more than this, some of them seemed to feel that it would be dangerous to provoke the citizens of St. Anthony in such a ridiculous manner. They were afraid that some of St. Anthony's residents might not appreciate this violent intrusion into their private lives and would react severely. The agents were afraid that IRS management might be pushing them into an extremely dangerous confrontation with innocent but enraged citizens, possibly jeopardizing the lives of agents and taxpayers alike.

A few days before the trap was to have been sprung, it appears that at least one of the agents refused to participate in the foray. The National Treasury Employees Union (NTEU, an organization which represents lower-level IRS personnel) became involved in the dissension. Union leaders feared for the lives of the agents involved in the plot.

The following cryptic remarks from a local NTEU bulletin a year later—dated October 22, 1976—refer to the RCP armed search:

MANAGEMENT PRACTICES
Took position that NTEU #5 takes offense and totally disagrees, with the below remarks:
(1) Mr. Hobson (Manager) blaming over-zealous employees for past IRS mistakes and therefore bringing about new collection of initiatives. (What a bunch of bunk.) Managers are the ones who pushed rules of seizure in 48 hours and special projects which could put employees' lives in danger. (Employees and Union disagreed with both ideas.)

Pressure was applied at the regional and national offices, and, four days before the Fremont County RCP was to go into effect, IRS officials at the highest levels finally caved in, overriding the state director. The following order was given cancelling the ill-conceived project:

November 7, 1975

TO: All Participating Personnel
    Fremont County RCP

FROM: Acting Chief, CTS
      Boise District

SUBJECT: Total Cancellation of Entire Project

The decision has been made to cancel all plans for this RCP Program. Those individuals previously notified to attend an orientation meeting on November 11, 1975, and to

be present in Idaho Falls during the week of November 17,
1975 should cancel their plans and resume normal activities.
All reservations and transportation plans are also being cancelled as of this date.

Ralph Hutchinson

This cancellation is not to say that IRS leadership was in
any way repentant about its desires for an armed confrontation with the public as planned in the near incursion in St.
Anthony. In fact, just the opposite is true. The officials and
agents involved in planning and coordinating the project
were given commendations—many were promoted a short
time later.

This is the letter of appreciation given to the IRS agent in
charge of planning the operation.

November 14, 1975

Sherrill Ohman
Revenue Officer

Monte Hobson
Group Manager

Memorandum of Appreciation

I would like to compliment you on your performance in co-
ordinating the proposed Returns Compliance Program in
Southeastern Idaho. I was very impressed with the *Plan of
Action* which you originated.

You have demonstrated that you are fully capable of organizing and implementing a complex assignment. I have
complete confidence in your ability to handle any project
assigned to you, and I look forward to working with you on
future projects.

I sincerely appreciate your enthusiasm and dedication in this
project.

cc: Personnel

Monte Hobson

I acknowledge that this document
has been discussed with me and
will be placed in my Individual
Development Folder and that I
have received a copy.

(Initials)   (Date)

I recall my initial bewilderment over the preceding scenario. There seemed to be no reasonable purpose or goal that could be achieved in such an effort. Education? At the point of a gun? This was the gospel according to Stalin, not Jefferson. I quizzed an IRS official about the mentality behind this scheme.

"I don't know about some of these guys. I think some of them must like war. They must like pushing other people around," I said, probing for a response.

"Well, I don't think they like war, they are using it for a purpose," the official said.

"You mean they like to push people—to bully them?"

"That's part of the mentality, that's partially right. I'll just say this: You'll notice the people behind it certainly won't get on the front line—they are behind the scenes all the way. They like to pull our strings as they climb their career ladders. It's the power they're after."

I asked another official what kind of response I would receive by going to the people in charge of the armed raid, and he said, "[Name deleted] was talking about the door-to-door thing and he told me, 'Well, I'll just tell Hansen that all of this is just a survey, that we were just going out and making a survey. Hansen doesn't have anything.' And he ended up by saying that the armed search was still a good idea. He said that we ought to do it one of these times."

Two IRS district directors have passed from the scene since that statement, but the attitude of the agency remains unchanged—with their arrogant disregard for the Bill of Rights and due process of law.

The more people question the actions and decisions of the IRS, the more the IRS seems inclined to apply force and continue talking about the need to proceed with the armed search.

4

An Internal Police Force

Knowing the history and the structure of the Internal Revenue Service and how the IRS operates is an important first step in grasping the true nature of this agency and understanding its basic, day-to-day activities.

Under the burden of the American Civil War, an income tax was first enacted in 1862. Although it was declared constitutional by the federal courts, and in one year produced over 24 percent of the country's revenue from internal sources, this tax proved unpopular, and after undergoing numerous alterations was abolished in 1872. Again in 1894 an income tax was imposed by the Wilson Tariff Act, but the Supreme Court held it unconstitutional, and only after a generation of agitation and effort was the Sixteenth Amendment finally passed in 1913, stating that "the Congress shall have power to lay and collect taxes on incomes," which was then immediately enacted as part of the Tariff Law of 1913. The pressure for the income tax to supplement or replace property tax developed as commerce became more important to the economy than land.

The Commissioner of Internal Revenue

The office of Commissioner of Internal Revenue was created by an Act of Congress on July 1, 1862. This Act had the effect of making the IRS an independent arm of the Treasury Department. Today the Internal Revenue Service has three distinct operating levels:

1. *The National Office.* This level includes the Commissioner and Assistant Commissioners, who set procedures for the IRS and manage and monitor all IRS activities. The Commissioner is appointed by the President. The National Office is located in Washington, D.C.

2. *The Regional Offices.* The IRS divides the United States into seven geographical regions. Each region is governed by a regional commissioner who reports directly to Washington to the Commissioner of Internal Revenue. Most income tax returns are officially examined at the regional level.

3. *The District Offices.* The fifty-eight IRS district offices correspond, roughly, to the fifty states (some of the more populous states have more than one district). Each district is run by a district director who reports directly to the regional commissioner. The district offices are subdivided into divisions or groups (usually there are at least four groups in a district), which are each supervised by a group manager. These groups consist of several local IRS offices in a given area, and each local office is run by an office manager. In theory, at least, the local IRS office manager is two steps from the state (or district) director and four

steps from the Commissioner of the Internal Revenue Service.

The Major Functions of the IRS

There are numerous and often complicated threads of bureaucratic order which weave their way up and down the relatively simple organization just presented. For example, each of the eight Assistant Commissioners of Internal Revenue presides over several functions of the agency, and each of these functions are carried out by literally thousands of employees at the national, regional, district, and local levels. Five major strands crossing the levels of the IRS bureaucracy are of particular importance to the individual taxpayer, since they are the lines of authority that the citizen is most likely to labor under in his or her encounters with the Internal Revenue Service. A sixth area of primary concern to the taxpayer is the Tax Court, which is not a regular division within the Internal Revenue Service. The organization and operation of the Tax Court is discussed in Chapter 10.

Although the IRS makes specific internal distinctions to define the lines of authority of the basic functions of its tax collection procedures, the results are often very complex, with overlapping functions that are confusing to the taxpayer, as the following descriptions demonstrate:

1. *Taxpayer Service and Returns Processing.* This is the part of the IRS most familiar to the average citizen. Taxpayer Service personnel are, generally speaking, the front-office staff members in every local IRS office. They provide answers to basic questions about income tax and distribute IRS manuals, leaflets, forms, etc. Returns Processing is a function generally performed at a regional service center. It is to this office that the individual mails his completed

income tax forms and pays any taxes due to the IRS. For many citizens, their only contact with the IRS is in this area of Taxpayer Service and Returns Processing.

2. *Examination.* This is the area of the IRS charged with auditing taxpayers. The number of returns audited annually has been rising steadily for twenty years. It is projected that the IRS will "examine" over 2.5 million returns in 1981. Nearly 80 percent of these examinations will be either full-scale audits by IRS tax auditors, or examinations of tax records at homes and businesses by revenue agents. The reason for these audits, according to the Commissioner of Internal Revenue, is "to help insure a high degree of voluntary compliance."

3. *Collection.* The Annual Report of the Commissioner of Internal Revenue states: "The IRS collects taxes that are due but not paid, securing delinquent tax returns and payments, and preventing delinquency in the filing and payment of taxes. During 1979, the Service disposed of 2.1 million delinquent accounts." The IRS collects these taxes, some of which are unquestionably delinquent and some which have been arbitrarily determined to be delinquent, by seizing the property and wealth of the taxpayer or by harassing the taxpayer until he succumbs and makes the payment. Over 5,700 revenue officers, endowed with incredible police-state powers, enforce the often arbitrary indictments of the IRS.

4. *Criminal Investigation.* The IRS has created its own highly trained "hit team" composed of over 3,000 armed agents to deal with those taxpayers engaged in apparent illegal activities and other citizens who have the courage to stand up for their rights against arbitrary assessments and unacceptable collection practices. (In addition the IRS has the power to enlist federal marshals and FBI agents in its

various projects.) It should be noted that some of these special agents are involved in the IRS Special Enforcement Program, which works with other federal agencies in federal strike forces against organized crime, drug traffickers, etc.; but a majority of IRS special agents work in the area of General Enforcement, which means an assignment to a local IRS office to work in conjunction with revenue officers and revenue agents. In many cases, unfortunately, special agents do nothing more than intimidate innocent citizens into paying up on arbitrary assessments for the sake of "voluntary compliance."

5. *Data Services.* Perhaps the most ominous, and pervasive, element of the IRS is its gigantic computer and data-collection system. IRS uses not one but *eight* complete computer systems and three microfilm systems to process the "master files" on over 115 million people in the United States. The IRS also has extensive files on almost 25 million business accounts. In addition, the IRS keeps voluminous document files on millions of U.S. citizens. These files often include newspaper clippings, police reports, court proceedings, personal correspondence, and tapes or transcripts of conversations obtained through various forms of electronic surveillance; much of this material other agencies such as the FBI are now prohibited by law from collecting.

In short, the IRS is an extremely complex, carefully organized agency for tax collection, and perhaps the most sophisticated and least understood internal police force in the world.

5

The Bounty Hunters

The Internal Revenue Service has been able to preserve and expand its powers only by keeping those who could frustrate its efforts on a very short leash. Those most carefully controlled and selected are their own personnel. The IRS goes to extraordinary lengths to determine the "loyalty" of its employees to the corrupt system.

A news report from San Francisco dated June 18, 1980, showed how the power of the audit can be abusively applied to employees as well as to taxpayers in general and how the agency gets away with it by sidestepping the issue.

It was stated that "a union of Internal Revenue Service employees charged that the IRS has deliberately harassed and excessively audited its own tax examiners" and it called for a Congressional investigation.

The National Treasury Employees Union, which represents about 70 percent of the 86,000 IRS workers, contended the IRS initiated the National Coordinated Integrity Program shortly after the General Accounting Office recommended in

January 1979 that the duties of the agency's Internal Security Division be distributed to other agencies.

IRS officials scoffed at the union's allegation, saying the program was designed as "just a test" of a longstanding policy of "assuring that IRS employees don't receive preferential tax treatment."

However, a source with the IRS recently told me how its Data Service System is used against employees and taxpayers alike and described the procedure as follows:

"They have got a new system in . . . the supervisors have a little dictaphone, and if they are documenting a case against an employee, they will have someone in the office assigned to watch him when he goes in and out—or whatever.

"These things are called in on the phone and by dialing a certain code number you get the recorder and you feed your information in. It is kept on a spool and it is never typed up and by not being typed up it is not subject to the Freedom of Information Act. So they can store up information over a period of years on employees—every little piece of document.

"It is not typed out so their contention is that it is not subject to the Freedom of Information request. In other words, it is not finished documentation so it wouldn't be available to the employee. But if it ever comes down to a case, then they just pull all of these things out and transcribe them and type them up.

"This isn't any small thing. I would guess in our office we probably go through maybe one or two or perhaps even three spools a week.

"Now, as I understand it, each of the managers has one of these dictaphones and they also have a system where you can call in to headquarters. They use this system on taxpayers, too. Say you are a special agent, there's a number you call and it is put on the tape and you can make a little note—I don't know how they code these things or how the access would be to it—but there the information is in the files and then if you ever get around to a case, building a case, you can call all of these things out. And of course they are not typed out so if the taxpayer requests his file under the Freedom of Information Act he is not going to get all of these things, yet they are in the record."

Over the past few years, a number of upstanding individuals within the Internal Revenue Service have come to me with information on IRS practices. They believe that someone in Congress needs to know exactly how the IRS is attacking the good citizens of this nation.

But it is not an easy thing to blow the whistle on a government agency–especially on the IRS. I asked one agent, who had publicly discussed IRS procedure, if he was under investigation by the agency.

"Oh, yes," he said. "I have an appellate hearing coming up. They are doing the same thing to me that they did to [name deleted]. This is part of the service."

"Oh, they were auditing him too?" I asked.

"Yes, I understand for about the last three years they've been after him."

"Well, what in the world do you guys own except your car and your home?"

"Nothing, but it doesn't make any difference. You know, it's just like my audit. It came up five times and I had to take off a full day each time and sit here while the gal looked through my records. She looked at identical records each time and I knew what records needed to be kept and what substantiation is needed—it was all right there. Then she went back and wrote up her report. She apologized and said, 'I'm not doing this, I want you to understand that. I have four people writing the report and I don't have anything to do with it.' "

"You have four people doing what?" I asked.

"Writing the report. She said she didn't have anything to do with it, and when the report came out there was no explanation for the adjustments, they just disallowed everything I'd claimed right across the board with no explanation of why."

"And so then you have to, at your own expense, try to prove that they've 'Mickey Moused' you," I said.

"Well, you know," he continued, "if I want to pursue it, the records are there, they can't—somebody down the line is going to have to overturn them, but in the meantime I've had all of this hassle, you know, and other employees feel I'm under pressure from above so then they hate to talk to me—they're under the same pressure. They're afraid to talk to me, they're afraid that one of the managers is going to see them talking to me and that's going to hurt their career."

Dissent is simply not tolerated by the IRS. Agents are punished for showing any sign of leniency toward taxpayers. One agent who expressed his concern that the IRS was being excessively hard on a particular taxpayer was severely chastised. An official IRS reprimand to the agent stated in part:

> It is management's prerogative to issue open TDAs [Taxpayer's Delinquent Accounts] to you with specific instructions to follow. You have no authority to make a determination that you will not take the action deemed necessary to close the account. I strongly suggest that in the future, if you do not agree with instructions given you, you call your group manager and discuss the issue before assuming authority that you may not have in returning a case unworked.
>
> A copy of this memorandum is being placed in your Personal Performance Folder. Please acknowledge receipt by initialing one copy and returning to me.

In fact, IRS management has at times demanded that employees who balk at IRS procedures undergo psychiatric or medical treatment, as indicated by the following excerpt from an official IRS management memorandum:

PROBLEM:
3. Revenue Officer [name deleted] was not performing at an acceptable level.

SOLUTION:
3. Management required [name deleted] to undergo a complete physical examination which substantiated that he is capable of performing the Revenue Officer duties. Subsequent case reviews and performance evaluations resulted in improving [name deleted] performance to a satisfactory level.

On the other hand, the ruthless pursuer of the taxpayer is praised and promoted. Those who knuckle under, who obey the heavy-handed will of the IRS, become the kinds of personalities that the agency is looking for.

This is because IRS emphasis is not on collections and settlements under normal and acceptable business practices, but on levies, seizures, summons, prosecutions, and quotas.

As was stated in an NTEU memo in Chapter III, "Managers are the ones who pushed rules of seizure in 48 hours and special projects which could put employees' lives in danger."

The following memo entry by one IRS official as to what constitutes an effective agent clearly shows that the IRS wants bounty hunters with a hair trigger for a fast levy, seizure, or summons to bag a given quota of taxpayers,

I considered Caroline as being one of the most effective Revenue Officers in the group. She independently initiated appropriate enforcement action on her accounts. As an example, she seized three snow mobiles, a camper, and miscellaneous equipment from a taxpayer who has a long history of procrastination with other Revenue Officers. . . .

Caroline has developed excellent work habits. She documents all pertinent history and she records commitments on her desk calendar. She is punctual in keeping appointments and in initiating enforcement action (levy, seizure, summons, etc.) where appropriate.

Other employees frequently consult Caroline for her opinion and assistance in resolving difficult problems. Through her affiliation with Officer Branch and her knowledge of I.R.M. Part 5, she has gained expertise in handling varied and complicated issues. The employees respect Caroline for her mature judgment in weighing all the facts and alternatives before making a decision.

Caroline was one of the most enthusiastic Revenue Officers in the District. I have complete confidence that she will continue to be an outstanding Revenue Officer in the Seattle District.

Those callous enough to win appointments to management-level positions in the IRS soon learn that to continue climbing the ladder of success, one must create new and inventive ways of prying apart the taxpayer and his wallet.

One IRS group supervisor answering the question "How can we prevent taxpayer delinquency" wrote in a March 2, 1973, memo:

Marginal taxpayers in inefficient, non-profitable businesses are probably responsible for a larger percentage of delinquencies than any other segment of the tax paying public. The most apparent characteristic of these enterprises is the ability to start business with an absolute minimum in capital equipment, cash reserves and other assets, e.g. service stations, restaurants, and construction trades.

The Collection Division has been faced with a two-pronged problem for many years:

(1) Prevent delinquencies by stern, prompt enforcement action which forces the taxpayer to discontinue business.

(2) Accomplish the above without undue pressure from the public and the elected officials.

In my opinion, this cannot be done and we must realize that complaints will be an integral part and result of such measures. We must not be oversensitive to these complaints and requests for leniency.

Law addition and other approvals that would help in other areas:

(1) Require known prior delinquents to post a cash bond before commencing business (as does the State).

(2) Require farmers to withhold income taxes.

(3) In collaboration with the State, require license applications to prove filing and paying of HUT and liquor and beer stamps before a license is issued.

(4) Provide more man hours for cold canvass operation.

(5) A more religious and systematic use of P.L. 85-321.

The implication of item 1 in the second paragraph of the preceding memo is simply staggering. It states, in effect, that the IRS is in the business of putting people out of business. Farmers, lawyers, accountants, insurance salesmen, commodity exchange buyers, construction firms, lumber mills, motel owners, waitresses, portrait photographers, and real estate salesmen are among the professions singled out by the IRS as prone to delinquency. Apparently, these are for the IRS the marginal businesses and occupations easily "terminated." In fact, revenue agents are currently performance-rated by the numbers of businesses and persons that they are able to force into bankruptcy each month. The quickest way for an agent to close "delinquent inventory" is to close the doors of the business. Taxes, of course, are the first payments made upon a declaration of bankruptcy.

Driving individuals and businesses into bankruptcy is not only standard procedure, it is actually organized on a competitive basis between the various IRS districts. One official IRS memorandum states, "Certain cases must be closed in order to meet predetermined goals and to compete with other Districts."

Item 4 in the third paragraph of the memo above talks innocently about "cold canvass operation," but this can involve even door-to-door armed searches. And the use of the word "religious" in item 5 is ironic considering the basically hostile attitude the IRS demonstrates toward religion. The law, P.L. 85-321, which the official wanted used more religiously and systematically is an act giving the IRS special power to force faster payments of employee deductions by businesses than the general law requires to assure that the government is the first creditor in line.

My own experiences with the IRS (see Chapter 6) thoroughly "educated" me to the meaning of item 1 in the second paragraph. Public officials who complain about IRS outrages will simply be ignored; but elected officials, who protest too loudly, will find themselves audited, investigated, and even out of a job. If no one else can bag a politician, the IRS can, whether he deserves it or not—and it can be done wholesale. Recently, for example, the entire Pennsylvania General Assembly was audited! UPI carried the following account:

Harrisburg, Pa., June 22, 1980 (UPI)—Legislative officials say the Internal Revenue Service has been conducting audits for more than a year of all 253 members of the Pennsylvania General Assembly, concentrating on each member's $7,500 annual expense accounts.

One former House member, Charles Mebus, a Montgomery County Republican, said the audit cost him $900 because he claimed $9 a day too much for daily expenses on official business in 1977. Mebus is now the House chief clerk.

Mebus and other current or former members said the special audits were aimed at the 1977-78 session, when many lawmakers took a $44 unaccountable per diem expense payment while the IRS allowed only $35 without receipts.

"It was an honest mistake, speaking for myself and probably for everyone else," Mebus said.

Another IRS official developed a more sophisticated method of preventing taxpayer delinquency. Here are excerpts from a memo dated March 1, 1973, from a group supervisor to his chief of Collection and Taxpayer Service regarding trust funds:

The single most important method of preventing delinquency is through education. The taxpaying public must be aware of the tax law requirements and of the consequences for failure to abide by these laws.

Revenue Officers and Revenue Agents should receive adequate training so that they routinely indoctrinate self-employed taxpayers of their estimated tax responsibilities whenever a potential delinquency exists.

The tax paying public should be educated as to the severity of failure to turn over trust fund monies.

[There should be no] breakdown in enforcement . . . as a result of some menial technicality and/or a sympathetic judge who is reluctant to prosecute these tax violators.

When an employer fails to comply . . . the resulting penalty should be routine and automatic.

A delinquent taxpayer should have the impression that *immediate* enforcement will occur.

In other words, the public should be educated of the seriousness and of the definite penalty which will be meted out to ... violators.

This same IRS memo urges one type of action which is so incredible that I include it in its entirety:

II. EMBARRASSMENT
A proven method of preventing delinquency has been through embarrassment of certain taxpayers.

A. *Federal Tax Liens*
Many taxpayers never become aware that a tax lien has been recorded against them. Even though tax liens are open for public inspection, few people actually become aware that a tax lien has been filed against a specific taxpayer.
A method of preventing delinquency is to inform the public of the names of taxpayers against whom a lien has been filed. This could be accomplished by publicizing this information in the Vital Statistics sections of various newspapers. This method was utilized in Twin Falls, Idaho for a short period of time. It was accomplished by the Revenue Officer contacting and convincing the local newspaper reporter to pick up Federal Tax Lien filing information and publicize the names of these taxpayers along with other public information, such as marriages, divorces, suits, judgments, etc. It became immediately evident in the Twin Falls area that the word had gotten around and that certain delinquent taxpayers became embarrassed as a result of their tax liabilities becoming public knowledge. The Twin Falls newspaper discontinued publicizing tax lien information after a short period of time due to the numerous complaints and criticisms received from the delinquent taxpayers.

B. *Seizure Action*

Delinquency in the St. Maries area has been reduced through the ingenuity of a Revenue Officer. The Revenue Officer seized a car which was owned by a chronic delinquent in the St. Maries area. The Revenue Officer found this car parked on the main street of downtown St. Maries and proceeded to seize the auto by placing warning notices on the car windows. The Revenue Officer secured the car by placing a large log chain around the car's bumper and on adjacent parking meter. The local St. Maries newspaper became aware of this seizure and as a result, placed a picture and story on the front page of the newspaper.

C. *Attorneys And Doctors*

Six prominent attorneys in the Sandpoint area had repeatedly been delinquent in the payment of their income tax. A Revenue Officer seized the office of the Sandpoint prosecuting attorney. This seizure was consummated by affixing hasp locks to the doors of the attorney's office. Considerable publicity occurred through radio, television, and newspapers as a result of this seizure. Delinquency has been greatly reduced in the Sandpoint area as a result of this seizure and the embarrassment to the prosecuting attorney. A similar situation occurred when a doctor's office was seized. The doctor's patients could not keep their appointments, and as a result, considerable publicity was generated.

It has been my experience that seizures which result in "sensationalism" tend to remain fixed in the public's mind, and are a great deterrent of delinquency.

Such unwarranted and high-handed actions by the IRS are often not just embarrassing but very damaging to the victim. For instance, in a recent case, one person had a piece of land which he had received as a gift from a grandfather.

He sold the property, and, expecting to receive the proceeds of the sale, made some business decisions based upon the availability of the money. The Internal Revenue Service, however, stepped in and seized the property and blocked the sale, while it conducted a lengthy and time-consuming fishing expedition against the estate, to see whether or not the grandfather was liable for any back taxes (over sixty years back). The man was in his nineties and some of the property had been granted when the state in which he resided had been a territory. It was virtually impossible to trace back all of his transactions and tax status.

In the meantime, it was found that the IRS agent who issued the attachment had been bribed by a third party who wanted to block the sale for reasons of his own. The IRS did not admit fault for almost two years. The proceedings dragged on with the IRS getting postponement after postponement, almost bringing about the bankruptcy of several parties and causing great economic loss to all the parties concerned. Losses were probably in the hundreds of thousands of dollars, to say nothing of the legal fees.

Eventually the IRS was forced to capitulate and not only had to release the property but to pay damages and legal fees. During this time, the taxpayer had been forced to sell his business. This didn't seem to be a matter of much consequence or concern to the IRS. It simply continued its blundering, unethical, improper actions until it was forced by circumstances to back off. Other than the agent who had been bribed, no IRS official had any personal liability.

Now remember, right and justice were on the side of the taxpayer. Eventually he won but there were immense hardships in the meantime, which almost resulted in his total financial failure. The IRS has the right under the law to seize your property and hold it for years until a leisurely determination is made. And it exercises this power freely. Its position is, "It will all come out in the wash, so you are not damaged." They do not consider the consequences of having your funds tied up.

The amount of money the IRS can tie up in this manner can be huge. Everyone has heard how prizefighters have had their winnings of millions of dollars held up until the Internal Revenue Service has extracted what it feels is its due. It does this despite the fact that it may not know whether the fighter has tax shelters, or has large losses to carry forward, or even has any liability at all. It simply moves to protect its interest and tie up the funds, and then waits to see what the actual liability might be. All of this is done without any legal authorization or any court order. The IRS administers a tax system of voluntary compliance like Attila the Hun.

As government spending explodes and taxes increase, taxpayer resistance grows and stronger totalitarian methods become essential in order to collect the taxes due. Congress has hesitated to strip the IRS of its dictatorial powers, partly because many members are personally afraid of a confrontation and partly because they think they are caught in a choice between individual freedoms versus the necessity of government to collect the increasingly objectionable tax burden. Heavy taxation to raise money for social spending will always result in loss of freedom because of increasingly repressive methods necessitated by increasing taxpayer resistance.

The IRS has risen to the occasion with enthusiasm. The taxpayer is the enemy to be subdued, rather than a citizen to be served. Such is the mentality of the IRS—to freeze and seize and "put the fear of the Lord" into the taxpayer.

6

Rigging
Elections

The Internal Revenue Service works diligently to ensure that public officials toe the IRS line. Political leaders are quickly taught that complaints about the IRS are not allowed. The FBI, the CIA, and other agencies of government have been searchingly investigated from time to time, sometimes to damaging excess. But not the IRS.

The IRS has never been thoroughly reviewed by any other agency of government, or even by the Congress for that matter. And it has never been exposed by the press. The reason is simple. Everyone pays taxes. They are so complicated that even the use of 1040a (the simplest return form) is no guarantee that you won't be harassed, a fact demonstrated in cases to be presented later on.

Blackmail and extortion are ugly words. But they are the only fair words to describe why the IRS is alone among government agencies in not being subject to scrutiny. Anyone who complains—*anyone*—is a candidate for destruction.

In 1968, after Senator Ed Long's U.S. Senate subcommittee had completed its three-year examination of IRS tactics, his tax returns were leaked to *Life* magazine. The information illegally released during an election year by the IRS indicated terrible irregularities in Long's returns. Even though Senator Long was later cleared by an exhaustive investigation, and even though he had apparently paid all of his taxes, his political career of some thirty-eight years was in shambles. His home state of Missouri rejected him for Thomas Eagleton.

According to *Saturday Review* of May 1980, Bernard Fensterwald, chief counsel of Senator Long's committee, was also audited and harassed by the IRS. Fensterwald stated, "Senators and Congressmen not scared of looking into the IRS have to be crazy, because the IRS will just ruin your career."

Several years later, Senator Joseph Montoya took on the IRS in another subcommittee investigation. Sure enough, shortly before Mr. Montoya began his bid for reelection the IRS leaked erroneous information about his income tax returns and he went down in defeat. As in the case of Senator Long, no tax irregularities were ever found in Senator Montoya's audit. In fact, according to Montoya aide Doris Ulman, "The IRS discovered that they owed him money."

These examples represent the extremes that the IRS will go to in order to prevent close scrutiny of its operations. Usually such extreme measures are unnecessary. An administrative aide of a prominent Congressman tells how the Congressman, because of an extraordinarily large number of complaints about the IRS in his district, set up a series of hearings in his state on IRS abuses. After the Congressman held the first meeting he was informed by the IRS that his income tax returns for the previous five years were going to be audited. He cancelled the remainder of the hearings.

Having been an outspoken opponent of government harassment of citizens, I have also been given a thorough education in the school of hard knocks by vengeful bureaucrats. Any agency has the power to retaliate, but the scorpionlike IRS is unique in the breadth and depth of its ability to sting its victims. And the examples I have used, in addition to my own case, demonstrate that it is not a matter of partisan politics. It is a matter of whether the people will govern or the IRS will rule.

Three weeks before the general election of 1976, a friend of mine called me to report that the Lewiston, Idaho, *Morning Tribune* had printed a long and detailed article alleging certain irregularities in my income tax history. I had heard rumors that some of my political opposition and enemies in the press had been working with certain IRS people in an attempt to affect the outcome of the election. But up to now, the gossip had never really bothered me. The reason for this is simple. I had spent almost all of the previous twelve years on government payrolls, either in Congress or in the Agriculture Department, and my income taxes (like most taxpayers') were withheld from my paychecks. Nearly every year I had a sizable refund due to me. It had never occurred to me that overpayment of taxes was a political liability.

I had always paid my taxes. I knew it and I knew the IRS knew it. There was only one logical explanation for this disclosure—someone in the IRS was out to damage or even destroy my political career. The IRS had apparently had enough of my annoying complaints and pointed questions on the behalf of my constituents; they decided that Idaho's 2nd District needed a new Congressman. An IRS official put it to me this way:

"In your case, Congressman, this thing was all planned way back and they probably never even intended to develop a case on you. All they wanted to do was to have the special agents involved so they could leak it to the press. You know, just the fact that you're under investigation, that hurts your reputation, and, of course, with a few innuendoes and a few leaks here and there, they can convict you without ever doing anything."

Besides rigging particular elections, I learned that the IRS has two other purposes for engaging in this kind of activity: First, they "keep the fear of the Lord" in the people by dramatically showing that the IRS can and will get anybody; second, they instill enough dread into public officials that they won't tackle the IRS for getting out of line. An IRS agent told me:

"It still goes back to the fact that you were the most prominent person in the area and this is their philosophy—to make a case on somebody who's prominent. They don't have to convict you, they don't have to prove anything. If they go around to your friends, pretty soon your minister is embarrassed to be talking to you—everybody is afraid to be associated with you because they're afraid your bad reputation is going to rub off onto them. And, well, they just try you and convict you without a court or without any evidence, really."

During the next few days before the election the political heat generated by the IRS disclosure became all-consuming. Other newspapers quickly picked up the vicious story and spread it across the state. "Does George Hansen pay his income taxes?" soon became the central issue of my opponent's campaign. I was being tried and convicted, not by the courts, but by the media and the IRS. Most of the media demanded that I make my tax returns public. I refused.

The *Idaho Statesman* reported my position in an article dated October 27, 1976:

> Hansen said if he is reelected he will take immediate steps to ensure [that] the Internal Revenue Service is not used as a "tool by the media or politically designing persons to harass people, to defame them or to harm them."

"I think that is the big danger when information can be attributed to them that can be dangerous," Hansen said, pointing out, "It can happen to any citizen—and we sure better see that it doesn't happen."

Hansen said his taxes are paid and he is due a refund as has been the case for the past decade. He said the Tribune story was "based on distortions and half-truths."

We fought back in the only way left to us—by telling people the truth. I emphasized the fact that I had paid my taxes—usually overpaid my taxes—every year of my adult life, and that the right to privacy was a vital principle. I could not violate that principle under fire without undermining everything I stood for.

Nevertheless, my support was slipping. I could sense it in the reactions I was getting from some of the people I met on the streets—people who apparently wanted proof, not principles. Quite literally, I had been convicted without a trial.

If it had not been for offsetting weaknesses in the opponent's campaign, and the valiant last-minute efforts of my loyal friends and voluntary campaign crews around the district, I might well have lost the election. Thanks to these people, who stood by me and trusted in me, we won—by less than 1 percent of the vote. The IRS had rigged the election, and almost got away with it.

All the finger-pointing by my adversaries, prompted by the illegal disclosures of the IRS itself, apparently gave the IRS the license it wanted to open a full review of my tax records. One of my sources in the IRS later told me:

"I can tell you as anxious as they [officials in the IRS] were to cause you trouble, if it had been anything they'd have nailed you to the wall before now. They wouldn't have gone through the back door if they'd thought they had anything concrete."

"It wouldn't have lasted for over a year then—is that what you mean?" I asked.

"Right. They'd have crucified you immediately, and I think the fact that they did this leaking is a pretty good indication that they didn't have anything concrete. Somebody decided there wasn't anything there and the only way they were going to get you was to—"

"Just to say you were under audit?" I interrupted.

"Right."

"For investigation, in this case. That may be the only reason why they gave it to Intelligence. The difference is if you're contacted by the auditors you're under audit but if you're contacted by the Intelligence people you're under investigation. Isn't that it?"

"Right," he continued. "Well, when the special agent walks into the bank or to somebody you do business with and pulls out the badge and says I'm a criminal investigator, it makes a big difference."

"Yeah, because that's just like on that violence list they make it sound like the guy has committed a criminal act, they say this is taken from criminal files, people who have a penchant—possible penchants for violence—they make him sound like he's a criminal and violent."

"Well, part of the introduction of a special agent is to inform the person he is talking to that he's a criminal investigator, not an auditor."

That is just the type of circumstance I encountered until I warned the IRS that I wasn't about to become a victim of that kind of operation—normal audit procedures, yes, but intimidation and harassment, no!

Eighteen months later the "investigation" was over, my taxes were audited, and I received a nice refund for overpayment; but not nearly enough to pay for the lawyers and accountants I had to hire.

Looking back on those months, I find that what has happened to the careers of the agents involved in my disclosure case reflects, very well, the mentality of the IRS—the political manipulators are promoted and the professionals who get in their way are the losers.

One agent, who spontaneously stood up in a public meeting and tried to professionally clarify the position of the IRS to prevent the agency from being used for partisan political purposes in the issue of my taxes, was severely reprimanded, investigated, and disciplined for "becoming involved in political activities."

An IRS official who took part in the disclosure but who in seeing his mistake stepped forward to apologize and to try to help bring the perpetrators of the scheme to justice was transferred out of the area and demoted. He became the IRS scapegoat in spite of the fact that several other illegal disclosures were also made by the agency.

This official wrote the following letter to me:

September 7, 1977

Dear Mr. Hansen:

I am writing this personal letter to you, because I feel that I owe you an apology and . . . I feel obligated.

As [an IRS official] I confirmed some information in response to what I considered a legitimate inquiry about your filing record for 1966, 1967, and 1968. That information, I think, contributed in some way to an article that appeared in the Lewiston *Morning Tribune* on October 15, 1976. While I have not been approached by or talked to any newspaper people, I erred in my judgment of handling that inquiry. I have volunteered my total involvement to the Service, and am naturally suffering extremely severe consequences for my actions.

I apologize to you for my error in judgment and for any-

thing I may have done that contributed to the publicity concerning your tax affairs, and I seek your forgiveness. . . .
[Name and address deleted.]

These disclosures were made directly to my opponent's campaign. Except for the person conscientious enough to confess, none of the other government officials involved in the scheme were formally identified or disciplined by the IRS. This is most significant in light of an incident I learned about from sources within the IRS. It is reported that as early as December 15, 1975, District Director Howard Martin is known to have asked employees:

"Do you have any ideas on how we can get Hansen? A lot of heads of other agencies and myself are worried about Hansen and what he is doing to the government agencies. We've had meetings about it. Do you want to help us?"

Both Martin and a group manager were also reliably reported to have been in frequent contact with my political opponent during the election. We're still waiting for the promised grand jury.

On February 2, 1977, the *Idaho Statesman* announced that Howard Martin had been named head of disclosure for the entire Internal Revenue Service. Martin stated that he would "be responsible for administering the Freedom of Information Act, the Privacy Act, and the new disclosure laws."

Ironically, the man who had apparently involved the IRS in partisan politics and improper disclosures was promoted to head the arm of the IRS responsible for preventing such activities—a clear case of leaving the fox to guard the chicken coop.

The FBI, the CIA, and other agencies of the federal government have undergone the closest of reviews in recent years. High officials have been found guilty and punished for improper use of power and abuse of people's rights.

As a Member of Congress, I have taken the Occupational Safety and Health Administration (OSHA) to the U.S. Supreme Court to end its random searches in violation of the Fourth Amendment. I along with others have also exposed fraudulent and wasteful spending by the General Services Administration (GSA) and the questionable activities of many other federal programs.

No agency of government should be immune to investigation and review, not the Congress, not the President. Nevertheless there is one which enjoys the privileges of a sacred cow and behaves much like a mad bull—the IRS.

The FBI and CIA and other agencies had their confidential files on public officials and other prominent and active citizens outlawed, but not the IRS. The IRS can maintain an extensive clipping file on your activities—one that will cost you a substantial sum for copies if you wish to satisfy your curiosity.

Why does the IRS do this? The IRS likes to watch your activities, your trips, and your acquaintances to be sure you and your family and associates are not getting away with anything under our great "voluntary compliance" tax system.

And if it becomes disturbed enough with you the IRS can always use what it has even more effectively. In my case, the Special Investigations Division of the IRS in Utah leaked illegal and erroneous information regarding my taxes to my political opposition in Idaho and to the press. Then, in addition to the bad publicity assault I had to endure as a candidate during a sensitive election period, the Special Investigations Division of the IRS in Idaho used the illegal and erroneous Utah leaks as reason to investigate my taxes, while sweeping the agency's illegal activities under the rug.

They didn't get away with it. I won the election, received a substantial tax refund, and have exposed their scandalous activities.

In a six-year period involving three elections I had the privilege of proving my integrity at great personal expense to the FBI, the Federal Elections Commission (FEC), and committees of Congress as well as the IRS as enemies illegally invaded my personal credit report, my bank accounts, and my tax forms.

These "full circle" assault tactics on targeted citizens are deadly. All it takes is an enemy leaking information charging you with illegal or improper activities. Then one of his "friends" reports you to the government agency concerned while another of their "friends" tries to find and forward personal information on you to stoke the fires.

In the *Congressional Record* of July 13, 1978, U.S. Senator Orrin Hatch of Utah used my story as a case in point to strongly condemn the misuse of government agencies like the IRS for rigging federal elections.

INJUSTICES TO A GOOD CONGRESSMAN

Mr. HATCH. Mr. President, agencies of government are often in a position to assure the election or defeat of Senators and Congressmen and State and local officials. Designing politicians and politically motivated agency personnel are all too frequently engaged in the misuse of government power, which could, in effect, rig elections and destroy opposition. These shocking conclusions are the result of a year of effort, in conjunction with my colleague, Congressman GEORGE HANSEN of Idaho, in working with a constituent who was experiencing problems with the Internal Revenue Service—his employer. Apparently, this individual had been involved in the scandalous and apparently illegal leakage of the Congressman's income tax information during the 1976 general election campaign. This key IRS official had written a letter of apology to Congressman HANSEN but was being disciplined by the IRS. To assure impartiality and fairness and because this IRS employee was residing in Utah, the Congressman turned the case over to me.

Our further investigation revealed what appeared to be a vendetta on the part of some IRS official or officials with respect to the Congressman when this improper action was exposed by this letter of apology. It seems that this IRS employee was made the scapegoat. Apparently tax information from the Congressman's files was improperly revealed to his political opponents and such information was then publicly disseminated. It also appears that certain elements of the press in Idaho also improperly received the same information.

It is my understanding that this latter incident has been under investigation by the IRS Commissioner's Office in Washington, D.C., and that the matter has been referred to the Office of the Attorney General. Under such provocation it appears to me that Congressman HANSEN has acted fairly and judiciously with respect to the handling of my constituent and encouraging the legal system to do its job without political fanfare.

I was disturbed by the initial series of events but what disturbs me more is an apparent failure to aggressively pursue these investigations. Furthermore, it appears that these abusive practices are continuing. Obviously such practices could influence or "rig" the current election the Congressman is facing. It seems to me as I have watched from next door in Utah, that the Congressman is being pushed into investigation after investigation at the behest of politicians when the original investigation if completed promptly would have resolved the whole matter. The Department of Justice should move swiftly to put an end to these practices.

Beginning in 1974 the Congressman has been subjected to what appears to be politically instigated or politically motivated investigations of the House Administration Committee, Clerk's office, and even the FBI and the Department of Justice. It appears a Democratic Party official improperly forwarded the Congressman's credit report to the above-mentioned committee as well. Furthermore, other complaints from political partisans caused a Federal Election Commission investigation. When the improper disclosures of IRS were revealed, it appears that rather than correct errors of fact and/or attempt to suppress such confidential information, these officials engaged in open speculation. This confidential information became so available and well known, it was finally utilized as a basis for a demand for investigation and prosecution by the U.S. attorney's office, even though it was improperly secured and was substantially erroneous.

Just recently I have learned certain elements are again pressing new complaints and charges which are similar to the same old tired charges despite the fact that some of these elements are under investigation themselves for their earlier improper activities. It would appear that Government agencies are being and have been used improperly in the harassment of a Congressman, who probably works the longest hours on Capitol Hill, meets all his obligations and even has his wife serve as his full-time administrative assistant at no cost to the taxpayers.

Through the years I have observed the occasional manipulation and misuse of Government agencies by ambitious, unscrupulous or designing persons but the degree to which this can now be done to influence and warp the political process and prey on those who wish only to serve their country, as evidenced by the Hansen history which I have briefly recounted, is indeed shocking. Every Member of the House and Senate should take serious note of what might be in store for them or for public officials at any level. Who would want to undergo that which GEORGE HANSEN has experienced—and why should anyone have to?

Elections should be decided on the issues and effectiveness of the individual, not on character assassination and the manipulation of Government agencies to harass, bankrupt, or even destroy those aspiring to serve.

We had better make early adjustments in the system to assure that Government agencies are not improperly used and that the rights of candidates for public office are protected, or no one will care to run for office and self-government will fail.

The following information relative to page 76 is excerpted from an IRS memo included in a letter to U.S. Senator Steve Symms, of Idaho, dated October 25, 1983. The memo dated January 20, 1981 was to the IRS State Director from a Senior IRS auditor.

---

to: ▆▆▆▆▆▆▆▆▆▆▆▆▆▆▆

from: ▆▆▆▆▆▆▆▆▆▆▆▆▆▆ January 20, 1981

subject: Litigation following arbitration action

Today is the final day for the instituting of litigation action on the 1976 disciplinary action instituted by then Director Howard Martin as a result of my hinderance of his efforts to influence the 1975 Congressional Campaign, and to provide him with a scape-goat should his efforts ever come to light. . . .

To present my case in court it would be necessary to disclose and document Martin's clandestine meeting in an Idaho Falls motel room with then congressional candidate Stan Kress. Also present during the early stages of this plotting session were an Idaho Falls Agent and his supervisor. . . . The supervisor was removed the week following his admission during the arbitration hearing to two additional such meetings with Candidate Kress.

Also required would be disclosure and documentation of the subsequent after hours meeting at the Pocatello IRS office between Mrs. Stan Kress and that supervisor for the announced purpose of preparing news releases. Present at this after hours session was the group secretary who performed the typing . . . .

You will recall that these efforts resulted in the improper disclosure of tax information concerning Congressional Candidate George Hansen and ultimately resulted in the public outcry against IRS which I attempted to answer. I felt that a statement of the truth might aid IRS. Unfortunately, Howard Martin viewed my efforts as an attempt to hinder his efforts to influence the congressional election against George Hansen and the disciplinary action was proposed.

Internal Revenue Service

7

Overkill

The IRS tax scandal of that 1976 election had its positive points. First, I was, as a result of these experiences, beginning to see precisely how the IRS operates. Second, the media coverage of the event, biased as it was, brought my name as a public figure to the attention of many other conscientious citizens in and out of Idaho who had problems with the IRS. Taxpayers who had been and who were being intimidated by the IRS wanted someone in government to whom they could tell their story. These people, and their lawyers and their accountants, started bringing their cases to me. What follow are brief accounts of a few of the cases in which I was involved. These stories demonstrate that the intended victims of IRS Gestapo tactics are not just IRS employees who sometimes refuse to knuckle under, or elected officials who sometimes get in the way, but America's taxpayers.

Here is an incident, told to me by an accountant, in which a farmer was audited because he refused to give the IRS information regarding his neighbor's finances.

"So the IRS goes to this man who is my client and asks him for information on—well, let's call him 'Mr. X.' My client told the IRS that he wasn't going to give them any information relative to somebody else. 'That's a bunch of nonsense,' he says. Two weeks later my client gets a letter in which he is required to bring in all his records since 1969. We did. We went to the IRS and took his records in because we didn't have anything to hide in that case. It was no problem. I wasn't afraid of it at all. I mean he was a good, clean, honest man. He didn't have any back taxes to fuss with and we had done a good job, so we took it all in there. In twenty minutes or a half hour of auditing, the agent went all through my client's taxes and said that all he was concerned with was what he could get on 'Mr. X' out in [address deleted]—not with my client."

"Why was the IRS after this man?" I asked.

"I don't have any idea why they were after him. All I know is they were after him and my client told the IRS it was none of their business what his relationship with the other man was, which is true—it isn't their business.

"He shouldn't have to rat on his neighbor, and because he didn't rat on him, we had audits from 1969 on," the accountant explained.

"And you feel that there's every reason to believe that this is true—I mean, that you were audited simply to harass your client into talking about his neighbor?"

"Well, it was a blatant situation. I mean, you might talk with [name deleted] out in [address deleted], it happened to him, too. There's no ifs, ands, and buts about it."

These overkill tactics of the agency are not necessarily deployed just against the rich or middle class. An IRS agent told me this one:

"There was the little janitor who they convicted for failure to file. The total tax was somewhere in the neighborhood of

$800 or $900. The penalties and the fine and everything were under $3500.

"On two different occasions they brought in witnesses all the way from Anchorage, Alaska. They brought in attorneys from San Francisco and Salt Lake. That $3,000 or $3,500 probably cost the government $20,000. He was employed by the local church and very active in its activities. He was just the kind of nice guy they were looking for. Now you can't tell me that somewhere they couldn't have found a more lucrative case than that. They took him to court strictly as an example.

"They could have just taken the information off of his W-2s and filed tax returns for him and assessed the tax and that would have been it.

"But what they did is like bringing in a tank to kill an ant. These people in the IRS have their own little empires and they have a lot of employees underneath them and if they went that route and just assess him the tax, what would all those people do for a living? These people live and grow off of the taxpayers. That's why they're increasing the number of special agents tremendously. Special agents aren't auditors, they're a police force."

The IRS is notorious for its arrogant abuses of power. In the following instance an accountant relates the attitude made famous by the bureaucrats in the Internal Revenue Service:

"I represented a crop duster. He'd done a good job in earning a living, made quite a little bit of money—he sold out a year ago.

"He had an excise tax auditor from the IRS come about three years ago trying to collect a three-cent-a-gallon excise tax that goes onto the aircraft. There's a tax on the act of putting gasoline from a bulk tank into a noncommercial aircraft. Well, we looked the thing over and decided we were commercial and we didn't have to pay it so we didn't fuss with it.

"Now along comes the auditor and we get ourselves a bunch of affidavits from FAA and we've got tax returns showing him paying taxes on $40,000 and $50,000 and we kind of thought that made those planes commercial. I don't know whether they are or they aren't—and they never did decide for sure—but the auditor went through the books and he came up with $184 tax bill out of it. When he finished, of course, my client and I sat there and smiled at each other because we weren't going to worry about $184. We were going to tell him that we were commercial and we figured he would go along with that after he thought about it for a minute.

"But first I asked him to define commercial aviation and noncommercial aviation and this was his comment. He said, 'You're noncommercial because I define you that way and if you don't like it, sue me.'

"I guess we should have sued them—but who do you sue for $184?"

Confiscating a person's wages is another favorite weapon of the IRS. In the example below an employer's view of the problem is presented:

"Back in about October of 1976 we received a notice of levy ordering us to pay all the salary owed to one of our employees until some back taxes he owed were paid in full. And, of course, I didn't know he owed any back taxes so I called our employee and asked him if it was true. He said, yes, he did owe some and they were due. So, I asked him if it would really work a hardship on him if I took all of his salary for the next month and a half to pay his back taxes—they wanted the whole thing. It was a notice of levy and they wanted the whole thing and I was to pay all the salary until it was paid off.

"Naturally, I was concerned for our employee and what he was going to live on so I decided to go to bat for him. I called the IRS and talked to them about it and they were really quite uncooperative at first. So I pointed out to them that, as a private citizen, if someone owes me money and I would go to court to collect, I would not be allowed to take their entire salary but would only be allowed to take a certain part of it and leave him enough to live on.

"So they agreed then that, yes, he could come in and they would make arrangements with him. He went in and talked to them and I don't know exactly what happened, but when he called back, he said, 'Just go ahead, just pay it all. Somehow we will get along. If my wife weren't working we'd starve, but somehow we will try to get along until that is paid off.'

"And so until that entire amount was paid, he didn't get any salary from us. It was all given to the Internal Revenue Service.

"I just can't quite figure why they can do that and a private citizen cannot. I don't think any of us should be allowed to do that to a person. I have no quarrel with the fact that he owed the taxes and I said, 'Pay your taxes.' But just the same, I thought what the IRS did was wrong."

8

Pouncing upon Disaster Victims

Those who can afford accountants and attorneys often fight and win against the Internal Revenue Service, but for the millions who cannot it is a different story. IRS quotas make the defenseless taxpayer all the more susceptible to IRS inspection. This point was dramatically demonstrated in my own Congressional district when the IRS pounced upon the victims of the devastating Teton Dam flood—a $400 million disaster in eastern Idaho.

The "roof" fell in on the massive earthen Teton Dam located in Fremont County at 11:57 A.M., June 5, 1976. As fate would have it, I was in the midst of a twenty-six-county airplane blitz of my district campaigning for reelection and found myself just sixty miles from the dam site when the alarm went out. Minutes after the dam burst, our twin-engine plane was above the giant expanse of churning water and debris.

As we flew over Rexburg, I watched in horror as the mammoth wall of water picked up hundreds of forty-foot logs from a sawmill on the north edge of the city and drove them like battering rams through the walls of Rexburg's homes and businesses. Over Sugar City only the tops of a few houses could be seen sticking up through the deluge. All in all, several cities and towns were rendered uninhabitable or were severely damaged by the flood waters; 20,000 head of cattle were lost; thousands and thousands of acres of prime farmland were covered by silt and mud and rocks and gravel. Nearly a half-billion dollars' worth of property was destroyed. Only the quick action and resourcefulness of the residents of the area held the number of fatalities to nine.

I landed at Idaho Falls in the path of the flood and stayed there day and night helping coordinate relief and rescue efforts between federal agencies and state, local, and private organizations. I then flew to Washington to get relief legislation moving in Congress to compensate flood victims for the devastation caused by the failure of a federal project.

In just days I was able to secure an amendment to an ongoing appropriations bill getting the first $200 million on line for the flood victims. Another $200 million followed in timely fashion in other legislation.

In the meantime, specific legislation authorizing more current provisions for relief payments to injured parties was introduced in both the House and Senate by members of the Idaho delegation.

The legislation soon moved through the Senate and into the House, where we quickly added the final necessary provisions. We sent it to President Ford for signature and implementation in record time.

Soon emergency measures gave way to actual reimbursement and rebuilding programs with government relief agencies generally providing good performance.

But the other side of government also began to appear.

The waters from the deluge had not even subsided before government bureaucrats swooped down on the hapless prey.

The worst culprit in this bureaucratic aftermath was the Internal Revenue Service, which hesitated only briefly before it resumed collection activities against the still-dislocated flood victims and even prepared to tax the disaster payments. It seemed that there was little sympathy for the fact that records, as well as sources of income, were destroyed by the flood and people were desperately busy with clean-up and rebuilding efforts.

A report from Group Manager 1100 Boise to Chief CTS Boise District dated August 10, 1976 (just two months after the disaster), states, in part, "The majority of taxpayers who were involved in the Teton Dam disaster have been identified."

On August 25, 1976, another report between the same individuals stated:

> The Teton Dam disaster has created numerous problems which will require ingenuity and finesse to resolve. The Revenue officers must analyze each separate case and exercise good judgment before *proceeding with collection activity.* The Revenue officers must also be fully aware of the numerous tax ramifications concerning casualty loss deductions and the *taxability of disaster fund payments.* [Emphasis added.]

IRS officials viewed the reimbursement payments as a literal grab-bag for capital gains taxes. Because of an aberration in the law, the IRS was able to pursue an extremely narrow interpretation of the meaning of "replacement with like kind." Farmers whose fields had been ruined as potato ground were not allowed to switch their fields to wheat or alfalfa without paying an excessive capital gains tax on the new farm equipment. Farmers, if they wanted to remain farmers, coughed up the taxes. To show how ridiculous this interpretation was, these farmers could only escape the capital gains tax by replanting potatoes—which was impossible.

Any other use of the money resulted in the levy of a tax. I think of it as a "flood tax"—farmers paid for the "privilege" of having a lifetime of work and dreams washed out by the U.S. government.

An accountant involved with helping flood victims offered the following example of the same capital gains problem:

"We have one man who called to report that he had a license in the State of Idaho to operate a shelter home and this shelter home, he said, could not qualify for a license today because of its locality, the manner of its construction, and so on. Nevertheless, he was able to operate that shelter home under a grandfather rights provision of the law. When the flood came it destroyed the shelter home and so to build it back would not have been possible because he couldn't get his license.

"So he said all right, I'll build back an apartment house. It is still to shelter people. But he said that he was advised by the Internal Revenue Service that that would not qualify as like property and, therefore, he would have to pay the capital gains tax on the proceeds received from the destruction of his shelter home.

"Now that creates a problem because he is either out of business, pays tax on the gain on the money he received, or if he reinvests, you see, it is going to take the same amount of money to build the apartment house and then he has to pay the tax on top of that and he is in a bind. There is no way he can do it."

The list could go on and on. My constituents appealed to me and I strongly complained to the IRS regarding their ruthlessness in dealing with these good people. As I told an IRS officer, "I will not stand by and allow the Teton area people to be further victimized. If the IRS plans any kind of tax auditing to reduce the reimbursements granted by the Bureau of Reclamation, I will seek immediate passage of appropriate legislation to obtain necessary relief and fair treatment. All I'm saying is, don't take away the government reimbursement money we've already given them for damages suffered."

I pressed a high-ranking IRS official in Washington on the matter of allowing local agents some leeway in the application of the law to the victims of the Teton flood. I insisted that the IRS has made such policy adjustments at other times and could do so again to give needed relief. Here is the response: "Capital gains—well, that's the damn law! If we do it [i.e. compromise with the taxpayer] in one case then we are opening the door, so our people are told that they don't administer the law. Sure, you may sympathize with these poor jerks out there, George, the poor farmers who are going through this sort of thing. But you just—there is no way you can help him because the law can't help him. My gosh, your interpretation of what is right and wrong is different than mine."

I rolled up my sleeves and dug in my heels. I was determined that the IRS would not treat my people in this manner. And, finally, under great pressure, they backed off—a little.

9

You're Being Watched

RS harassment often takes on subtle forms. Approximately fifteen years ago radically new trends of enforcement, as well as new methods of collection, were developed by the IRS. These tendencies were undoubtedly spawned by the covert activities of the FBI and CIA during the same period of time. However, during the 1970s, these legitimate intelligence agencies were dangerously throttled by Congress, while the IRS continued to set aside acceptable accounting procedures and tax collection practices and employed cloak-and-dagger methods to humiliate and even destroy taxpayers.

Fear of retaliation has severely retarded organized opposition to IRS abuses, as has previously been pointed out. However, movements to challenge these high-handed methods have begun to stir through scattered groups of tax protesters and, more recently, through a strange fusing of political elements from left and right having a common concern for citizen rights, whether under the guise of "human rights" or "constitutional rights." Beyond this, the kneejerk preoccupation of political reactionaries still screaming about CIA and FBI "surveillance" allows the IRS to goosestep its way into the private affairs of U.S. citizens with surprisingly little organized opposition. For example, opening and monitoring mail is just one of its many tricks. An IRS source told me:

"I've heard of instances where the IRS recorded every piece of mail coming to a person and the source of it. Now I don't know whether it was opened or not, but I have heard of that being done, yes.

"They were talking about making someone nervous that they had under investigation by going through all of his mail and they would keep the pieces of mail for a week to make sure that he knew they were going through them."

Making lists of persons in attendance at political rallies is also a popular IRS activity. As one IRS official stated, "The IRS is so interested in tax protester groups, and in right-wing organizations like the John Birch Society, that they go to their meetings and take their names and license numbers and put them on watch lists."

In an Associated Press story of November 3, 1978, the IRS district director for Montana stated bluntly that the Internal Revenue Service was sending agents to Montana taxpayer meetings to collect names and that the IRS would then run tax checks on those who attended. "An IRS spokeswoman in Washington [D.C.] acknowledged such monitoring." The article continued, "The agents [hiding behind a partition] were noticed by reporters, but refused to give out their names . . . the agents remained [hidden] because they were known to several in the audience and were fearful of causing a disruption."

In the area of religion the IRS is even more abusive with the rights of both taxpayer and employee. Its axiom seems to be that a compassionate person makes a bad bureaucrat.

For instance, eastern Idaho is heavily populated by Latter-day Saints or Mormons. Like the Catholic and Jewish religions in the East, or the fundamental Christian sects of the South, the Mormons form integral religious communities in many Western states. In Idaho, Mormon agents are routinely transferred out of the areas of the state which contain a large percentage of Mormons. Apparently, the IRS is afraid that a Mormon agent will not deal ruthlessly enough with the members of his own church.

A sworn statement by an IRS agent contains the following:

> Shortly after Dee Brady was promoted to a GS-13 position in the Boise District Office, I had an occasion to have a conversation with Gus Santilli, the Audit Division group manager in Pocatello. Gus and I were talking in general about who would be applying for the GS-12 revenue agent vacancy in Idaho Falls created when Brady left. We were discussing this topic briefly when Gus asked me to go to coffee with him at JB's. While we were having coffee, the discussion continued, and Gus made the remark, *"I know one thing for darn sure. I'm not going to put another Mormon in Idaho Falls."* He elaborated on this by mentioning the Mormon employees currently stationed in the Idaho Falls post of duty.
>
> Sometime after the first conversation with Gus Santilli, I had occasion to have another conversation with him over a cup of coffee. This conversation took place at Elmer's Pancake House in Pocatello, but I do not recall the specific date. The topic of who would be selected for the GS-12 position in Idaho Falls again came up during this discussion. *Gus Santilli again stated that he was "darn sure that he was not going to put another Mormon in Idaho Falls."* [Emphasis added.]

A second testimony provides corroboration of the first:

When I first started working for the IRS, I was an office auditor in the Pocatello office. I subsequently transferred to the Idaho Falls office when I was selected for a revenue agent position in that post of duty in June, 1973. *When I transferred to the Idaho Falls office, Dean Bigler, the former group manager over Pocatello and Idaho Falls offices, mentioned to me that he was concerned about having three LDS revenue agents in the Idaho Falls post of duty due to the number of Mormons in the Idaho Falls area.* [Emphasis added.]

Two Mormon agents, denied promotions in the IRS, took their case to the Office of Equal Employment Opportunity (EEO) and won. The national NTEU Bulletin contained the following article, dated December 31, 1975, on the discrimination case:

Race discrimination may catch the media's attention one day, sex discrimination the next. Yet, despite the fact that one of these may dominate the public eye, other brands of prejudice still linger on.

Ask, for instance, two GS-11 Revenue Agents in the Boise District Office of the Internal Revenue Service who were victims of religious discrimination. The employees, both members of the Church of [Jesus Christ of] Latter-day Saints, applied for a GS-12 Revenue Agent position in Idaho Falls, Idaho last May. Both were ranked "highly qualified" for the position and made the best-qualified list with three other employees—two of whom were also Mormons.

Through the office grapevine, the employees learned that Mormons would not be considered for the vacant position since "there were too many Latter-day Saint Agents in the Idaho Falls area." To no one's surprise, the one Revenue

Agent on the best-qualified list who was not a Mormon was selected for the promotion.

Obtaining assistance from NTEU, the two employees immediately filed an equal employment opportunity complaint, charging religious discrimination. The Boise EEO Investigator assigned to the case found that the two employees had actually been ranked first and second on the best-qualified list.

In addition, on interviewing the employee's supervisor, the Investigator learned that the group manager strongly believed that both employees were well-qualified for the post and was surprised that one of the two was not selected. Completing his study, the EEO Investigator concluded that the employees would have been promoted if not for management's discriminatory attitude toward Mormons.

Following this report, Boise District Office officials met with the employees, Chapter 5 leaders, and an NTEU National Field Representative in an effort to resolve the matter. In the October 1 meeting, the Boise District Director openly admitted that discrimination had occurred but initially refused to grant either employee an opportunity to receive a GS-12 promotion. NTEU persisted in its demands, however, and ultimately the Boise District Director backed down, conceding that both employees will get a fair opportunity to receive a GS-12 Revenue Agent position.

Another agent, who was suspected by the IRS of making telephone calls to members of his local parish on IRS time, had two Internal Security agents assigned to his case. According to a source within the IRS, these professional finks clumsily trailed their prey every working day for two weeks—during which time the agent under investigation made a few phone calls to his fellow church members but only in his break periods. The ensuing harassment from IRS management drove the agent out of the Internal Revenue Service.

The taxpayer is similarly subjected to religious bias and discrimination. Automatic audits frequently await those of all income levels dedicated to making large church contributions. The IRS computer system is specifically designed to "kick out" these returns for audit. Unrealistic assessments and deduction allowances also reflect definite religious bias, as exemplified in distorted definitions of who is a clergyman. The IRS took the tax-exempt status away from Seventh-day Adventist churches because some of their ministers were not licensed to perform marriage ceremonies. Such mentality is now unfortunately spreading through government, as illustrated by a November 1977 criminal trial in Maryland which involved two Catholic priests as witnesses for the prosecution. The defense argued that all Catholics should be removed from the jury because "no Roman Catholic is or can be neutral as to the credibility of a priest."

In a typical case, IRS officials arbitrarily assigned a value of 25 percent of the commercially assessed value to an expensive painting being contributed to a church school; in so doing, they rejected repeated evaluations of the work by well-known art appraisers. The IRS agent making the reduced assessment had no qualms about expressing his dislike of the religion and the notion of charitable contributions to religion.

"Let's get down to business," the agent is quoted as saying. "You have one of two choices, either pay your taxes due or take it to Tax Court."

And the Internal Revenue Service is no stranger to legislative maneuvering. When H.R. 7583 came up in the 96th Congress, the IRS lobbied for expanded powers to deal with "religious cults." Little noticed was the fact that the powers sought were equally available against every religious organization, both the mainstream and the less accepted. The IRS thinks so little of the First Amendment right to religious freedom that it never even bothered to prepare a defense of its proposals on Bill of Rights grounds. Some defenders of the

IRS even suggested that only approved religions were entitled to religious freedom.

In 1978 I conducted *ad hoc* hearings on IRS abuses in Idaho. During those hearings the following instances of deception, fraud, and attack on the freedom of speech by the IRS were related by a young man named Larry Fullmer.

Mr. Fullmer: First I would like to say that when I was going to high school we used to talk about Russia occasionally. I don't think I got a very good education about the situation there and how it is supposed to differ from the situation here in the United States. But one of the distinguishing characteristics that I heard often was that in Russia people inform on other people and it is government policy to get private citizens to inform on each other and to get children to inform on their parents and that sort of thing. The KGB keeps citizens under surveillance at all times, keeps lists of people.

Well, we've got that developing here in the United States, the same kind of situation, I think. If children inform on their parents to the IRS, even the children can receive the monetary reward for doing so. We've got lists, we've got surveillance, we've got all of that on the part of the IRS. A lot of that we've heard about today.

I didn't used to be very paranoid about the IRS. I figured they just collected taxes and most of them were accountants and that was about all that it came to, but a number of things have happened to me and have happened to other people I know that have caused me to become very paranoid. . . .

An acquaintance of mine in Utah a couple of years ago published a book called *Taxation and Tyranny*—it was a small book, not many pages, but it was full of quotes from Jefferson and Washington and Hamilton, our founding fathers. . . .

I wanted to look at it. So I sent a check to him for about $3.00 and he sent me the book and that was fine. Then a friend of mine, who has told me that he would just as soon that his name not be mentioned today . . . wanted a copy of the book himself so he sent cash in his letter and used a phony name, but gave his correct address. He got his book and I got my book. About a month later the Internal Revenue Service in Utah called a press conference and said that they had gone to the bank, seized Carl Bray's records, made photocopies of all the checks, made a list of the people who had purchased the book, and announced that they planned to audit every person who purchased the book.

Now they didn't audit me and they may not have had the manpower to audit all of those people, but it was clearly, in my mind, an attempt to prevent communication of ideas. People are already upset about whether the IRS is watching them, making lists. People are certainly not going to order a book if they think they are going to be audited by the IRS and their name is going to be put on a list.

Anyway, by the time this happened, another friend of mine in Salt Lake was arrested and charged with conspiracy to create public havoc. The reason he was arrested is the IRS has a little pink document that they put on the doors of business establishments when people don't voluntarily pay their taxes—it says we have the greatest tax system in the world because it is a voluntary tax system. (We all send our money in because we want to, right?) [Laughter]

But if you don't send it in voluntarily, they put this little pink sticker on your door that says, "This property has now been confiscated by the United States Government." Well, it's a nice funny little sticker. I'd like to put one on the front of my door just for the fun of it, although I have paid all my taxes.

My friend in Salt Lake was arrested and subsequently sentenced to six months in jail for having in his possession one of these stickers. He didn't use it for anything. He had it in his possession. He was charged with conspiracy to create public havoc because they thought that he might conspire with someone else to put these stickers on doors.

The main encounter that I have had with the IRS happened after some of these other things. A couple of years ago, when my particular story started, I had started to get upset about the level of taxes and all. I wrote a letter to the editor of the *Idaho State Journal* and that letter was published. It was a short letter, I won't read it right now, but it discusses the level of taxation in the country, the fact that according to the U.S. Census Bureau the poorest of all taxpayers, those that earned $2,000 a year in 1971 paid 50 percent of their income in taxes—

Mr. Hansen: It was a political letter regarding the levy of taxes.

Mr. Fullmer: Sure, that's all it was.

Mr. Hansen: I have copies. In fact, to assist a little, another member of Idaho's delegation and I wrote letters in your behalf to the Internal Revenue Service in Boise with regard to this problem. We received an acknowledgment from the IRS which you will tell us about. I just wanted to be sure that people understand this is a long problem that you asked help on over a period of several months—in fact, several years now—

Mr. Fullmer: Yes, it has been a couple of years now, really. So it was a letter about taxes, statistics and that sort of thing and I admitted that I was upset about the level of taxes and that I would like to do something about it and that I hope there were other people in town that would like to do something about it, too, and I hope to make contact with them and talk about it. I also suggested in my letter that if there was anyone who wanted to do something who didn't know quite what to do yet, that I could send them some information.

[Note: The letter reads as follows:]

Fellow Tax Slaves,

So you have paid your taxes for the year, complained to your friends, and now you can forget about them until next

April. Don't rest so easy. The politicians and special interest groups who want your money won't rest.

According to the April 19th issue of *The Wall Street Journal,* government at all levels now takes 43 percent of the gross national income. That money is not being taken from someone else, it's being taken from you! For instance, a study recently released by the U.S. Census Bureau reported that the poorest of all taxpayers (those earning less than $2,000 a year) lost 50 percent of their income to government in 1971.

Because of the hidden nature of most taxes the actual size of the burden is not immediately obvious. And this illustrates why more taxes on corporations won't help. The price of any product is set to recover the full cost of producing that product. Taxes are a production cost. If you pay the price, you pay the hidden taxes. In the final analysis, it is the individual, as an earner of income and a consumer, who pays all taxes.

If you are upset about the growing size of the burden that you carry for the politicians and want to do something about it, then write to me and I'll put you in touch with others who are already doing things. If you are not upset, then you deserve the slavery you will get (remember, if you are an average taxpayer you are 43 percent a slave already).

Laissez-Faire,
Larry Fullmer

Mr. Fullmer: Time passed, a week or so, and I didn't get any letters. I was a little bit disappointed, and then one day I got a letter and was really excited.

This is the letter I received, if you can see it. It is handwritten on plain white paper. Nothing official about it at all, just a short note, and it says, "Dear Mr. Fullmer, I read your letter of May 28th, copy enclosed, with interest. I am interested in learning more about what can be done with the tax situation. Sincerely, Ray Boone."

Well, I was really excited about it. I got all my stuff and wrote him a three-page letter about the different things that could be done and different organizations that could be contacted, and told him how I felt. And all this time acquaintances of mine would come up to me on the street and say, "Aren't you a little worried about having that letter published in the paper? Your name is probably on a list by now and you'll probably get audited." They'd say, "How do you know that letter that you received isn't from an IRS agent?" I would joke and laugh about it a little bit, but a number of people asked me that and I started to wonder—how do I know? So I called the IRS office and asked for Ray Boone and he answered the phone. [Laughter]

He didn't identify himself as an agent for the IRS in the letter. As a matter of fact he did everything that he could do to indicate that he was a sincerely concerned private citizen who shared my views and responded to my letter. In principle, he could have come to my home and identified himself as someone who was concerned, sat down on my couch and talked to me for hours. It would have been the same kind of thing.

Okay, so I sent him some information. Some of it was valuable to me. When I found out he was an IRS agent, I called him back and asked that my material be returned to me. He told me he couldn't, that it had been thrown away, and that he couldn't return it. That upset me a little bit. I would like to have had it back. That got me thinking about lists and I decided to write to you, Congressman Hansen, and find out about these lists, to find out if my name was on a list, if it had been on a list, if they had been destroyed or whatever. I did write, and was informed they were supposed to have been destroyed in January, I wrote in April. Senator Church and yourself wrote the IRS office in Boise and I discovered that three months after the lists had all been destroyed and the files all had been destroyed, they still had a file on me. They also had all the material in it that they said had been thrown away. This was three months after the National Director said the lists had been destroyed. And now, you know, you've had people here talking about lists right now—and they said three or four years ago that they were never going to keep them again.

I imagine my time is about up. There are some other things I could say, but I'll cut it off here.

Mr. Hansen: I think it is important that you read the letter that the IRS sent to me: because they not only admitted that your material was still available, but they said right in one paragraph, "We didn't find anything significant so we have closed the investigation." Obviously you were investigated.

So, I guess what it really boils down to is write a letter to the editor, complain about your taxes, complain about the expense of government and you get yourself investigated by the Internal Revenue Service. That is, I think, the bottom line, isn't it?

Mr. Fullmer: I really hate to make this public because I am afraid a lot of other people who might otherwise say something about high taxes are now not going to do it. I'd just about like to keep it a secret so at least some people keep talking about how they don't like the level of taxes in the country.

There is one last thing that I would like to bring out here. In the *Idaho State Journal* on the ninth of January, we have Leon Levine, the Public Affairs Officer in Washington, D.C., defending past Idaho Director Martin. He says that agents absolutely have not contacted individuals who complained of high taxes or placed them under investigation—which they certainly did in my case. Levine says, "You can say that while Martin was Director in the Boise District, he certainly did not engage in any way, shape or form in activities that could have been labeled improper and he could in no way have condoned such actions."

But I have a letter here from Martin which was written in 1975 about my situation, and in order to condone IRS action, he says, "This was in a period when various tax resistance movements were growing in Idaho and considerable areas of noncompliance with tax laws were being discovered." He also says that literature they took from me was considered by his office to be without value (which is interesting since they had had it in a permanent file for almost two years).—They just keep lists. They keep files. This letter entirely represents an attempt to condone Ray Boone's activities. There is no indication that it was an incorrect activity on their part, no indication that Ray Boone had been censored, nothing like that. It was Martin condoning what Levine says the IRS does not condone.

Mr. Hansen: What it boils down to is the doctrine of entrapment, I think, where you induce people under unknowing circumstances to give information on themselves that they possibly would not have done if they had known who they were dealing with.

Mr. Fullmer: That's right. If there's an IRS agent in the room right now, he won't identify himself because there are a lot of people here (and he might want to get their names on a list) who might not talk if they know that he is here.

Mr. Hansen: Larry, I appreciate very much your appearing. I think this testimony was significant in the attitudinal situation we are trying to establish and I guess it gets around to the point again that it is one thing to have a law, it is another thing to have a regulation, but we still have got to have balanced people administering the law.

10

An Ounce of Justice and a Pound of Flesh

In an effort to provide an independent, neutral "arbitrator" or judge in disagreements between taxpayers and the Internal Revenue Service, the Congress in 1924 established what was then called the Board of Tax Appeals. This board was reconstituted in 1926 and in 1942 was renamed the Tax Court. The Tax Court is located in Washington, D.C., but its sixteen judges travel "circuit" or hold hearings in various localities throughout the country. The Tax Court judges are appointed by the President but have, themselves, the power to appoint "special judges" to serve in their place. As originally envisioned, the Tax Court was to have functioned much like a small-claims court. It was, basically, an informal hearing wherein an impartial judge would listen to both sides and then try to strike a compromise solution between the taxpayer and the IRS.

But those days are long past. Now the Tax Court is a sophisticated legalistic nightmare. Many taxpayers who enter the Tax Court expect to be judged by a jury. This never happens. The Tax Court is regulated by a special branch of civil law which, contrary to all Western legal tradition, denies the citizen not only his right to a jury but also his right to appeal to a higher court of law. Once the taxpayer is in the Tax Court system he usually discovers that "this is it." The decision of the judge of the Tax Court is final unless the citizen pays the (often arbitrary) assessment of the judge and then sues the government to have his money refunded. The citizen can, if he prefers, refuse to pay the tax assessed in Tax Court—but in this instance the taxpayer is hauled off to the criminal courts. He finally is able to get a trial by jury—but not for his disputed income taxes.

Refusal to pay taxes assessed by the Tax Court is a felony. The taxpayer who has taken this course of action stands accused as a common criminal for refusal to obey the orders of the Tax Court. Even if the citizen is able to win his new case in the criminal courts, rarely will the fees of his lawyers and accountants be reimbursed to him. In any event, his reputation and standing in the community, after the long ordeal, are always diminished or destroyed.

The IRS has done its best to take advantage of a system already heavily weighted in its favor. Tax Court judges, far from being comfortably impartial, have been, in every instance I was able to determine, previously employed by the federal government. *Ten of the sixteen Tax Court judges today are former employees of the Internal Revenue Service.* Four other former IRS people are special hearing judges. Citizens who believe that they are assured of fair treatment in a Tax Court have been sadly misled. They may indeed find evenhanded consideration or they may find kangaroo justice with no real appeal rights—it's a grotesque game of making people play Russian roulette with their own rights.

Furthermore, the Internal Revenue Service sees the great potential of the criminal courts in the harassment of taxpayers. The funds available to the IRS for prosecution are, practically speaking, unlimited, while the money on hand to the taxpayer to defend himself is usually scarce. In the following interoffice memo, an IRS official reminds an IRS tax lawyer of the power of the agency to "litigate" or to keep an innocent citizen in the courts.

November 19, 1976

E. Clay Freed, Attorney
Regional Counsel, Salt Lake City Office
Group Manager, 1004
Boise District Office

[Name deleted]
We have received your disagreement as to the issuance of statutory notices and request that you reconsider.
[Taxpayer information deleted by source.]
It is stated that you do not wish to litigate a case you may lose. However, failure to attempt litigation will foster their program far more than a loss in court. *At least by litigating, the Taxpayer is forced to produce the necessary substantiation. In addition, the Taxpayer is committed to spend time and money defending his position. Perhaps the inconvenience alone will inspire future compliance.*

If this case is rejected, we will be at a loss as to where to proceed. Further efforts by us will result in an incomplete and inaccurate profit and loss. The bank would have to be summoned for copies of all cancelled checks which would be futile, costly, and a waste of Audit resources.

If Regional Counsel will not back us on this case, the only reasonable solution would be to give this Taxpayer a complete victory and throw in the towel.

Hoping you will reconsider your position.

Trenton Fewkes
[Emphasis added.]

There is another upshot to the arrogance of the Internal Revenue Service which needs public airing. The frustrations and hardships caused by this agency have now been discussed at length; but there are also painful personal and emotional consequences which result from a "close encounter" with the IRS. People, decent people. are often terribly hurt by these bureaucratic brutes.

The testimony which follows, taken almost verbatim from transcripts of my *ad hoc* hearings on the IRS in 1978, provides a typical example of the gross injustices too often perpetrated by the Tax Court on American citizens and a stunning instance of the cruelty of the IRS. I might add that this case is not unusual. Almost identical situations have been discovered in another area of Idaho, in Salt Lake City, Utah, in Arlington, Virginia, and in other cities across the nation. One cannot adequately express the anguish and despair I detected in the faces and the voices of these good women during these hearings. Perhaps their own words will convey these feelings.

Statement of Dorothy Rutledge

Mrs. Rutledge: Thank you, Mr. Hansen.

I am not used to talking to an audience with the exception of the one experience I had speaking in front of the judge in Pocatello last Halloween, which seemed quite an appropriate day.

The first thing that I might say is that I have come here with a bunch of legal documents. I might also say that these legal documents have had to be done by we girls ourselves. We have not had finances to have legal counsel so we've had to do a great deal of learning and studying in order to be able to prepare these legal documents ourselves. I do want you to know that everything I'll testify about I do have personal firsthand knowledge of. It is a long story—it has gone over three years now and there have been over three Christmases involved.

It started out when one gal came to work one day. (We knew we were being audited. They had been doing this for a period of probably eight or nine months since the first assessment.) IRS agents came into the cafe that morning, and caught a new waitress who was sixteen years old and demanded that she empty her pockets. One of the other girls saw this happening and informed the new girl that she didn't have to do that.

A few days later, another one of the girls came to work very, very upset. She had just received an assessment from the IRS for $3,200 for taxes on alleged tip income for two years. The girl had claimed her tips and she had paid her taxes. She worked eight, ten and sometimes twelve hours, six days a week, very hard. She would go home with her knees swollen up so big she could hardly walk. She has a son who has a serious case of diabetes and takes care of a young daughter as well. When I saw the ridiculously large amount that the IRS demanded I knew something had to be done. I knew that it was wrong.

If they had come in and said, "You owe $300 or $400," we would have given in. We were scared enough. We would probably have run right down and paid it. But $3,200 was just so far out.

We began looking for help. We knew there had to be help when there is something that wrong—you've got to have some way to make it right.

Mr. Hansen: How many of you are there that are involved?

Mrs. Rutledge: We have—counting our husbands who have never received tips in their lives except when you tell them it's time to wash their hair or something—[laughter] 24 persons. There were many more involved at that time. We sat out in the coffee shop just now figuring in five cases our total bill from the IRS was $12,000, George. That is for five of us.

Mr. Hansen: That was their assessment?

Mrs. Rutledge: Their assessment against us. Some of us work part-time. Their assessment against us is more than our total wages for the three years combined.

Now one day we did this, we wanted to ask Bruce Dopp, an IRS agent, some questions. We sat for an hour waiting for him. None of the other agents there wanted to talk to us. When he finally came into the room, he sat down and he said, "Now, if you want to talk about the Constitution, I have nothing to say to you. If you have something else you want to talk about, fine."

It became quite apparent and quite frustrating to realize that you were innocent and there was absolutely nothing you could do to prove it.

About this time we found that there was no way that we were going to be able to come to a settlement. We weren't going to admit to having made more than we had made, so we asked for our appellate conferences and at that time they were denied because there were not 180 days left on the statute of limitations. We wouldn't sign the waiver, which would allow them to go back into our taxes as far as they wanted to—we felt that we couldn't sign that waiver form. Our only alternative at that time was to have them issue the ninety-day letter, which you must have in order to get into the Tax Court.

When you read the Tax Court petition, and you've never had any legal experience in your entire life, and you get a ninety-day letter that says you owe $3,200—it is a very frightening experience. We found that it also was a very costly experience. Now it is very costly to hire a lawyer, but believe me, when you have to buy this book and that book and this rule book, and 101 other things to defend yourself—that is costly, too. We all donated some money so that some of us could go to seminars, and do a few other things, so that we could learn. We crammed it in so fast there was a time I thought they could just haul me off to the asylum. I think that I would really have been happy there because I soaked up legal information until I could speak "legalese" just about as well as the lawyer could. [Laughter] The ninety-day letter came and it cost us each about $55 apiece by the time we got our Tax Court petitions filed and our filing fees for Tax Court and so forth.

Then sixty days later here came their answer to our petitions. They charged each and every one of us with fraud—out-and-out fraud. We lived under that charge for a year's time and then at stipulation conferences almost a year later, the attorney sat in front of us and said, "Oh, I dropped those charges because we think they exist but we can't prove them." So, a year later the fraud charges were dropped.

Then under the Freedom of Information Act, I wrote a postcard and asked for all the information they had in their files on me. Oh here came my ugly flyer that they had in their files on me but they also said they had a form 3949, which is a *criminal* form, which I was denied access to. I would like very much to know what is on that criminal form for Dorothy Rutledge.

The form 3949 didn't mean too much to me at that time. I found out more about it later and then I became even more concerned about it—what it did actually say about me. However, in order to find a few of these things out—and we've been told other things and I can't go into everything today, though I'd love to—we filed sets of interrogatories, which are questions that they are supposed to have to answer fully and completely. Of course, when one of us did one thing we all were in the same position, so naturally, you file fourteen sets of interrogatories—it's not our fault that we got fourteen identical ninety-day letters, that we were charged fourteen identical times with fraud. So fourteen sets of interrogatories went, fourteen answers came back that didn't answer anything.

We couldn't get the court to set a place of trial or anything. I'm sure that the Tax Court does not have a "granted" stamp because everything came back *denied, denied, denied, denied.* Everything. [Mrs. Rutledge began crying at this point.] The only thing we ever had granted was what I call my "damn dam" petition, and I filed a motion for an extension of time to do something for the following reason: the damn Teton dam broke, [laughter] and that was back in five days stamped "granted."

Okay, we got nothing out of the interrogatories, but there was another route to go, request for admissions. Here you make statements and they can either deny or admit. The IRS didn't like it so they put in a motion for a protective order to protect them from us and our harassment or coercion. [Laughter] And it was granted—with no hearing. (Now that is not a proper exercise in law. The civil rules of procedure show that protective orders are almost never granted and never without a hearing, and in the [unintelligible] trial in Denver, Colorado, Judge Winter absolutely denied a protective order to stop them.)

They granted themselves a protective order and denied us any further discovery at all. Period. No more discovery under Rules 70 through 72 inclusive and Rule 90 and Rule 182 would not apply in this case. And then they assigned a special judge. Now I had been assured by one of our Congressmen, not yourself, that the judge at the Tax Court would be fair because the President of the United States appoints him, but he failed to tell me that the judge he appoints can then send anybody he wants to act as judge that day. The man we saw hadn't been judge before, they even forgot to call him judge. They called him "Commissioner." More often he was Commissioner than they would remember to call him judge.

That's the judge that was sent to take care of our case after we had been denied discovery completely and totally. He set the hearing at the time of trial on the 18th of July in Pocatello, Idaho. Everything had been granted the IRS and denied the waitresses.

Now we knew at that point we had been denied discovery. We tried three different times to take that protective order off. (Judge Winter absolutely denied it against Grand Rush's in Denver, Colorado, as an insult to the court.) But in our case, it was granted to the IRS.

At this time I want to tell you something about stipulation conferences that they forced us to go to and then said we did not even try to comply with. I will tell you about one—the first waitress who went in for the stipulation conference met with Ralph Jones who was the attorney for the IRS. She sat down at the table. (We had learned by this time that you take witnesses. We had learned that under their own rules and in their own confidential tax law guide you do have the right to a tape recorder and if you go in with it and they know you are going to use it they don't try to stop you.) We had our two witnesses and this girl came in and sat down, scared as she could be. Sure, we always were scared. It's frightening, specially for women. I happened to be the witness at that case and she sat down and the lawyer for the IRS took his pad of paper and a pencil and he threw them at her and he said, "You sign me a waiver of your rights to privacy or I won't talk to you." Well, she sat there so upset she didn't know what to do and so I said, "Surely, she has a right to a witness in this room, doesn't she?" And he said, "No, this conference is . . ." [Mrs. Rutledge crying at this point.] I've got it on tape, George, I've got a whole bag full of tapes. This man told me that I had no rights in Tax Court that a criminal would have in a criminal trial. I'm sorry I can't continue with this. I am going to call Marilyn Giles up here because the tape we have on their conference is a horror story. It couldn't be any worse if we were in Russia.

Mr. Hansen: Marilyn, come on up.

Mrs. Rutledge: This is Marilyn Giles. Now I want you to know right now, they've combined our papers, they've combined our suits, but my name is Dorothy Rutledge and this is Marilyn Giles, but in the newspaper I was Marilyn Rutledge. [Laughter and crying] When they combine your names, then I object.

Statement of Marilyn Giles

Mrs. Giles: As Dorothy said, we learned very early to protect ourselves with tape recorders, with the witnesses, because we have found them to be liars. They often tried to entrap us by the way they made their questions—I'm sorry my voice is shaking like crazy.

Mr. Hansen: Marilyn, I'm not hostile, so don't worry—

Mrs. Giles: I think it's the microphone, I'm not afraid of you, George—even though you are big. [Laughter]

You know, early on this became a moral issue with us or we would never have been able to proceed, because from the studying we did, the things we learned, we found out what jeopardy our Constitution was in. We each knew in our hearts it is our duty to God to protect this Constitution or then we would be the ones at fault, not those who have violated the Constitution—we who did not protect it. So this became a moral issue and I resent very much being labeled as a tax protester when what I am protesting is procedure, their methods of operation, so every time it comes out in the paper "tax protesters do this," and it is always us labeled protesters—I wish some of you other guys would get your name in the papers. [Laughter]

One of the first things that I asked in my hearing is that we should have a word of prayer. Mr. Jones informed me he didn't give a damn (I'm sorry, that's what he said) what I did, he was an atheist. We wished we had been sharper on our feet and asked him how he took his oath of office if he is in fact an atheist, but we forgot to ask him that little question.

We didn't realize what a Pandora's box we were opening when we started this. When we got our assessment for John and I it was only $875. I was working part-time. It would have been cheaper for us to have paid it, but, like I said, it then became a moral issue and we couldn't do anything but fight and then still face our children.

I, incidentally, have ten children and I could have used all that money that they said I made. [Laughter]

Mr. Hansen: You had ten children at that time under age?

Mrs. Giles: Oh, I've got them all ages. [Laughter] But Mr. Jones said a few interesting things at that stipulation conference. He said that he had been warned about us before he ever got here and that he knew how these conferences were going to go before we ever walked in the door.

I'm going to read a conversation that I took down from the tape we made of that. It starts out with my saying,

If you have drafted your stipulations, may we see a copy of them, please?

Mr. Jones: I have mailed them back to Salt Lake to be typed.

Myself: Then we will receive a copy?

Mr. Jones: You will receive a copy very shortly.

My husband, John: You mean, they will be the same as anyone else's? How did you know what they were?

Mr. Jones: How did I know what what was?

John: The stipulations, you said you just mailed them back.

Mr. Jones: I drafted them based upon how I knew these conferences were turning out.

Myself: Then we were prejudged before we got in here.

Mr. Jones: No, because of the stipulation on how each person was coming in.

In fact, that's double-talk. I had trouble taking it down it was such double-talk. But you realize what he is saying here—that though they've claimed all along that we were not ready and would not cooperate during the stipulation conferences, that we in fact were ready. One of our stipulations on our list of stipulations was in fact that the Constitution is the supreme law of the land. He would not even stipulate that the Constitution was the supreme law of the land.

Mrs. Rutledge: Well, I forgot to mention the fact that in my assessment I was assessed for tipping during the three months when my right arm was in a full-length cast. I had not even been able to work as a waitress, plus many, many hours that several of us worked in the capacity of hostess or cashier where there were no tips involved. We were charged straight through 12½ percent, the IRS claims, of the total intake of the West Bank Cafe.

Mr. Hansen: I saw affidavits in your material to the effect that you were not in a tip-gathering circumstance for periods of time like this. When you brought that to their attention, what happened?

Mrs. Rutledge: They denied all of our affidavits. Can you believe it? We have sent affidavits to the effect when we tried to get into the Appeals Court. I know what they rely on is the fact that you don't have the money to fight them and at this point they pretty well had us broke, so we filed affidavits with them hoping we could get into the Appeals Court without having to pay all the sums first. There are other reasons why we should have been allowed that.

They would send them back, "They have no bearing in this case. We have filed them in your correspondence file."

Now we come right up to the time of—by the way, Mr.

Jones definitely did tell us that the Constitution did not apply in this case. On more occasions than one he told us that our interpretation of the Constitution and theirs was entirely different and that justice had no bearing in this case. And those statements we do have on tape.

Okay, now, we're within two weeks of the time set for trial. We have been denied discovery. They've granted everything to themselves and denied us everything. We know that summary judgment is set for the beginning of the trial session in Pocatello on the 18th of July. We have one thing we can do and that is hope that another court will rule that if we haven't been allowed equal and nondiscriminate use of the rules of the Tax Court that we shouldn't be forced to go into the court under those situations. There is no way you can protect yourself in that situation.

As a matter of fact, if they would have looked at the government's case against Judge Ritter, the government ruled that your trial was actually without a court because of Judge Ritter's action and we felt like this certainly applied in our case, too. So here, again, we dug deep. By this time girls were beginning to borrow money to be able to help pay their share of expenses and we went to Boise. By this time I also had to quit my job, although I couldn't afford to do so, in order to pursue my "legal profession" full-time. [Laughter]

We ran to Boise to file a suit saying, hey, look, somebody at least help us get our constitutional rights reinstated so that we can go into that court with the full use of the rules of that court. So at that time the suit was filed, we had filed a motion with the Tax Court to vacate or set aside that trial date until such time as this other issue could be litigated.

The first semblance of due process we ever experienced was when Judge Callister said, okay, we'll have a hearing.

The IRS immediately filed a motion to dismiss our suit against them. Judge Callister says, okay, let's have a hearing.

That's the first semblance of due process we ever saw. I went down there, and I spent six solid weeks getting ready for that until I hurt all over, and, believe me, when you talk about financial problems, we were all experiencing them by that time. I think I was able to effectively hit everything—everything that they cited in their motion to dismiss had to do with cases where people were trying to move a tax question from the jurisdiction of the tax court to the jurisdiction of the federal district court.

We did a beautiful job of discounting any of their arguments and yet the day before Christmas I got a notice that Judge Callister had granted their dismissal. I have now put in a notice of rehearing. I hope that it is because I didn't make my position perfectly clear and that we will still have that opportunity, because there is no judge, there is no court, there is not one person who has the right to deny a Constitutional right.

Mrs. Giles: Right now I might add a little story. There are so many I'd like to but I won't have time. We have one little lady involved in this case who is sixty years old who has a husband on a kidney machine. She is the only one working in her family. The ninety-day letter itself says if you petition-the tax court then they may not go ahead and assess or collect any taxes.

Mrs. Rutledge: That's right. In this particular instance, even though she was in the Tax Court at that time and they had guaranteed that they could not then assess or collect any tax—the refunds this lady and her husband had coming for the next year were withheld. It was not returned to them although they needed that money very badly. They had a statement come from the government saying IRS had applied it to this alleged tax due for 1972 and it had cleared that up and part of it had been applied to 1973 and instead of almost $1,200 she now only owed them a little over $300. Now, mind you, they still haven't even proved that she owes it. But the day before Christmas she got a bill from the IRS and they were billing her for the full amount again. They hadn't even given her credit for the money that they had held out illegally.

Now, let me tell you another thing. I know of three instances where there was not Christmas this year in these girls' homes. I know it for a fact because I've got a friend living in my house because she can't heat her house. I had a friend bring me a car the other day to drive because I didn't have any way to get around. We have gone through everything we had to fight this, George, and I know you can understand this because you face the same thing, but I'd like these people to know how easy it is to get in that position so quickly.

Well, these girls have gone through this without ever complaining. They've told no man, they've just done it because we know the Lord wants us to do it and we know we will win because it is Him that wants us to do it. We knew that—and it was known in the beginning, we just had to decide what side was wrong. And I can't even say it without chills going through me because we have such a testimony of that.

They can't stop me by threatening me. They can't stop me by putting me in jail. But two days before Christmas when I had to go to those girls and say we've each got to raise $35 more in order to have this in time so we won't default, that almost stopped me. That's the hardest thing I ever did. I would like to have taken some money to those girls but I had to go tell them I needed more. [Crying. End of Testimony.]

[Note: Some of the waitresses in this case have settled with the IRS; other cases are still in litigation. Dorothy Rutledge's name appears on an IRS violence list I have in my possession.]

As was stated earlier, the waitresses in Idaho Falls are not alone in this fight against the rough-riding bureaucrats of the IRS. I have heard the same touching story from waitresses in Boise to Arlington, Virginia. The "little people" are being bullied by the tax collector. One of my sources in the IRS, familiar with the case of the Idaho Falls waitresses, stated:

"Just like on these waitresses, you know, why pick this area when this is probably the lowest tipping area in Idaho? Doesn't seem to make good sense unless the IRS wanted to create a problem.

"Now I made a special point to check on the waitresses, which is a matter of public record, it is in the courts and in the newspapers. I don't know how many waitresses there were—probably about forty waitresses. Apparently from what was said in the Tax Court proceeding and in the district courts, there are about forty or so waitresses now who have just quit filing tax returns and are filing what they call "vacant tax returns." If anyone defends these women then the IRS is likely to come back and say, 'Well, these people haven't even filed tax returns in the last three or four years.' The thing is, they were all good, honest taxpayers, and they were filing tax returns before the IRS came in and rode roughshod over them.

"Now they have no more faith in IRS. If IRS has done this with forty waitresses, then they come in and ride roughshod over all the Teton flood victims, instead of forty tax protestors, you're going to 8,000. It is perfectly obvious that somebody back there has decided this is a good way to create tax protestors, and then they can create a problem.

"Then they can bring in enough agents to have an army of their own. The important thing is . . . their policies are creating a situation here that is harming not only the citizens, but it is harming IRS."

Further Injustices and Irritations

1. *The Appraisal Frustration.* In one case, a man who had acquired a painting for a relatively small amount decided to

give it to his church. Just as with money itself, he was entitled to deduct a charitable donation equal to the money value of the painting.

As is customary, he had the painting appraised. The IRS rejected his deduction. He had the painting appraised again. Again IRS was not satisfied. Only after multiple appraisals and a near approach to a court battle did he get his deduction.

In the same region, at the same time, another man was giving a similar painting away. He got his deduction without contest. Had the IRS reformed? If not, what was the difference in the two cases? The only difference was that the second man was giving his painting to a government agency, not to a religious group.

2. *Waiving Your Rights Under Threat of Extortion.* The use of extension of time (or waiver of the defense) of the expiration of the statute of limitations is both widespread and notorious in the IRS collection process. The classic case is one in which a taxpayer is under audit or investigation for a potential tax liability for years some time in the past. A year for which the IRS hopes to catch him in a tax deficiency is about to fall by reason of limitation of the time within which an assessment may be made.

The agent in this predicament simply offers the taxpayer a Catch-22 alternative. He can sign a waiver of the defense of statute of limitation or the agent will make an assessment for that year without reference to any evidence then in his possession. If the taxpayer signs the extension, he extends the time of his harassment by the IRS for at least a year with no guarantee that he will not later be asked to extend again on the same extortionate terms or that the assessment, when it is made, will be any less arbitrary.

To understand the process better, it must be contrasted

with regular civil litigation. If a statute is about to expire in legitimate courts, the plaintiff (the party in the position of the IRS) must make the hard decision whether to litigate with less than clear evidence and run the risk of being dismissed for failure to state a sufficient cause of action or to drop the cause of action. The IRS procedure reverses the normal relationship of the parties in that the IRS when faced with the same choice as legitimate plaintiffs, can merely act as though the case had already been tried and find you guilty, thereby forcing you to burn money to appeal an assessment (judgment) based admittedly on no evidence.

The principle of a statute of limitations is that no one should be subject to contingent liability for crimes or civil wrongs indefinitely. There must be a cutoff time when he can be sure of his position. It includes the idea that the plaintiff or prosecutor has a duty to pursue his remedies within some reasonable time. For this purpose, Congress put a time limit on tax liability.

It is this fundamental and valuable idea which the IRS destroys by the coercion of extension. Were it not for the IRS preferred situation in which it has its own process, its own courts, and its own rules of collection, no one in his right mind would agree to an extension. If the IRS were forced into a legitimate court either on arbitrary assessment or on the issue of the voluntariness of the waivers, it would lose hands down every time. A consent based on the threat of extorting money from the signer of the waiver probably could not even be litigated by the IRS.

3. *The Let-You-Hang-Twisting-in-the-Wind Syndrome.* No single case could exemplify this technique. It has a thousand forms. A taxpayer receives a notice from the IRS. Usually it says that the addressee owes the IRS money. The taxpayer writes and asks for particulars. Months usually pass. Finally

an answer comes. It usually does not answer anything. The now-worried target writes again. More months. Then a response which puts the victim to more anguish. Sometimes these writing bees go on literally for years.

Among the variations of this device is the you-owe-us-money ploy. In one recent case, a taxpayer got such a notice. He sat down and immediately wrote out a check for the amount demanded and sent it to the IRS. He got his return receipt and then relaxed. But the IRS had other ideas. They sent him another letter announcing that they were deducting the amount from his refund check for the current year. When he got his checks back from the bank that month, the victim found that the IRS had cashed his check more than a week before they sent him the second notice. As I write, he is still trying to get back his double payment—and he still doesn't know what he owed the money for in the first place. Oh, by the way, he filed his return on the short form 1040 and the amount involved was considerably less than $100.

Another is the don't-catch-them-in-an-error problem. If the IRS sends you a bad-news letter in which they say that you owe them $10 plus $2 interest and $2 penalty for a total of $12, don't tell them that they are wrong in their math. You may go into the computer for permanent annual audit. Call and ask them to compute the total because you are about to write out your check. Help them to find the error by themselves.

The technical-question variation is also bad news. In one case, a man had his sewer repaired when it broke. The IRS said that the repair was not a repair, that it was a capital improvement. At the lower level, he got two different determinations. At the appeal level, he was put back to square one with a reassertion of the repair as capital investment. In support of that, the IRS man was careless enough to send a part of the IRS manual to support his determination. As you might guess, the manual supported the taxpayer, which he was not slow to point out. As you might also guess, no change has yet been made in the determination. But the worst of the story is not the incompetence. Everyone who deals with government expects that. It is the sloth. In our little sewer story, the most important element is that the victim always wrote back within a very few days, never even as long as a week. The IRS let as long as seven months go by between answers.

It was pointed out earlier that hiring lawyers and accountants to do battle with the IRS is a very expensive undertaking. Therefore, this course of action is usually open only to a person of some means. At this high-powered, big-money level of operation, the IRS and the legal/accounting profession cooperate quite well. IRS civil procedures, which are so flexible as to vary from case to case (even in nearly identical cases), keep hundreds of well-paid attorneys and CPAs busily employed creating tax hedges for America's affluent. In these instances the IRS and the tax professionals usually get along just fine. When differences do appear the wealthy do not hesitate to engage the IRS in lengthy court battles—after all, the legal and accounting costs are likely to be deductible as business expenses.

On the other hand, the IRS can, and does, bring enormous pressure on the lawyers and CPAs who handle the tax cases of America's lower- and middle-income citizens. An attorney defending a victim of IRS intimidation must ask himself how far he is willing to go to defend this particular client. The lawyer or accountant who goes too far soon discovers that the IRS is auditing his other clients, family, and friends. When the IRS, with all its totalitarian methods, finds that it is still unable to convict the taxpayer, it begins to strike out at the people around him. There are several such incidences, but one tells it well. The typical trials of one taxpayer, as seen through the eyes of his accountant and his attorneys, is an interesting case in point. This is the story of Jack Wright.

Statement of Jack Wright's Accountant

Mr. Merrill Rudd: At the time Mr. Wright was being audited a revenue agent from Idaho Falls came to my office unannounced and demanded that I show him what I had in my file to do with Jack Wright. In talking with the agent, I asked him if he had talked to Jack yet to let him know that he was being audited and he said no, he hadn't. He had come directly to me because he knew I prepared the return.

So I said, "Well, I feel like I owe enough respect to Jack to let him know he is being audited and so—"

Mr. Hansen: You mean Jack didn't know at that time?

Mr. Rudd: Not according to the revenue agent. I didn't talk to Jack. But the agent demanded what I had in my file and I said, "I have nothing in my file except my pencil copy of the return that you already have a copy of." And he said, "I want to see your file anyway." And because of his attitude, I refused to show him the file, except I did assure him that he already had everything that was in my file. He returned to Idaho Falls at that time and told me that I would be subpoenaed to appear in Idaho Falls and repeat the same things down there. This was during tax season and I didn't have anything to give them. I did not respond—I didn't go to the Idaho Falls office. When I didn't appear, they called and said that I had missed the appointment. I again told them that I had nothing to show them, they already had everything that I had. I just figured the thing was dropped.

About six months later I received a letter from the Director of Practice from Washington, D.C. He said that my right to practice before the Internal Revenue Service was being challenged. I wrote back to him and explained the situation and made several telephone calls and tried to get him to understand my position. All I got was that I had violated a section in the law that regulates a person's right to practice with the IRS. I requested a hearing in this area so I could talk with them face to face. I got nowhere. They said, "If you want to appear you will have to come to Washington, D.C."

Mr. Hansen: At your expense?

Mr. Rudd: Yes. And a country boy in Washington, D.C.—you know, I've been there, of course, but I didn't know my way around or anything so I didn't go. They then suggested that I subject myself to a voluntary suspension to practice for ninety days. This really didn't mean anything to me because all this covers is my right to appear and discuss a client's case with the IRS. At that time, I had no cases to discuss, I had no clients that were being audited, and so I said, well, what the heck. I would rather do that than take the time and expense to go back to Washington, D.C., and heaven knows what I would run into there.

So I agreed to the ninety-day suspension. After the ninety days they wrote and said, "You are now allowed to practice again."

Mr. Hansen: The Lord hath spoken. [Laughter]

Mr. Rudd: In December of that year, twenty-five, or at least twenty-five, of my clients were audited. Twenty-five of my clients received on the same day a letter saying they were being audited. It was right before tax season. I asked one of the IRS auditors one time who was ordering these audits and why they got this list of my clients. I explained to him what had happened to me. He said, "It's possible that is the reason they got the list."

Mr. Hansen: Isn't this an unusually high—in your visitations with other accountants—percentage of audits among your clientele?

Mr. Rudd: Yes. Particularly on one day. [Laughter] It was

just the harassment of going to the client and the client on being audited saying, "What do I do?" And so I had to take the time and effort to present a case for each of them.

Mr. Hansen: In other words, you obviously had done the job pretty well if there were no changes but it was the idea that they just keep coming.

Mr. Rudd: Right.

Statement of Mr. Wright's Attorney

Mr. Gordon Thatcher: I have been authorized by one of these gentlemen to tell a little bit about his case. This is Jack Wright. We became interested in the case (and I guess I'll just talk very frankly) from two situations, one from a religious point of view because I held a position in the LDS Church and one from a legal point of view. There had been information which had come to local church leaders, like myself, that some tax protesters had used the Mormon Church as a justification for their tax protest. So officials in the church called some of them in to make unmistakably clear that the church in the bulletin had said, pay your taxes (which was my position), file your returns, pay your taxes, obey the law.

Jack Wright came in later to the law office. Now because of IRS harassment, he had filed a withholding statement which claimed thirty exemptions or something, I don't remember the details, and then stated right on it that this was a protest. It was a withholding statement, not a W-2, so that they would not withhold tax. Now Jack felt, as some protesters did, that it was unconstitutional for the government to require an employer to withhold. He didn't like the withholding. His method of getting the attention of the government was to claim excessive exemptions. But he put right on his exemption form why he was doing this so there was no deceit or fraud or subterfuge in it. And then he went to the IRS after there had been a meeting in which the church's position had been stated and said, "Look, if my church leaders feel I'm wrong on this, I want to get out of the lawsuit." (The status of the lawsuit was that he had been prosecuted criminally and had been convicted by a jury—found guilty. He had appealed, himself as attorney, to the Court of Appeals in San Francisco, the Ninth Circuit Court of Appeals. The appeal was pending. He had come into our office and asked that we help him put a brief together.)

Mr. Hansen: May I interrupt?

Mr. Thatcher: Yes.

Mr. Hansen: At whose expense did he carry forth all this effort in this protest to make his point?

Mr. Thatcher: Well, at his own. So Jack came in to our office again and said, "Check with the government and I'll dismiss the appeal. See if they will eliminate the jail sentence. They've made the point. They've convicted me; there's a fine." So we called for him. I talked to (I think it was) an Assistant U.S. Attorney who checked with Internal Revenue Service. He came back and said, "All right, if Jack Wright will go on television and over television will announce to the public that the Internal Revenue Service was wholly right in this matter and in essence had not made any mistakes"—I mean they wanted him to say that the Internal Revenue Service never made mistakes, as I remember—"and will admit that he was wholly wrong and apologize for what he had done, then they would drop the jail sentence and he could dismiss the appeal."

I've got to say that I presented that to Mr. Wright and, of course, he said, "It would be lying for me to say that." He refused to do it and I've got to be frank with you, I didn't think he ought to have to do that. In other words, it's one thing to—

Mr. Hansen: For what other crimes do you have to do that? Usually you take your penalty, you go to jail, or you pay your fine or something, but to have to do on TV and say the Bureau of Reclamation is right, for example, or somebody else is right—

Mr. Thatcher: That's what they required in the deal. That was the condition that was laid down. So I told Jack, "I don't think you ought to have to do that." He then carried the appeal himself—and lost.

11

Are You
on Their
Hit List?

The most damning thing the Internal Revenue Service has done is to maintain fabricated "hit lists" of people prone to violence. These lists are not just "enemy lists" like those in the White House which caused such a stir during Watergate days. And they are not just lists of people to be contacted for a tax audit.

These hit lists are the trigger for the Gestapo mentality of the IRS to justify violence against American citizens. To get on the list, people don't have to be violent, the IRS just has to say they are.

A "violence list" gives the IRS an excuse to institute armed searches, send out SWAT teams, and provoke dangerous confrontations which could get a few or even a lot of people killed.

And don't think that enterprising bureaucrats haven't thought of the idea that these so-called violence lists are a ticket to getting more personnel and building a bigger empire. especially if an emotionally charged incident of bloodshed just happens in this kind of government-contrived pressure cooker.

The worst part of the whole thing is that these IRS violence lists are manufactured and phony. As I have already said, I have yet to find a known violent person among the hundreds of names on the IRS lists.

In Chapter 2 it was clearly established that the IRS keeps such hit lists. Anyone who disputes or criticizes the IRS is likely to end up on such a list, but you can also get there without any involvement at all.

These lists perform two functions. First, just by their existence, they intimidate the citizens. But they serve an even more ominous purpose—they are advance justification for the day when IRS agents adopt violence as a primary means of achieving total power over the taxpayer.

This is a fraudulent but highly explosive tactic which should scare Americans into cleaning up the IRS now. The planned armed search on St. Anthony and the violence portrayed in parts of Chapter 1 show the IRS drive for power at any cost is not a pipe dream, but a very real nightmare.

I invited several of those enrolled on one IRS violence list to testify at *ad hoc* hearings on IRS abuses. The incredible stories of two of those placed on the list are told here in their own words along with my observations at the hearings.

Statement of Del Ray Holm

Mr. Holm: Well, Congressman, I was shocked to find my name on the list because I have never failed to pay my taxes. I've paid them every year, been audited twice in the last few years; I've been a member of the NFO [National Farmers Organization] and been a bishop for the LDS Church and I am chairman of the Democrat Central Committee in Jefferson County. (I see one other Democrat on that list, so I suppose it isn't a political thing.) And as to why I'm on there, I have absolutely no idea. It is a shock to me that things like this are going on in the country and I object to it.

Mr. Hansen: Let me just ask you for the record, have you ever had any complaints against you registered any time with any law enforcement agency, or anyone else that would constitute some kind of civil or criminal authority, about your behavior toward your fellow man?

Mr. Holm: No, I have never had anything but a traffic citation, quite a few of those, but outside of that I have never been involved in any criminal action in the courts and I haven't packed a loaded gun on my person since I was in the Korean War. I don't threaten people and I don't carry guns with me or anything. I have no idea why I should be on that list.

Mr. Hansen: I've known you for years. We ride different political animals, but we go to the same church. We have some things in common and some things not in common. The only thing I could see, and I have reason to believe this from some law enforcement files I have examined, is that you were involved at one time with a group of people who didn't care to have the general public treading over your land on some kind of entry that you had considered to be trespassing. Maybe you would like to tell us about that because I think, from what I could gather, the files that I saw would suggest that the IRS was making a clipping file. They were saving newspaper clippings in order to identify you in some way, to put you on some kind of a list.

Mr. Holm: We live in an area out in Bonneville County where we don't have any law enforcement. We have a lot of trouble with vandalism and we have a lot of problems with thieves. In fact, only recently they broke into my son's house and took everything he had in the house and those things go unanswered. Even when we have caught people in the act, nothing is ever done in regard to punishment, and we have had the same person doing the same thing over again.

So, we formed an organization out there, a kind of a group that patrolled the area and helped each other out. I think that this is still being done in this particular area, but we don't shoot people. In fact, I wouldn't shoot anybody for stealing anything. I would have to have a little better reason than that to shoot anybody.

I don't advocate violence—and never have—or the violent overthrow of the government or anything else. I think I have a right to protect what is mine—even with a gun, I suppose, if it came down to that, but like I say, I wouldn't shoot anybody for stealing gasoline or shooting a hole in my sprinkler pipe. I might feel like it but I certainly wouldn't resort to that sort of thing. I am not of that nature, never have been and probably never will be.

Mr. Hansen: Isn't it true that sometimes because, just like you are saying here, people get a little upset at the way some of their fellow men act and sometimes people use a loose word like saying, "They better not come on my property or I'll shoot anyone who trespasses"—or something. It is possible that people use those phrases occasionally; but it is seldom that anyone follows through. How could anyone construe that as being some kind of an act of violence?

Mr. Holm: Well, that's the thing. I suppose we've said things like that (as President Nixon found out) which really shouldn't be made public. I am sure we have all said those things. I see no reason why there should be a list published on anyone for that. I know a few of these other guys on this list. I have known them for years and I don't see any reason, while I may disagree with them politically—there is no reason why they should be on that list.

Mr. Hansen: Doesn't the First Amendment of the Constitution guarantee the right of free speech?

Mr. Holm: Well, I think so. It's supposed to. If we say

what we think there is no reason why we ought to be put down on a list. For what reasons we are on the list—and why we are harassed or whatever—I don't know. I don't like it.

Statement of [name withheld]

Mr.   *:* I was just going to say as big as I am and as violent as I am supposed to be, this microphone shouldn't scare me, but it does. [Laughter]

Well, I was really surprised—it was the night before last, wasn't it?—when I got the telephone call from Congressman Hansen. I was laying on the couch almost asleep and my wife answered the phone—

Mr. Hansen: I'll bet you laid awake the rest of the night.

Mr.   *:* Yes, I did. [Laughter]

But, anyway, she told me it was Congressman Hansen, and he addressed himself as such, and I said, "Yes, I know of him." I didn't think it was really you. [Laughter] But anyway, after talking to him for a while I realized that I was talking to the Congressman. But it confounds me that I am on this list. I spent almost three years of my life in the United States Navy. They asked me to be violent in war and I did it. I still think that we've got the greatest nation on the face of the earth, bar none. And I would defend it today. But for me to be put on such a list, I don't understand. I have no criminal record, none whatsoever that I know anything about. I have stood up for what I believe and I think our Constitution was divinely inspired. I definitely think that.

Why am I put on this list—maybe you can answer it. Have you got any information on it?

Mr. Hansen: That's why you are here—I don't know.

Mr.   *:* Well, to me, it nauseates me. I cannot for the life of me understand it. As far as an arsenal of guns, I've got an old worn-out .22—that's all. The ammunition—I don't think I've even got any shells for the rifle.

To be put on a list like this, it makes me wonder if our country has really gone to that level. I don't think being put on something like this could be any worse than something like this in Russia or any Communist country. If we have this sort of thing, I don't know what I'd just as soon move out to some other country if this is what we've got to put up with.

I have always paid my taxes. I've paid my honest share of taxes every year. My local property taxes have been paid. They're paid now. I don't consider myself better than anybody else. I've paid my taxes. I consider myself as good a citizen as anyone else, that's all. I don't know that I have any more to say, but I do hope and pray that this bunch is brought out into the open that they have to answer to this, that they have to tell me why. I appreciate your efforts, George.

Observations of Congressman Hansen

[Note: At this point in the hearings I read the names of the so-called violence list and had those on the list move to the front of the room.]

Mr. Hansen: I'd like all of those I just called—I would just like you to stand and turn around and look at the audience for a second and then sit down. I would like to tell the audience something. These people, ladies and gentlemen, comprise the IRS violence list in this area. [Laughter.]

From the Floor: Should we applaud? [Laughter]

Mr. Hansen: I don't know what you should do. I really don't.

From the Floor: What date is that?

Mr. Hansen: This particular list is December 31, 1975. I have newer ones.

I have given each one of them a copy of the list—I think this is the first time you have seen it, isn't it?

From the Floor: Yes.

Mr. Hansen: I informed all those in this area on the list. I have not yet informed those who are out of my Congressional district, but I want you to know that I have made this known to several key people. This has been an ongoing project of the IRS. This list has been in my hands for some time, and I have a lot of other documents. The IRS would like you to believe that every time you find something like this it's the only thing they ever did like that, you know. But this document proves that they are lying.

This document speaks for itself. It says, "We are currently in the process of identifying other individuals in your district who may have a propensity toward violence. Additional information will be forwarded periodically." So this isn't a one-time thing. This is ongoing. They are still busily assembling lists.

And then the paragraph goes on, "We are transmitting a list of individuals in your district who may advocate violence toward government officials including revenue employees. The list was compiled from a system of records dealing with criminal law enforcement." The suggestion is this—unless I don't know how to read—the suggestion is *violence.* The suggestion is that IRS agents couldn't get around these people without expecting violence. These lists are supposedly compiled from records dealing with criminal law enforcement, so the lists also suggest *criminal actions.* Now, that doesn't mean just holding the idea of a little mayhem in your hearts once in a while; it suggests—it almost indicates—that there must be a criminal record of something somewhere, or that the IRS is pretty firmly convinced that these people are criminals. This is what I think needs to be explained by the Internal Revenue Service to the public, to the public who pays the taxes and supports them and expects a clean operation, a decent operation. I am concerned because when the IRS says *violence* and *criminal,* to me what they are saying is if they go to see somebody on the list they had better go armed. It suggests that if they are going to be armed they had better be willing to use those arms. If somebody from a federal agency comes up to your door and shakes you up a little, makes you nervous, points a gun at you, does this mean that your civil rights have been violated, maybe even your life jeopardized? I don't know. It concerns me. It concerns me as a citizen, it concerns me as an official of government very, very much.

We talked about this earlier today. It seems to me that when the IRS is working, they ought to be dealing with you as an individual. If you don't abide by the law, they should take you to court and prosecute you under the law. But I don't understand this idea that they think they can circulate lists on people. I don't understand why they think they can make people go on television and apologize to them and say they are right. I guess the IRS would claim that those of us who say that there is something wrong with the IRS are paranoid. But I wonder if the IRS isn't paranoid. It seems to me that they are the ones who are nervous. They are the ones who always want to prove they're right. If you wrong anybody except the IRS you take your lumps—you get fined, you go to jail, or whatever. But if you wrong the IRS, you do all of these, and then you get up and apologize. And then you certify that they are right. This doesn't make sense.

So I guess the point that I am getting to is that I am going to demand an explanation—in fact, I have already asked for it. Now that the matter is in the open I am going to push for answers. This has been long overdue. I have already had a verbal justification from a high IRS official—but it didn't make sense to me at all. I'm determined to get a valid explanation for these violence lists.

[Attorneys Gordon Thatcher and Ray Rigby expressed similar concern at the hearings.]

Mr. Thatcher: The whole concept of this [violence list] is just really chilling to me. It's frightening that if somebody wants to protest, which is part of our system, they have nowhere to go to complain. They can't say a word. I think it is a healthy situation to have a group that has courage enough and the strength of conviction if they feel something is wrong in the government to go protest. I think it is a way to help government officials be informed and keep them in line.

Mr. Rigby: The thing that is sinister about this [violence list], Congressman, is the secrecy of it all. Now, for instance, if a person is considered for an appointment in the government they check basically with the Internal Revenue Service and the FBI. Isn't that true? Those are the agencies that would have something to do with your character. In other words, they check us out so that we don't embarrass the government if the government hires us. Well, if this record of a "protester" is kept, the protester is rejected for whatever position he wants, maybe even a private position. Somebody who has made that kind of a record with the IRS is accused without a hearing, without that individual having been given an opportunity to be present to present his own witnesses, to be represented by counsel, to have his day in court. They have gathered their own evidence, made their own findings and judgment, and determined that he has violence in his nature and is considered to be dangerous. So it is more than just the IRS record, it is everything that he does from then on.

Mr. Thatcher: For instance, if you wanted to become a lawyer, a doctor, any professional man—

Mr. Hansen: You can't get cleared for security since the government—

Mr. Thatcher: That's particularly the one I was talking about—any security for the government, you would be checked through those agencies. This really becomes scary to me.

12

The Cover-Up

Late in 1977 I began pushing the Internal Revenue Service in an effort to learn more about IRS Gestapo tactics. I was specifically concerned about the so-called violence lists I had discovered and about the armed raids the IRS had planned or undertaken. On December 13, 1977, I sent a letter to Jerome Kurtz, Commissioner of the Internal Revenue Service, outlining what I considered to be major problems with the IRS. The text of the letter, included in an excerpt from the December 15, 1977, *Congressional Record,* and his answer to it, appear in the documents section in the back of this book. I repeat here the final two paragraphs, which summarize my concern:

> The power of the arbitrary audit, the possibilities of intimidation over filing details and judgment factors, and the required waiver of Fifth Amendment Rights make IRS, if used wrongfully, the most dangerous threat of destructive

cancer to our system of self-government and our individual rights and freedom. IRS must be totally objective, color-blind, non-political, and religiously and philosophically neutral. The virtual impossibility of your task makes your challenge great and the consequences of your failure a "hell" for the victims.

I am alarmed that too many have already been irrepara-bly harmed by IRS abuses, both employees and taxpayers. I am concerned that confidence in government has eroded to such dangerous proportions. I am hopeful that you can give assurances that strong corrective steps are being taken and that you will make proper recommendations to me and my colleagues in Congress as to what legislation is necessary to get the nation's tax collection system out of the gutter and on to the high road.

Soon after, I again invited Warren Bates, Assistant Commissioner in charge of the highly secretive Internal Security Division of the IRS, into my office to discuss IRS procedures.

"First of all," I began, "I'd like you to try to be more specific in describing the violence lists for me. Especially any you are keeping on my constituents. There are—"

"Refresh my memory a little bit with what went on out there," Bates interrupted. "There was one letter prepared, I guess you have a copy of that, that went from Fred Rowe [commissioner of the IRS Western Region] to several of the district directors in that region. And that is the only letter, by the way, the only list that has ever been prepared as far as I can determine right now. I'm sure that's the case, there has been none since then and there is no indication that there were any before then. The reason—"

"Which date was that one?" I asked.

"That would have been in December of 1976, I guess, no, '75. December '75 . . ."

"Well, I'm not sure you are right because I have reason to believe there were several," I said.

"If there are, they would have acted—"

"In fact, it was rather periodic," I interrupted.

"Nope. There is no indication that that is true," Bates said.

At the time that Bates made this assertion that there was only one violence list, I had three in my possession. One was dated before December 1975 and one was dated after December 1975. Everything that Bates had just told me was a lie.

I changed the subject to the armed raids:

"You and I discussed the other day this proposed armed search you fellows cooked up in eastern Idaho. You said that you had turned it off."

"Yeah, they had some problems out there. I really don't think it was an armed search, George. I think it was a compliance check where they were going to go verify whether or not people in that area had filed their tax returns and just ask them to see copies of their tax returns," Bates replied.

"Was that on a door-to-door basis?"

"I don't know exactly how they were going to do it. I would assume that would have been a possibility. It didn't come off so I don't know what they would have done. Of course, this is not an armed search and if the taxpayer said, 'I'm sorry but I don't have copies of my tax return and I don't feel I want to show them to you under the circumstances,' that would have been the end of it," he said.

"Trouble is, most people don't understand their rights under the law and that is the problem. Plus, at least some of your people *were* carrying weapons," I asserted.

"That is part of the problem. I would assume that this is not entirely a new kind of thing. The Internal Revenue Service has done this over a number of years in many many areas," Bates conceded.

"Now on this door-to-door compliance check or armed search or whatever anybody wants to call it, is there an inspection [investigation] report available?" I asked.

"No, there would not be on that, George, because it never occurred."

"Well, I understand that there was an inspection made on that which was made by an inspector by the name of Higgins, I believe," I said. I had to smile inwardly at the continued evasive answers of this man who was the "chief cop" of the whole IRS.

"An inspection of that matter? I'll check it out but I don't think so," he responded.

"Sometime in early '76 or thereabouts. Probably out of the Ogden office."

"Let me check it. Higgins. Okay. And that was on the compliance check?" Bates asked.

"As I understand it, there were thirty or forty agents going out on some kind of door-to-door check and that at least some of the agents would be carrying arms and it was a random check where they would be asking for tax returns," I said.

"What area would it be in?" he asked.

"In the Upper Snake River Valley. Rigby, Rexburg, along in there," I replied, not wanting to be too specific in order to find out what he knew.

"Okay. I'll check and see but I don't recall. I have never seen a report, but that doesn't mean that one doesn't exist. I can't take time to look at all the reports. But I'll check and see if there was any report. And that was in early '71? I mean '76?" he asked.

"It would have been February, March, along in there of '76, give or take a few months. I'd like to know more about what is going on—half knowledge is dangerous for anyone."

"Well, let me see what went on there," he said.

On Bates's advice, I wrote a letter to his office under the Freedom of Information Act requesting documentation and information on the violence lists and on the armed search planned in my Congressional district. A month later I received the following reply, dated January 24, 1978, from Bates:

> With regard to your request for information concerning random search, collection or taxpayer compliance projects and operations, please be advised that these activities do not fall within the jurisdiction of the Inspection Service. I did not forward this portion of your request to the Office of the Assistant Commissioner (Compliance), which has jurisdiction in these areas, because your request did not reasonably describe the records you seek.
>
> The Freedom of Information Act requires that all requests submitted for access to Service records should reasonably describe the records sought. This enables the Service to properly and more expeditiously respond to requests for information. Attached is Part 601—Statement of Procedural Rules, as published in the Federal Register, to assist you in preparing your request.

Clearly, this backtracking and evasive letter told me that anything I wanted to know about the internal workings of the IRS, I would have to learn for myself.

On February 24, 1978, I finally received a reply from Jerome Kurtz. This letter was either written by an innocent but ignorant bureaucrat (perhaps by a subordinate of Kurtz) or was an outright lie intended to cover up the gross injustices being perpetrated by the IRS on U.S. citizens. Even at that, Kurtz admitted, perhaps inadvertently, some of the shocking tactics of the IRS as these excerpts from, and my remarks about, his letter indicate:

High level Internal Revenue Service managers were seriously concerned that certain tax protestors belonging to organizations . . .

Point: The concern that prompted the creation of hit lists was registered all the way to the top of the IRS; it was not just a local phenomenon.

. . . our Inspection Service [the secret police] began to gather information on various tax protestor groups which, in their organizational documents or other pronouncements, advocated violent interference with the administration of the tax laws.

Point: This sounds reasonable on paper, but the IRS did not confine itself to these guidelines, but instead conducted a witch hunt into every group who complained about taxes, either out of anger at IRS collection practices or because of other political considerations, and it was an organized nationwide effort.

Some of the information obtained by Inspection from the sources described above did include license plate numbers of individuals who were attending or were parked in the vicinity of SPC [tax protester] meetings.

Point: Parking a car in the wrong place might get a person placed on an IRS hit list.

In keeping with our *established procedures,* the Internal Revenue Service gathers directly tax related information from a *variety of sources, including newspapers,* concerning possible failure to comply with tax laws. [Emphasis added.]

Point: People who take trips, win contests, or receive business appointments or promotions which are announced in the paper will likely make the IRS clipping file. Through the Freedom of Information Act, I recently obtained the huge newsclip file that the IRS keeps on me and was interested to see how many items were included which were related to my job as a public official rather than to my personal taxes. The very act of keeping such files on citizens seems to be in flagrant violation of the Bill of Rights and the new restraints placed on the FBI and the CIA.

> . . . the waitresses in eastern Idaho have not been subjected to *special* scrutiny with respect to tip income. [Emphasis added.]

Point: In other words, waitresses across the country, not just in eastern Idaho, are also being unfairly hounded by the IRS—IRS tactics are uniformly bad.

> Among the compliance techniques occasionally used by the Service are canvassings of areas by revenue officers who knock on doors and ask occupants to produce a copy of their tax return as evidence of their compliance with the tax laws.

Point: Any first-year law student could tell Mr. Kurtz that producing a copy of a tax return is not evidence of anything, particularly not evidence of having filed the original. On the other hand, there is no requirement of law that such returns be kept available and failure to produce the tax report copy is not evidence of failure to file. The IRS goes door to door searching for evidence? What ever happened to the Fourth and Fifth Amendments?

My reply to Kurtz's letter was tough but unspecific. The precise nature of the armed raids was still out of reach and I did not know how or why the violence lists were being made. Still, I had one advantage. The IRS believed that the only information available to me was the violence list of December 1975 to which both Bates and Kurtz constantly referred. They were trying to explain their devious activities in my Congressional district solely on the basis of that one list. This proved to be a decisive mistake.

Unsatisfied by the nebulous response I received from the IRS hierarchy, I returned to my two-pronged probe for answers: the quest for documents under the Freedom of Information Act (FOI) and procuring additional evidence from my sources in and near the IRS.

My requests under the FOI were either ignored entirely or shuffled to another branch of the agency. Bates referred my requests to the Idaho state director, who, in turn, referred me to the regional office. Then the regional office sent me back to Bates. The following memo explains my attempts to retrieve information from the regional headquarters:

TO: Congressman George Hansen
FROM: [Name deleted]
DATE: February 19, 1979
SUBJECT: IRS

The following statements were made during the meeting between me and Bob DeBoer (Western Region IRS official) at the IRS Service Center in Ogden (Utah) this date:

Bob DeBoer did help formulate the plan. [The armed raid on Fremont County.]

Bob DeBoer decided it was a bad plot and discarded it and stopped the plan.

Bob DeBoer forwarded the case file to D.C. the Disclosure Section.

Bob DeBoer couldn't give any information to me from the file because the Disclosure Section had the file and that they had already responded to the request from you.

Bob DeBoer called *Howard Martin*, Director and clued him into the plan and the *disposal* of the plan.

Bob DeBoer assured me that he would respond to the Office of Assistant Commissioner of Inspections; ATTN: Chief, Disclosure Section [i.e. Howard Martin] re: your request of this date. [Emphasis added.]

The armed-raid file and the violence lists thus ended up in the lap of Howard Martin—the very man who had originally approved the plan. The wheel of bureaucracy had turned full circle.

I learned from an IRS source what was really going on inside the agency during this period from late 1977 to early 1979. One IRS official stated:

"DeBoer put it this way, he said to me, 'What we have here isn't a problem in interpreting the record, it is a problem of missing records.'

"So by that I assume that a thorough search had been made of the records in Boise and they are now missing. And I said, 'You mean to tell me with all the copies of everything in the government that there wasn't a copy anywhere?' He just kind of smiled and he wouldn't say any more. So apparently the records are gone and maybe there was some hanky-panky.

"They weren't in [name deleted] office either. I talked to him again Friday morning and asked him if he'd ever found any records and he said, 'No, I don't know whether they are misfiled or thrown away.' So I know there are none there.

"That shredding machine, I have an idea that's where they went, but records are not supposed to disappear like that. In my own mind I'm sure that part of what was shredded was their enemies lists [or violence lists] that came out."

IRS officials apparently thought that they were keeping one step ahead of me by shredding some documents, forwarding others to Washington, D.C., and "losing" the rest.

Fortunately, my contacts in the agency were able to salvage a few of the records before they were destroyed. With those records I eventually was able to reconstruct IRS procedures in several key areas.

As another agent told me in a conversation:

"Well, there are a lot of things I would like to give you but I am afraid I can't."

"That's privileged information. I understand that," I replied.

"I'm sure they went to great lengths to get rid of every shred of evidence. If you got anything, I think it was just probably sheer luck. This shredding has been going on for the last two or three years."

By 1979 my investigation of the IRS was complete. Documents I had been able to gather proved that the IRS did, in fact, engage in enforcement procedures which grossly violated civil and constitutional rights. Furthermore, the documents proved that IRS officials at the highest levels had lied to me and kept information from me in an attempt to cover up their misconduct.

In February of 1979 I took my findings to Congress, to the Ways and Means Committee's hearings on the Internal Revenue Service. In conjunction with several other Congressmen, I presented a well-documented case against the IRS. I also placed extensive material on the subject in the Congressional Record. Again in 1980 a few of us spoke out sharply in opposition to the machinations of the agency. But so far the Congress has turned a deaf or, at least, disinterested ear on our evidence. The power of the IRS to destroy a public official's career does not go unheeded in political circles. Congressmen may talk about cutting taxes (even if they never *act* on their rhetoric) but rarely will a Congressman stand up against the Internal Revenue Service. It is simply too dangerous; it is inviting too much trouble.

Probably the only thing that frightens or disturbs an elected official more than the IRS is an enraged electorate—a constituency demanding to be heard, or else. Certainly, the creation of such an uprising is one of the goals of this book.

13

The Nature
of the Beast

Having witnessed the true and varied stories of a
few of the victims of the IRS, and having seen the design of
IRS operations, we can now draw some general conclusions
about the nature of the IRS beast.

First, Internal Revenue Service procedures are set up to
intimidate, to harass, and to drive individuals and businesses
into bankruptcy. The IRS contends that this is the most efficient way to collect taxes.

Second, the incentive system for promotions within the
agency is based on strict adherence to IRS procedure. Ruthlessness is the most important character trait for an up-and-
coming IRS bureaucrat. The Internal Revenue Service feels
that the unmerciful tax collector is the best tax collector.

Third, the IRS goes to great lengths to prevent the taxpayer from seeking redress outside of the agency. It is almost
impossible for the taxpayer to be judged by his peers, unless
he pays up on arbitrary assessments or willfully commits a
crime in order to force his case beyond the *civil* laws which

have been manipulated to serve the whims of the IRS. In other words, because the IRS can seize property, confiscate records, and levy bank accounts, all without accusing the taxpayer of a *crime,* the IRS tries *not* to allow the taxpayer to move outside of IRS civil procedures. The IRS, in its own bureaucratic sphere, can arraign and convict a taxpayer while acting as judge, jury, and prosecution, but it has no official unit charged with handling taxpayer complaints.

Fourth, the IRS goes to great lengths to hide its abuses from the public. It does this by ruining the careers of elected officials who try to expose IRS atrocities. In addition, the IRS either destroys the documents which would prove its pettiness or keeps them in files which are not accessible to the public. When the IRS is "caught in the act," it claims that the incident uncovered is a fluke—a once-in-a-lifetime goof-up. IRS officials might blush a little, and even apologize, but they repeat the same thing over and over again. In 1976 IRS officials told me that they had stopped making lists of tax protesters in 1974. In 1978, they said 1976 was the last year. In 1980 they claim to have ended the practice in 1978. In fact, the oppressive tactics are getting worse and worse. The IRS is on a rampage and is determined that nothing will stand in its way. I recently asked an IRS source about the current status of the violence lists.

"The tax protester lists are super-secret. I've only seen one in the past year," my source said.

"Oh, you've seen one this year?" I asked.

"Yes, about a month and a half ago," he replied.

"You didn't get a copy of it, did you?"

"No."

"Do you know the date on it?"

"It was dated in March, it was an update or an addition to the list."

"March of 1980?" I asked.

"Right. The main lists are kept by the criminal investigators. They're super-secret. One criminal investigator is assigned to keep the list and it is under lock and key at all times. It probably has about 200 pages."

(Note: The violence list of December 1975 had twenty-five names on three pages. The IRS is obviously achieving its goal of alienating the public.)

Fifth, IRS procedures produce a kind of cloak-and-dagger mentality which in and of itself becomes a source of harassment to the taxpayer. "Power corrupts," Lord Acton told us, "and absolute power corrupts absolutely." I have been told that the IRS has severely cut back the hiring of professional auditors in the last few years and now takes on partially educated people who are more readily taught IRS "audit procedures." The IRS is, literally, creating its own "goon squad."

Sixth, the IRS has lost all perspective of its *constitutional* role as tax collector. The Sixteenth Amendment reads:

> The Congress shall have power to lay and collect taxes on incomes, from whatever source derived, without apportionment among the several States, without regard to any census or enumerations.

By what possible stretch of the imagination can current IRS procedures be justified under this Amendment? Does the Sixteenth Amendment repeal the First, Fourth, Fifth, Sixth, Seventh, Eighth, Ninth, and Tenth Amendments? Certainly the examples in this book would indicate that the IRS seems to think so. At least it acts as if such is the case—which prompts such typical American sarcasm as seen recently on a bumper sticker, "Fight Organized Crime—Abolish the IRS."

The IRS, in its drive to overcome and destroy the will of the American people, has burgeoned into a fearful *master.* It takes its pleasure, it sustains its existence, through the process of overcoming the will of the individual taxpayer by means of the will of the bureaucrat backed by the full power of the establishment. The life of the bureaucrat, indeed the life of the bureaucracy, is an ever-growing circle of struggles with and victories over the citizen. When the IRS wins its case and extracts its tribute, the agency swells in numbers and becomes more powerful.

Seventh, an expanding Internal Revenue Service does not loathe tax resisters, it needs them—so it creates an atmosphere of intimidation and abuse in which fear and hate are cultivated which drives people into resistance to the system. To repeat, the IRS creates and encourages confrontations between itself and those who must struggle against it.

It is for precisely these reasons—power and empire building—that the IRS has recently chosen to pursue and destroy America's private schools.

IRS regulations for Revenue Procedure 75-50, FEDERAL REGISTER, Vol. 43, No. 163, state in part:

> . . . schools in the community. *Generally, the Service will consider these schools to be racially discriminatory unless the schools can show that they now have a significant minority enrollment* or that they are in good faith operated on a non-discriminatory basis. If the schools cannot make such showings, the Service will consider the schools to be racially discriminatory, and tax exemption will be revoked or denied. In certain cases, schools may be allowed a grace period to bring themselves into compliance with the guidelines. [Emphasis added.]

These institutions provide a new source of confrontation, new victims, for the IRS. The IRS assertion that all private schools are presumed to have been established for racist purpose unless proved otherwise serves two purposes in their scheme for domination:

One, the assertion creates a confrontation. It gives the IRS an excuse to expand, a reason to escalate the conflict between the agency and the American citizen. Those who believe that they have a right to educate their children as they see fit constitute a field ripe for harvest by the bureaucrats. The *belief* of the taxpayer that his rights are more fundamental than the authority of the government stands like an enemy before the IRS.

Two, this assertion provides a kind of ethical justification for the IRS. It vindicates the IRS in its efforts to impose its "morality of leveling" or "equality" onto the public. Individual rights, attitudes, and customs must be brought into line with the will of the bureaucracy. Thus, "equality" is always expressed numerically by officialdom. The IRS measures what is right and wrong by the *quantity* of students of a particular sex or race or creed attending a school. The *quality* of the education is a criterion which is beyond the brute mentality of the bureaucrat. The "moral" person is defined by the IRS as a person who is willing to subjugate himself to the mind of the bureaucracy.

The persistence and arrogance of the IRS on the matter of the regulation of religious schools have earned the active enmity of Congressman John Ashbrook (R. Ohio), Robert Dornan (R. California), and Philip Crane (R. Illinois), who, together with those of us who have been warning about these abuses for years, succeeded in passing a prohibition against the rule in the Treasury appropriation for 1980. The same prohibition is pending for 1981.

The abuses of the Internal Revenue Service have become so rife and widespread that there is scarcely a Congressman whose office has not received constituent complaints. At a recent Ways and Means Subcommittee hearing, Congressmen Don Young (R. Alaska) and John Rousselot (R. California) and former Senator Eugene McCarthy testified as to specific IRS abuses in their personal experience.

The Senate also held 1980 oversight hearings on IRS excesses because of public pressure regarding abuses. Republican and Democrat, liberal and conservative, the Congress is visibly becoming agitated over the problem of this runaway agency. Continued public interest and pressure can bring needed corrective action, but it has to be maintained and significantly intensified.

The medieval tactics of the IRS must be abandoned. We live in an age of computers, not inquisitors. Surely there are more humane and efficient methods of tax collection than smashing the Olivers' car windows or attacking and looting the Snyders' home.

Wouldn't certified letters to taxpayers requesting a meeting be more reasonable than random searches and armed confrontations?

Wouldn't a quick computer check, to see if the Larry Fullmers of the world have properly filed and paid their taxes, be much less expensive and time-consuming than an "investigation" conducted as a result of a political letter to the editor?

Wouldn't understanding compassion have saved the IRS both money and prestige in its dealings with the waitresses and the janitor?

Wouldn't standard business collection practices have been better in the Jack Wright case than extralegal actions of vendetta and humiliation?

Wouldn't fair play on capital gains have speeded recovery and given IRS more tax potential among Teton flood victims than anything they collected in taxes by swooping like vultures among the suffering?

Wouldn't a professional and honest application of the law elicit respect and confidence instead of fear from the smallest taxpayer to the highest public official?

Wouldn't straightforward answers, instead of lies and cover-ups, better earn the trust and support of the taxpayer and of conscientious IRS employees?

Wouldn't it be best for all Americans if the Internal Revenue Service would strive to serve instead of dominate the citizens of this great nation?

The answer is, of course, a resounding "Yes!"

But our return from the brink of totalitarianism will not be as easy as our journey there has been. Other federal agencies have followed the IRS through the cracks opened in civil and constitutional law by the excesses of bureaucratic regulation. We are now fighting on more than one front and stand in danger of being outflanked. OSHA, EPA, CPA, ICC, and hosts of other acronymic monsters, along with IRS, are busily regulating America into another "gulag."

The time for a revolution, if it is to be a peaceful revolution, is now at the ballot box and at the mailbox. It is extremely important to elect right-thinking people and then follow up strongly with cards and letters. Government of, by, and for the people only functions when an alert citizenry resolutely makes its desires felt.

Some of us in Congress have charted a responsible corrective course. We have offered proposals; we have solutions.

An explanation of how to fight back and a strategy for an ultimate victory make up the final chapters of this book. As you read the next few pages, ask yourself, "Where does my Congressman or Senator stand on these issues?"

14

How to
Fight Back

According to the Internal Revenue Service figures, in 1978 U.S. citizens failed to report approximately $125 billion in income. There are over 2 million people in this country who have simply stopped filing income tax returns. About 10 million more are professional tax evaders who file but use a number of methods to avoid paying a "typical" amount of income tax. Some of these people are successful in their struggles with the IRS—others are not.

This advice on how to fight back will *not* be addressed to these individuals. They are called tax resisters, and their weapons include nonfiling of returns; filing of returns which refuse information on constitutional grounds; claims that the income tax is illegal or that, if legal, it does not reach wages; or claims that wages are not subject to tax because wages are paid in money which is not supported by hard metals.

Many of those who follow this path are more familiar with the relevant law than most tax lawyers. The only aid that will help them is the total repeal of the income tax itself. I feel that most of this group, whatever the merits of their individual claims, are a symptom of a serious defect in our tax system. They represent a group that feels that the government is the enemy of its citizens and that guerrilla warfare in tax matters is the weapon of an occupied people. And this group is unfortunately growing in numbers.

Legislators ignore such a phenomenon at their peril. It arises out of a perception that taxes are an unfair burden and worse, that the government doesn't give a damn as long as it gets its pound of flesh. Tax resisters cannot be helped until the government is willing to reexamine the bureaucratic structure and how it came to be estranged from its own people.

While one can sympathize with many of the perceptions and views of tax resisters and even accept the argument that most are protesting the unfairness of the system and not dodging their fair share of the cost of government, the courts (state, federal, and tax courts) have generally continued to rule against these people and in favor of present revenue collection procedures. I recall visiting with a seventy-year-old man who had stopped filing his income tax returns because he claimed such returns were unconstitutional. He was not a wealthy man—he was acting on what he felt were good principles. This man was recently sentenced to a six-month term in a federal prison. Unless the reader is willing to take this kind of risk, he is better off to fight "within the system."

Protecting Your Rights

It is to those who wish to protect their rights *within the system* that the following information is dedicated. The means are through application and alteration of law rather than the challenge and defiance of authority. The best weapons of the average citizen are to be well informed, firm in his convictions, prepared with good records, and determined to defend his rights.

First, and most important, *keep good records*. Unless you are fighting the IRS for the fun of it, limit the range of your potential dispute by maintaining a thorough and accurate system of records. Your records should include the obvious items like receipts of all purchases and deposits, and documents showing wages, interest, and other earnings. But they should also include a personal record of spending and earning. A diary is a valuable asset in determining deductible items. (For example, when properly kept, a diary can tell you almost exactly how many miles were driven for business purposes.) In some cases, you can even document income from your own records. A day-to-day entry on such things as tips can be very persuasive on the amount of unrecorded income on which taxes are due. And keep records of improvements to your house; they can increase the tax-free base when you sell.

Plan all of your expenditures with an eye toward a hostile reception from the tax people. If it doesn't happen, you have lost nothing. If it does, you are prepared.

Find a checklist of deductions. If you can't find a reliable list, the instruction book from the IRS for 1040 forms is at least a basic start. Paste it on your desk on January 1 of the year and keep it before you every time you spend money. Get receipts for everything.

A good accountant can be a valuable friend in your struggle with the IRS. Often the accountant will serve as an "objective" third party in a dispute between the taxpayer and the IRS. If you can afford to hire a reputable accountant, do it. In fact, it may well save you money if better handling of your accounts and taxes helps you avoid audits. Professional help also relieves you significantly of legal questions of "intent" in tax disputes with the IRS.

Think defensively. You are going to be dealing with an agency which has a philosophy alien to the American spirit in that you will be considered guilty or liable unless and until you can *prove* that you are innocent and free of obligations.

Keeping a clear set of records will do two things for you. One, it will give you confidence when, and if, you are called in for an audit; and two, it will let the IRS know that you will be able to quickly spot any unfair assessments by them. *Good records are a must.*

Second, when you are called in by the IRS, go to the meeting with a good attitude. Know what you want to accomplish before you meet with the agent or auditor. Be prepared to argue for your deductions—know what you are talking about. Be polite, but do not be afraid to contest a determination of income.

Once you are at the meeting, act in a businesslike manner. Don't start with a chip on your shoulder. Most IRS contacts with taxpayers are ordinary matters which can be handled without confrontation. Do not assume the worst until there is a reason to. Retain your poise and be professional. Even if you are resisting an assessment, let the IRS act the villain. If you act responsibly, it will strengthen your position and emphasize any churlish conduct on the part of the agent.

Do not volunteer more information than the point in question requires. Talking too much may resolve one issue and open many more. Or worse, it might solve this year's tax problem and create a new and larger one for next year.

If the interview seems to be getting out of hand, terminate it. Become ill; remember a dental appointment; announce that by accident you have forgotten a key record. Just get out, compose yourself, and figure out what was going wrong. Never participate in or continue an interview in which you have lost the initiative.

Third, if the IRS gets rough and makes unreasonable demands, insist that the agent provide you with the statute and the regulation pursuant to the position he is taking on your tax problem. Remember that there is a big difference between a *statute* or a law passed by Congress and a *regulation* or a bureaucratic ruling devised by the IRS. The taxpayer *must* obey the law, but he is not necessarily bound by IRS internal regulations. IRS agents and auditors may try to bluff you on this issue. Be prepared to study the relevant tax laws. Ask for a copy of any memorandum or correspondence in which the subject matter concerns your particular controversy and obtain the instructions given by the IRS to your agent regarding your case. Request all materials compiled by the IRS on you by audit or any other means. (This information should be available to you through the Freedom of Information Act.)

If the IRS agent asks you to show him documentation that you think will cause you problems or damage your case, you have the technical legal right to refuse to show it on Fifth Amendment grounds. The Internal Revenue Manual (242.12) states in part:

(1) An individual taxpayer may refuse to exhibit his books and records for examination on the ground that compelling him to do so might violate his right against self-incrimination under the Fifth Amendment and constitute an illegal search and seizure under the Fourth Amendment. However, in the absence of such claims, it is no error for a court to charge the jury that it may consider the refusal to produce books and records, in determining willfulness.

(2) The privilege against self-incrimination does not permit a taxpayer to refuse to obey a summons issued under IRC 7602 or a court order directing his appearance. He is required to appear and cannot use the Fifth Amendment as an excuse for failure to do so, although he may exercise it in connection with specific questions. He cannot refuse to bring his records, but may decline to submit them for inspection on Constitutional grounds.

You *must* bring your records with you to the audit, but you may refuse to show parts of them. Be sure to cite the

Fifth Amendment and to have your interview on tape if you pursue this route. In any event, do not bring unnecessary records to your interview.

If a tactic you try irritates the IRS and its agents, you can assume it is legal—remember it for future use. You *can* tape-record your interviews with the IRS. (It is perhaps better not to do so at the initial informal stages, however.) You *can* bring a witness. You *can* demand policy clarification on "borderline" issues. Be very careful in signing any waiver of your rights and waivers of statute of limitations, particularly under inducement or coercion.

Don't give up your negotiations with the IRS too quickly. There is a multilevel "review" system (in effect, an appeal to the supervisors of those at the lower IRS echelons) that you should use. If you are refused at one level, demand a hearing by an IRS official higher up. But beware! One of the most abused and dangerous weapons in the IRS arsenal, and one, therefore, to which you must be alert, is the request by the IRS for extension of time within which to make a determination of your tax assessment. There is a statute of limitations on back taxes due. After a certain amount of time (three years for certain back taxes and five years on others) has gone by, you are no longer legally responsible for taxes incurred in that fiscal year. The IRS gets very nervous about this law, which prevents them from digging deeply into your tax history. An extension of time is usually offered by the IRS as an alternative to an immediate assessment at the highest possible arbitrary figure. As stated before, do not sign an extension form unless you have clearly determined it is to your advantage.

Fourth, if you are unable to settle with the IRS and if you feel that some type of litigation is your best bet, decide whether you want to go to Tax Court or to pay the assessed tax and sue the government in U.S. District Court. It is important to reemphasize that most people are ill equipped to be doing legal battle with the tax establishment. Sometimes you can do the overall cause of getting a just tax system harm by fighting the wrong fight at the wrong time. Tax Court is a highly technical procedure in which the final decision rests with a judge (see Chapter 9), while the taxpayer's case when he brings suit will be heard by a jury in the district courts.

If you have any energy left after fighting with the IRS, use it to let your elected representatives know what needs to be done about the tax system. Remember that the tax rebellion was fueled by a people's movement in California, not by the federal government. All elected officials are proper targets of your opinions.

You will notice that I have conspicuously avoided mentioning retaining a lawyer. It was not an oversight. Although the right attorney can be an invaluable aid in beating the IRS, the average taxpayer is usually unable to afford the costs of extensive and ongoing litigation. In many cases, legal fees will soon outdistance the questioned amount of taxes assessed by the IRS—then, of course, the taxpayer is fighting merely for the satisfaction of whipping the government. Furthermore, few practicing attorneys specialize in tax law, and hence few lawyers are readily prepared to adequately defend their clients in the Tax Court. If you can find and afford a lawyer who is both willing and able to fight the IRS, you are one of the fortunate few.

Assault on Religion

Foreword

This section—*Assault On Religion*—brings to the attention of the nation the alarming assault on freedom of religion in America.

For the first time in our history, governments of the United States—national, state and local—are taxing churches; imposing fines on churches; and even padlocking churches.

Ministers and church officials are being fined and thrown in jail.

Government is jailing fathers and hunting down mothers to put them in jail and make their children wards of the state.

Freedom of religion is at stake as arbitrary social demands and government "policy" invade the First Amendment sanctity of the pulpit.

Civil and Constitutional rights are a federal issue, and it is vital that steps be initiated by the federal government to end this terror which government at all levels is bringing on religion.

We cannot sit idly by while churches are locked and fined, and while ministers and church members languish in jail because of their religious beliefs.

We cannot remain passive as churches lose their tax exemptions and ministers are jailed by the IRS for political reasons.

We cannot tolerate the IRS making churches into tax collectors and the mandatory new unconstitutional Social Security tax on churches must be repealed—repealed before ministers in large numbers are forced to the jailhouse door for refusing to pay.

It is time for action. America must not endure the shame of destroying churches and jailing ministers—nor the shame of jailing church members, and driving women and children from their homes as fugitives.

Introduction

Just a Pinch of Incense

At the end of the Third Century of the Christian era, the Roman Emperor Diocletian began the seventh and, by some accounts, the bloodiest of the Roman persecutions of the infant Christian Church. He introduced a new concept into the Empire's attempt to crush Christianity.

Instead of commanding that all Christians be killed, the Emperor issued an order that, if Christians would throw a pinch of incense on the fire before a Roman idol and give up their sacred books, at the time principally the Sacred Scriptures, he would allow them to continue to practice their religion.

This tactic gave him two benefits. First, it caused a lot of Christians to come forward; and second, it created dissention among the Christians. Some said it was a small price to pay for freedom from the threat of death. Others said that it was an acknowledgment that the state had control over religion and that the Empire could control its content and functions.

Certain people in Washington and other areas of the United States seem to have been reading the story of Diocletian. Whether by design or coincidence, our government at all levels has begun a campaign quite similar to his. Some religions they attack straight ahead. Some they ask for the pinch of incense. And some, they ask for control over the Sacred Books. Following are some case histories on how the "empire" is conducting the "eighth great persecution" in the 1980's with techniques developed in the 280's.

Subchapter 1

A Thing Called Public Policy

In other chapters and documents of this book, I have outlined the assault on small educational groups by the IRS and the fight to keep those schools free of government domination. These preliminary skirmishes are now developing into war between church and state with major battles raging on several fronts.

We recently lost one of those battles which has left many religious groups vulnerable to attack by the government. This was the Bob Jones University case won by the Internal Revenue Service in the U.S. Supreme Court. In that case, which was unfortunately obscured by racial overtones, we have a major escalation by government forces in their campaign to limit the free exercise of religion in the United States.

The elements of this attack are quite simple. First, the defendent is small. Bob Jones University is an unaffiliated school without the backing of a large religious community, like the Catholics or the Lutherans. This is a crucial element in the plan. Government forces have no intention of awakening the giants of the religious community to what they are doing until it is too late to mount a defense.

Equally important, the issue must be one which can be framed in a way which mutes opposition. In the Jones case, that issue was race. Bob Jones University is a religious school to which admission is open to all races. The authorities at the school, however, hold it as part of their religious faith that interracial dating and interracial marriage are forbidden by God. It is here that the IRS found its weapon.

Before going further, let us get the case analyzed. Many of us may disagree among ourselves about a large number of issues concerning the divine dispensation. Nevertheless, a sincere attempt by a religion to live up to what it considers God's commands is the crux of the Jones case.

It must also be clear from the outset that there is no issue of government funding. The sole consideration evolved on whether this school would lose its tax exemmption because of its beliefs. Would donors to Bob Jones be entitled to deduct their contributions just as those who give to other religious enterprises?

The shocking answer in the Jones case is **no**, donors may not deduct donations to that school. We might anticipate that the Court would have cited a statute prohibiting such tax exemption. This did not happen. We might expect that the argument might have been that the Constitution forbids tax exemption to such schools. We would be disappointed here also. What the Supreme Court tells us in the Jones case is that tax exemption for a religion which forbids interracial dating and marriage is contrary to a thing called "public policy."

Now, in searching out the limits of religious freedom, we are not surprised that one is not free to violate criminal law on the grounds of religious beliefs. And certainly no one objects that religious freedom cannot be the pretext for harming other members of society. But now, we are introduced to a new limitation. You may not hold religious beliefs which are at variance with so-called public policy.

That may sound reasonable until one asks himself what is the public policy I must adhere to in order to obtain the protection of the free exercise clause of the First Amendment? Is it definable in clear and consistent terms and who sets such policy?

We all understand what is meant by foreign policy, farm policy or economic policy. These mean the measures taken by a particular government administration to deal with continuing problem areas in society. They last as long as the administration is in power and then give way to the next set of policies. But this is not public policy.

Public policy has the ring of permanence. Yet where is it to be found? The answer, of course, is that we citizens are to find it in the latest statement of those in power. By its very definition, then, there is no such thing as the official public policy of the United States, nor has there ever been.

Therein lies the real monstrosity of the Jones case. If our religious beliefs displease the current public policy of our masters, we will be punished. One can be safe in his religious beliefs only if he reads the morning papers to keep in tune with today's public policy. So much for subjecting religious principles to the arbitrary and changing policies of the mighty IRS.

Under such political circumstances few felt inclined to come to the defense of the school in the Jones case because they found it impossible to defend the principle of freedom of religion without being castigated as racists. The IRS had gotten its pinch of incense and created the dangerous precedent that no religion may without penalty hold beliefs which are at odds with the public policy of the United States. Put another way, certain religious beliefs may now be taxed.

This unbelievable restriction now imposed on the free exercise of religion opened the door to alarming questions about what other public policy demands might follow.

Would all-black educational endowment funds also be deprived of their tax exemptions because of public policy on racism? Would Jewish charitable funds be deprived of their tax exemptions because some of the funds might be used contrary to U.S. public policy on colonization of the West Bank? Would the Catholic and other churches with all-male clergy be deprived of their tax exemptions because of public policy against sexual discrimination? The list goes on and the targets for government action against religion have been multiplied massively because of the disastrous precedent set by the Jones decision.

And more frightening yet is the question of who declares public policy for the government? There is no such thing as an office of public policy. The Bob Jones policy was derived by the IRS. Who would decide the next one? We did not have long to wait. The Department of Housing and Urban Development (HUD) and the Department of Education provided the answer in the cases of Grove City and Brigham Young University. If you didn't subscribe to the current government demands for equal treatment of the sexes right down to putting both in the same college housing facilities, then you had to be punished.

In the Grove City case, the issue wasn't even a tax exemption. Here the government has decided that no one who receives government assistance may even go to the school without forfeiting their government assistance. No GI bill beneficiaries, no recipients of government loans, no grantees of aid to students in higher education may go to Grove City.

Does Grove City endorse the wholesale use of drugs? No, but that's not necessarily true at several other universities which receive millions of dollars of your tax money. Does Grove City encourage promiscuous sex on campus? No, but you can be sure that many universities which do will continue to have your tax money shoveled at them. Grove City concentrates on education in the classic sense, and that might be its greatest crime.

The reason given by the government for punishing Grove City is that it refuses to sign a paper agreeing to treat both sexes exactly the same in physical education matters. Why the government is out to harass and even destroy churches and highly respected schools, like Brigham Young, Grove City, and Hillsdale College, is difficult for people to understand.

These are schools with outstanding records for maintaining high standards of academic excellence and moral codes, but they have independent ideas about education being a process of developing the person, body, mind and character which do not conform to the government policy straitjacket. Unfortunately, because of their differences, the academic community has largely stood by silently or cheering while the government presses its attack.

The administration now in power opposes the use of "public policy" against Grove City, yet it continues to be the stick with which the school is being beaten. This makes the situation even more frightening because it then becomes clear that public policy is not even what the President says it is. So who does dictate this phantom called public policy which is being used against our churches and schools to disrupt our lives and those of our children?

Subchapter 2

Nebraska—
The Disease Spreads

In Nebraska a seven year holy war has been raging between church and state over the operation of Christian schools. Preachers have been jailed repeatedly and their churches fined and padlocked. Fathers have served months in jail while the wives with their children fled as fugitives of the law from their homes, from their jobs, from the state itself.

One father in jail said, "I went 10,000 miles to the Far East to fight for freedom and I end up in jail when I came home to practice it." For all who cherish liberty this spectacle is becoming a nightmare in the American dream. Here's the picture.

A number of small towns in the state of Nebraska have Baptist Churches which until recently were just another part of the mid-America landscape. Each of these small churches had attached to it an equally small church school. Through this combination came the beginnings of a controversy which has shaken the nation and reached to the White House itself.

Nebraska has a law which requires all private schools, including church schools, to have their students taught only by state certified teachers. Nebraska also requires that all private schools submit for approval the curriculum of studies to be used by the school. Therein lay the seeds for a church-state confrontation.

Now you may wonder why such a story is in a book about the Internal Revenue Service. The answer is really quite simple.

The techniques, ingredients and targets of the school controversy are so similar to those which we have been discussing that it appears that the State of Nebraska might well have learned how to oppress and destroy religions from the IRS. First, there are the small unaffiliated churches unlikely to be noticed or defended by the larger affected population. Second, there is a cover issue which tends to make the small church schools look like villains or intransigent hardheads. Third, there is an issue which, once imbedded in the public record, can be used anywhere against all similar organizations no matter what their size or prestige.

Add that all the elements of the IRS targetry are in place. Religion as we have come to understand it; ministers thrown in jail; resultant disruption of family and religious life and you have a pattern which is too close to our subject to ignore.

The final element is the involvement of the federal government in creating the opportunity for mischief and then ignoring the consequences of its conduct. Federal money is the name, counting children is the game. As usual in these stories, the love of money is the root of all evil. In Nebraska, as in other states, public officials contend that each child who is placed in a private school represents a loss of thousands of dollars in subsidy from the federal government. Thus, as with the IRS cases, the government sets in motion a chain of events related to the desire for money, and nature and greed take care of the rest.

The problem will repeat similarly in the situations we report, greed coupled with the growing tendency of government to bring everything under its control, conspire to create a scenario for the state to usurp religious independence.

An intransigent Baptist preacher set the first match to the Nebraska tinder. Everett Sileven, an independent Baptist pastor, was ministering to his small flock in the small town of Louisville, about 20 miles southwest of Omaha, in a Church called the Faith Baptist Church. Literally in it is the Faith Christian School. The basement of the Church houses a modern facility which accommodates some thirty students placed in the charge of Pastor Sileven and his daughter, the school principal, Theresa Schmidt, who is married to the assistant pastor.

Both Pastor Sileven and Mrs. Schmidt refused to even attempt to qualify under the Nebraska "accreditation law". His grounds were simplicity itself. The state had no authority to intervene in or overrule the parents' decisions on such crucial and personal matters as the upbringing and education of their children. In addition, to submit the teachers and the curriculum to the state for approval would be tantamount to admitting that the state had authority over the church.

Reverend Sileven rightly contends that both the Constitution of the State of Nebraska and the Constitution of the United States forbid such a result. More disconcerting yet to the civil authorities was Dr. Sileven's position that even if there was no such Constitutional prohibition, the Law of God made such a usurpation unacceptable. They could not subject "God's will" to the approval of the state. The battle was on and the results have created an unending list of unprecedented problems.

Lest someone think that Pastor Sileven is just using religion to cover slipshod education, let the record show that the State Education Department of Nebraska has painfully admitted that the school principal is eminently qualified under the state law, having taken the requisite education courses and passed them. Even less appetizing for the State, the Faith Christian School children were independently tested and scored an average of a year and a half to three years ahead of their state school peers.

So the Nebraska fight does not really involve the issue of adequate education, but it is rather a naked drive for power. The state, like Diocletian, issued its fiat and good reason or no, the church school would obey.

The battle has continued for close to seven years and is not resolved to this day. Reverend Sileven lost in every court in which the case was heard in Nebraska and the United States Supreme Court refused to hear it. At one point, the doughty pastor was thrown into the county jails for four months because he insisted that his school would remain in operation.

When classes were again resumed for the fall term in October 1982, the local District Court ordered *the Church padlocked* to prevent the use of the school. On a cold Sunday evening the Sheriff, with a number of deputies and several state troopers, arrived and threw scores of Baptist preachers, who were praying in the church to express their solidarity with the pastor, out into the snow. The officers then padlocked the church, the first time such an alarming act has occurred against religion in America in recorded memory.

Up to this point, to demonstrate its dominion over religion, the state of Nebraska had closed the school, padlocked the church and jailed its pastor. And still the state had not won. Ministers and other interested people from all parts of the nation came in by the hundreds to help. The more State and County officials persecuted Faith Baptist and its people, the more resilient they became, and the more people everywhere came to understand that Reverend Sileven and his allies were fighting their fight.

Nebraska is only one of thirteen states with such laws and the situation has provoked considerable interest among those who hope to exert similar government control over church schools. With such attention and pressure from special interest groups like the National Education Association, Nebraska authorities pressed their attack. And the more Dr. Sileven resisted, the more the naked face of government hostility to religion was exposed.

By the beginning of the school term in September, 1983, it was evident to the state that it had a tiger by the tail. Sileven was getting stronger. His school reopened and hundreds of his brother unaffiliated Baptist preachers were flocking to Louisville to give their visible testimony that they stood shoulder-to-shoulder with him.

The state was not prepared to back off. A new District Judge, with the unlikely name of Ronald Reagan, was sent in from an adjoining county. Judge Reagan, a man of obvious pre-formed opinions and limited sensitivity, indicated on his arrival that he was prepared to use the law to subdue this pesky preacher and break the back of the rebellion.

The series of events launched by Judge Reagan might well enshrine his name with boycott, lynch and Judge Roy Bean. His first step was, with the compliant cooperation of the County Prosecutor, to issue orders for the Pastor, the Principal, and seven sets of parents who had enrolled children in the school to appear in his court to "show cause" why they should not be cited for contempt for continuing to operate the school and send children to it respectively.

The cited group was forewarned that the plan of this infamous pair in the Cass County Court was to jail everyone and to put the children of the cited parents in foster homes from which homes they would be sent to state schools. If anyone doubts the bad faith of the State of Nebraska, let him reread that sentence. In the name of protecting the children of the State of Nebraska from their parents, Judge Reagan planned to put *16 people in jail* and *24 children in foster care.*

On November 23, 1983, Thanksgiving Eve, the seven male parents appeared in Court. The wives and the Pastor and his daughter fled the state, with the 24 fugitive children in tow.

And the warning was right on the money. Judge Reagan trumped up an excuse to send the fathers to jail. If the others had been there, they too, would no doubt have been jailed. That was the sole and entire purpose of the November 23rd legal charade.

There has been a lot of nonsense floated around about these people being guilty of disobedience to the law, or to the order of a judge, or to the spirit of the times. Most of this propaganda has been put out by the State of Nebraska, and, like its judicial system, it is a fraud.

The seven men were ordered by the Judge to take the stand and to testify about the Faith Baptist School and their involvement in its operation. Now there are a number of things wrong with such a proceeding, even by the twisted system which goes by the name of judiciary in the State of Nebraska.

1) The seven fathers and mothers were not parties to any pending case in the court. As such, they were not even properly before the court on a show cause order.

2) The men pleaded the 5th Amendment. For almost two centuries, both the United States Courts and the local courts, *even in Nebraska*, have recognized the right of a person in a civil case, as this case is, to claim the 5th. Judge Reagan denied that this is the law.

3) Very late in the game, Judge Reagan changed his story and began to allege that he had granted these fathers immunity, thereby overrriding their claim of the 5th Amendment and requiring them to answer. His last minute switch sounds fishy enough without more, but there is a great deal more.

4) A grant of immunity under Nebraska law must be based upon a formal motion of the prosecutor and must be invoked only on a specific order of the Court. You guessed it. Neither requirement happened in that court on that day. THERE NEVER WAS A LEGAL PREEMPTION OF THE

5TH AMENDMENT RIGHTS OF THE FATHERS IN THAT COURT ON THAT OR ANY OTHER DAY.

5) Judge Reagan then issued bench warrants for the arrest of the seven mothers. Under Nebraska law, he is without power to issue such warrants in a civil case, especially against non-parties, as described in item number one.

The Judge can have it only one of two ways. Either he is ignorant of the law or, in aid of his publicly expressed intention to break the back of the rebellion, he ignored the law. In either case he held the men in contempt of court and jailed them until they agreed to testify.

The story gets even worse. On December 6, 1983, this same Judge held a continuation of the hearing on the case of Faith Christian School and Faith Baptist Church.

At that continued hearing, I offered my staff legal assistant who, although not a Nebraska attorney, is a practitioner with experience in education law of some twenty years. The Judge refused to let him represent the men. (Later the Judge also denied a request from the men for a court-appointed attorney.)

Judge Reagan then outdid even himself. He left the seven men in jail, all dressed, shaved and expecting to appear in court, and commenced the hearing without their presence. *They were not even allowed to attend their own hearing.* I am no lawyer, but you don't have to be to know better than that. I was stunned; I hadn't seen such a kangaroo legal procedure since the movie, "To Kill a Mockingbird."

The Sheriff testified that he had interrogated the men in the jail which is a few yards from the courtroom and had gotten each to sign a statement that they continued to refuse to testify. That was the entire hearing. The men were to remain in jail. Then, as if to emphasize who was the real party in contempt, the Judge closed the hearing with warnings and insulting remarks to the spectators who were quietly sitting in the courtroom.

With the exception of one man who, as a result of a later threat from the court, testified, six are still in the Cass County Jail as I write these words.

Although these political prisoners are illegally detained in jail as hostages to Judge Reagan's effort to close the school, the judges of Nebraska have turned down three applications for Writs of Habeas Corpus. Do not misunderstand. They did not deny release after a hearing. These judges have all refused to sign even the Writ which would authorize a hearing. Bail requests, motions to void the warrants against the women and a host of other moves, have all been rejected by both the highest court in Nebraska and the local Federal court.

By the time you read this, these men may be free. Hopefully so. However, that will not change the horror of this story nor the injustice. These men have been in jail for two months. They have committed no crime, yet they have not seen their wives and children since they were jailed—not for Thanksgiving, not for Christmas, not for New Year's. They have lost their jobs. Their families are broken and fugitives. Their children are guests in friendly homes, but they are living out of suitcases denied their own homes and their own school.

The sole issues are and will remain whether the state of Nebraska or the parents are the best people to raise these children and determine the type of education they will receive; and whether these people's belief in God has any claim against the state's general educational responsibility to the public and its seeming commitment to a labor union, the NEA, to take such children to enforce job security for the teachers in the state system.

If enough Americans are not indignant at this kind of action by government, there will be many more fugitives in our nation. If enough Americans do not demand that the heavy hand of government be lifted from our families and our consciences, big brother will become even stronger and we will get the stifling overdose of big government we deserve. If enough Americans do not raise their voices to Washington, demanding the Congress and the President enforce the Constitutional rights of parents against the usurpations of the state, then the authorities will continue to do nothing and the next cases we face will surely become even worse.

Half a dozen years ago, a California judge, in a case involving money, told us what the battleground would soon be. We did not hear or believe him and we got Nebraska. That judge declared that the child is an asset of the state. If that seems right to you, then do nothing. Bit by bit, the new paganism will close your churches, jail your pastors, forbid the operation of your church schools and throw the dissenters into jail with their leaders.

After Nebaska, we don't need to appeal to some prophetic visionary like George Orwell. It is already happening. But if you do not think that Nebraska is right, tell your leaders in Washington, that you will not tolerate any more Nebraskas. Tell them that you will look closely at what they do to defend the Constitution and the rights of religion and of the people.

It took a thousand ministers descending on a small town in Nebraska to get a non-binding Governor's Commission to even admit that a valid problem existed. Such small relief cannot be allowed to put us back to sleep or the state for sure will finally own our children and grandchildren.

Excuses by public officials do not protect the "Nebraska 7." Either our national government is on the side of the parents and on the side of protecting the constitutionally guaranteed free exercise of religion without government interference or it is not. Either it acts or it does not. Six men are still in jail. Their pastor and their school principal are fugitives. Can America continue to allow such abuse of human and civil rights?

Subchapter 3

Selective Targeting

How does the government select a person or organization for tax audit? Is it done scientifically, arbitrarily, or at random?

Naturally, the Internal Revenue Service will look at returns with a substantial income, those with large and unusual deductions, and those with big refunds. Other concerns also receive special attention, all of which the IRS collectively refers to as the DIF technique, or "greatest audit potential".

Translated into English, this simply means that the IRS programs a computer to sort out returns with certain characteristics for review. Conveniently, this process also provides the appearance of complete objectivity and scientific precision enabling the IRS to discount complaints by taxpayers of mistakes involving human error. Unfortunately for the public, however, this system provides an illusion which is deceptive and even dangerous since the machine can be blamed for selection of certain targets for audit—targets which are actually chosen arbitrarily by IRS officials for reasons of their own.

These reasons include a hunch by an IRS officer, complaints from other citizens, and information from anonymous sources. Prejudice and political motives, either within or outside the Agency, can also cause targeting of a taxpayer.

In other words, you can be selected for an IRS audit for no reason at all, or you can be selectively targeted because the IRS or someone else, particularly someone of influence, does not like you. Yet, when a taxpayer asks, "Why me?", the excuse most commonly used will always be the DIF program—the machine did it to you.

Several alarming examples of "selective targeting" of individuals and churches are discussed in various chapters of this book. But the problem is getting worse as the IRS invades the Constitutionally protected sanctuaries of the nation's churches with jail sentences and criminal penalties.

In the Western States, a senior Internal Revenue auditor has not only proven religious discrimination practices by the IRS in promotion and assignment policies, but he now details how the U.S. Treasury has recently lost what could amount to hundreds of millions of dollars in another case of religious prejudice.

In a letter of October 25, 1983 this agent wrote to U.S. Senator Steve Symms of Idaho with the following information.

Honorable Sir;

I am placing with your office all pertinent documents relating to the formal Complaint of (Religious) Discrimination which I, as an employee, had filed against the Internal Revenue Service and which included the reports of suspected religious bigotry on the part of IRS.

I am requesting that your office attempt to secure a copy of the formal investigation report resulting from my complaint and have authorized such a request by your office.

This appears necessary as I have been informed that the official investigation report, which was completed and ready for issuance, has reportedly been intercepted by the National IRS Office and I fear that it may be altered before final release.

In addition to the suspected tampering with the investigation report, I fear that the documents and records which I have and which support the reported religious bigotry in the conduct of the IRS national project known as the "Erickson Mining Claim Donation Project" may no longer be safe in my possession. I base this fear on a comment made by a regional IRS Official to the local IRS manager to the effect that, if they didn't start getting cooperation (in coverup efforts?) they had better plan on setting a house on fire and getting rid of some records.

I believe the comments which I overheard were aimed at me and I also believe they represent a very real threat to the pertinent records. Such a comment by any IRS officer would be a terrible travesty of his proper responsibilities, but this very same act of arson occurred on March 8, 1982, in which an unknown arsonist set fire to my home and nearly destroyed it and everything in it.

I might note that, in addition to the arson at my home which occurred shortly after I initiated my complaint of discrimination with a report of suspected religious bigotry on the part of IRS in the direction of its national "Erickson Mining Claim Donation Project", an act of sabotage occurred to my auto which was intended to cause a highway accident just days after I initiated the formal Complaint of Discrimination which resulted in the official investigation report discussed earlier.

Additionally, I was then suspended without pay for some 48 days on the charge of insubordination based upon my action in requesting an EEO Counselor to aid me in the preparation of my formal complaint and reporting the auto sabotage incident for investigation.

I might also note that the National Commissioner of the IRS has come to Idaho once this year, apparently to direct the IRS efforts to cover up the anti-Mormon bigotry involved in the previously named national IRS project, and he is due back again on Nov. 10th apparently for the same reason.

The desperation of these IRS officials can be understood

only in light of what occurred during the approximately five years during which the Erickson Mining Claim Donation Project was conducted, and during the court action by IRS against the L.D.S. Church which culminated that project.

By way of brief explanation, let me report the following: There were perhaps more than 8,000 mining claims located by geologist Einar Erickson with many, if not most, being donated by the owners to countless charities with an unsupported and unwarranted value claimed for each of $250,000.00.

If only half, or something in excess of 4,000 of these mining claims were donated to various charities, which include everything from state medical societies to the L.D.S. Church, then simple computation would indicate that potentially fraudulent donations were deducted on the owners' tax returns in an amount in excess of one billion dollars.

IRS could easily have identified all of the abusive donations and corrected every return involved and collected the full tax that was due. All the needed records which gave the owner's name and the date and recipient of the donated mining claim were on file in the Reno, Nevada, B.L.M. offices. Even the outside consulting geologist hired by IRS noted in his report to IRS that a large number of recipient charities were involved and that all pertinent records would be on record with B.L.M.

IRS chose to search out *only* those abusive donations which went to the L.D.S. Church (B.Y.U. and Ricks College), which donations comprised only a very small percentage of the total. So as not to include any of the mining claim donations made to all of the other recipient charities, IRS hand searched thousands of tax returns with the express purpose of identifying *only* those involving donations of mining claims thought to have gone to the L.D.S. Church. All the rest were purposely ignored and the taxes due lost to the government.

Even with the accidental inclusion of a few returns which contained claimed deductions for donations of these mining claims to non-LDS charities, the total number of donations challenged by IRS was only a small fraction of the total number of such donations with all such donations claimed as made to non-LDS charities purposely ignored by IRS.

The number of such donations challenged by IRS (which were those made to L.D.S. charities plus a smattering of donations made to other charities included by accident in the IRS project) have been variously reported to be from 300 to just over 600. Assuming that no more than 700 such mining claim donations were challenged by IRS, then simple math computation would indicate that no more than $175,000,000 of the total of more than 1 billion was challenged and the tax owing collected by IRS with the balance of something in excess of 825 million simply ignored by IRS.

This loss to the government of millions of dollars in tax from the thousands of donations of these mining claims to non-LDS charities would be terrible enough if this were due to a simple oversight on the part of the IRS officials responsible. That does not appear to be the case. IRS intentionally set out to identify and challenge only those abusive mining claim donations going to L.D.S. charities and went to a great deal of expense and trouble to omit all those abusive mining claim donations going to the multitude of non-LDS charities. To achieve this very narrow selection of returns involving only donations of the mining claims to L.D.S. charities took thousands of hours of hand sorting of returns and cost hundreds of thousands of dollars in salary. The absurdity of this effort is evident when one remembers that the complete record of all of the abusive mining claim donations—both those to L.D.S. charities and those to non-LDS charities—were already on file with the government's BLM Offices in Reno.

And why did IRS choose to identify and challenge only those returns containing a donation of such a mining claim to an L.D.S. charity while attempting to ignore all such returns with donations of such mining claims to all the other non-LDS charities? It appears that the sole purpose of this activity by IRS was to create false statistics which would be ultimately used to support a request to the Justice Department for a summons action against the L.D.S. Church in which IRS asked for the names and gifts of all who contributed to the L.D.S. charities. In short, IRS wanted the name of every individual who had supported the L.D.S. charities with any donation or gift of property.

And what would IRS have done with this list of supporters of the L.D.S. charity (BYU)? It seems logical that every name received by IRS would be targeted for an audit and somehow tagged as a person somehow evading his tax by supporting the L.D.S. charity. Such a large scale project by IRS in which a few questionable mining claim donations are used as a tool to present false statistics to secure Justice Department attacks against the L.D.S. Church and its supporters can be viewed only as a direct attack against one religious group—the L.D.S. Such can be nothing less than bigotry on a scale we have not seen since the days of NAZI Germany.

When this attack against the L.D.S. Church went to court, the Federal Judge asked IRS the reasonable question of why hadn't IRS gone to the BLM records rather than mounting a summons enforcement attack on the L.D.S. Church. To deceive the court apparently, IRS then went to BLM and asked for a list of all the mining claim donations which went to the L.D.S. charity (BYU). Had IRS not so restricted its request, BLM would have provided all of the names of individuals making such abusive donations to all of the many recipient charities involved and not to only the L.D.S. charities. Such a response could have greatly embarassed the IRS so it purposely secured only the slanted response it wished to continue its court attack on the L.D.S. Church. This was nothing less than perjury by the IRS before a Federal Court.

All of this activity by IRS had to have top IRS direction and approval and, as such, certainly must have constituted bigotry and other assorted illegal actions on a grand scale unsurpassed in U.S. History.

You can now see why IRS is so desperate to cover this matter up even if it must burn a house or two or sabotage a car and perhaps kill someone in the process.

If there was any way this information and my experiences might be presented to a committee or hearing, I would certainly cooperate. This must be made known and prevented from happening again. IRS has immense power and with that power it could destroy and control any organization or church through the very means it has used here against the L.D.S. Church and its supporters.

Even if I were not myself L.D.S., I would fear this example as IRS may next use the same illegal methods to control my religious group. And this can be viewed as nothing less than a direct attack with the obvious purpose of control or destruction of a specific religious group for no reasonable reason other than organized bigotry of the greatest magnitude.

With the desperation of the responsible IRS Officials evident, I am expecting more attacks and I fear for my safety and the safety of these records which I place with your office.

Your consideration and aid will be greatly appreciated.

> Sincerely,
> /s/ [Name withheld]

On January 5, 1984 an affidavit was filed with the U.S. Commission on Civil Rights at Seattle, Washington, including the following statements relating to religious discrimination:

(Paragraph 1)—My name is Douglas F. Rose, and I am an attorney and the duly elected prosecuting attorney in and for the County of Lincoln, State of Idaho. I am also a citizen of the State of Idaho and reside in the Second Congressional District of said state. My district is represented by Congressman George V. Hansen.

(Paragraph 2)—As a result of certain stories I heard, I began privately investigating and examining a series of acts and conduct by officers and agents of the U.S. Government which led me to believe that my civil rights as a citizen of said state and as a member of the Church of Jesus Christ of Latter-Day Saints (Mormons) have been and are now being knowingly, intentionally and unlawfully violated by officers and agents of the U.S. Government.

(Paragraph 4)—Finally, I have accumulated information which indicates that the IRS in Idaho and surrounding states is conducting a purposeful course of anti-Mormon discrimination. The IRS is investigating an alleged tax fraud scheme involving the Erickson Mining claims in Nevada. Basically, a mining speculator filed a number of mining claims on the public domain in Nevada. These claims were later transferred for consideration to taxpayers who were either interested in them for their investment or tax write-off value. Some claims were then donated to some 300 different non-profit organizations, including Brigham Young University, Rick's College, and Boy Scouts, etc. At the time the claims were donated, the donators wrote off the claims on their income tax returns, and the IRS alleges they did so at greatly inflated values. However, rather than go directly to the Nevada Bureau of Land Management for a list of the claims so that they could follow each and every claim, the IRS chose to attack only those donations which came directly to Brigham Young University and Rick's College, which are Mormon-owned universities. In fact, there is presently a case pending before the U.S. Supreme Court involving these donations. Even though I am Mormon, I am nevertheless outraged that the IRS would target one non-profit organization for attack. The IRS does not seem to be concerned about the other 200 plus non-profit organizations and donations. In my way of thinking, the IRS is willing to forego attacking other donations at the expense of another. In a sense the IRS is allowing the other donators to reap the benefits of what it believes to be illegal tax write-offs while concentrating its efforts on the Mormon donators. Not only does this course of action violate fundamental doctrines of fair play, but it also robs the national treasury of possible additional revenue (which may be in the millions of dollars). The selectivity of the IRS attacks which is directed exclusively at Mormon donators is clearly motivated by the IRS's religious bias and their choice of a religious beneficiary. I have documented evidence of established IRS discriminations against Mormons.

(Paragraph 5)—I am prepared to provide the Civil Rights Commission with documentation which fully substantiates my claims.

Among these documents is a March 31, 1981 memorandum from the Chief of an IRS Section in Idaho to his counterpart in Nevada pushing for a proposal to end the biased activity of the IRS against the L.D.S. Church which had been submitted in November 1978 by the agent who later wrote the letter of complaint to Senator Symms previously cited.

The memo expressed frustration that this proposal to provide equal treatment for targets in the questionable project and to stop the targeting of the Mormon Church had been sidetracked in official channels for 28 months.

The author concluded his urgent plea for a change in IRS procedures by stating, "If it is as relevant to the Erickson Mining Claims as the Group Manager and the Tax Shelter Coordinator believe, I want to give the appropriate recognition to [the agent] for his enthusiasm and foresight in generating this approach."

A later memo from the IRS tax shelter coordinator dated May 22, 1981 further establishes the credentials and credibility of the Agent fighting the Agency's bigoted and wasteful targeting programs.

This communication commended him for his "suggestion on tracing the Erickson Mining Claims from their source to the ultimate disposition" and concluded by saying, "I, as a tax shelter coordinator, wish to congratulate you on your insight and knowledge of the mining industry."

These crude targeting tactics of the IRS against certain religious groups have not gone unnoticed in Washington, D.C., where concerned agencies and several committees of Congress are currently reviewing and investigating these activities. One such investigation is being conducted by Congressman Charles Rangel, Chairman of the Ways and Means Subcommittee on IRS Oversight, who has demanded an explanation from the Commissioner of Internal Revenue, Roscoe L. Egger, Jr., in a letter dated December 19, 1983.

In my own communication with Chairman Rangel of November 14, 1983 regarding this case, I stated:

> There is simply no other explanation of the course of action against only LDS institutions than that the IRS planned its procedures to harm that group alone. Aside from the fact that, as a member of the LDS Church, I am keenly interested in protecting it from IRS religious discrimination, as a Member of Congress, I am concerned that this entire matter raises the specter of the IRS acting under this same anti-religion motivation against other religions in other circumstances.
>
> Like the LDS in minority status and with limited public acceptance, the Scientologists have also been under IRS attack for more than a decade. Since all anyone knows about such matters is what the IRS tells them, is it not possible that that they too are the victims of an agency answerable to no one and which has developed an appetite for the resources of religious groups once thought to be protected by the First Amendment and the Internal Revenue Code itself?
>
> Certainly credence is given to that view by the recent conduct of the IRS against the Unification Church. Their head

(to whom members of their religion look as Catholics do to the Pope) has been convicted of criminal tax evasion on a charge that involves under two hundred thousand dollars and a highly questionable interpretation of the law.

The enactment last year of TEFRA has now markedly increased the power of the IRS. Have their activities against these smaller religious groups been only trial runs in preparation for the use of this expanded power against the larger sects—Catholics, Protestants and Jews?

We have reached the point where the IRS is now, by its own claim and its regulations, the final arbiter of what is a legitimate religion in the United States. Can anyone think of an agency less appropriate to such an office? In truth, should there be any government authority empowered to certify religion? Has our lust for revenues led us to put these discreditable people in charge of who we worship, what we believe, and to whom we may give our substance?

Subchapter 4

Politics and Prejudice

Selective targeting of taxpayers by the Internal Revenue Service is a fact. It happens—sometimes legitimately and sometimes from prejudice.

The prejudice is the problem. Prejudice in the hands of unrestrained power does great damage to the people and institutions it targets. Injustice and fear are its byproducts.

Politics is an engine which too often uses prejudice as its fuel to create the policy of government and society. This is a fatal combination for democracy and genuine self-government in most areas of the world.

In America, where racial, ethnic and religious lines are not so clearly drawn, the politics of prejudice is not so constant, but the system still has its targets and can still be fatal.

Thus, when prejudice and politics combine to form so-called public policy, someone gets hurt. And that someone is usually the individualist, the non-conformist, the outsider, the one who looks different or talks different, and those who press hard for a controversial cause.

All of which brings us to another tax battle—a battle between church and state, one which also has gone to the United States Supreme Court. The Unification Church, and its leader, Reverend Sun Myung Moon, are under siege by the Internal Revenue Service with politics and prejudice carrying the offensive.

The Unification religion, often referred to simply as "Moonies," had its beginning in South Korea in 1954 and came to the United States in 1959. Reverend Moon and his followers moved aggressively into America with a strong and controversial missionary zeal and enthusiastic involvement in public and political issues.

These Unificationists were different, they were highly patriotic during the anti-war era, they were boat rockers on the American scene, they were easy targets for strong public opinion. And, naturally, the IRS was soon sent after them by their enemies for all the wrong reasons—reasons light on facts and heavy with social and political prejudice.

The Moon case has become the centerpiece for the IRS in its continuing battle against religious freedom in the United States. Though a worldwide church, the Unification membership in the United States was relatively small. It was unpopular in Establishment circles and it easily could be used to establish a precedent for later use against any church which reposes the ultimate trust of the members in the leader of the church.

In 1981 Reverend Moon was indicted for tax evasion and related matters. From the beginning, it was evident that the government was relying for its case on the most damning facts possible—the unpopularity of the Moon Church and the fact that Reverend Moon is an Oriental. Although not part of the indictment, it was these charges which the government proved without the slightest effort. The defendant didn't speak English. What evidence, after all, could be produced more damning than that?

What did they charge Reverend Moon with? Basically, that he put $112,000 in interest in a Chase Bank account and didn't pay taxes on that interest for three years in the early 1970's. Watch closely. The IRS and the Department of Justice are about the business of proving that assets held in his own name by the leader of a religion are his personally and therefore he owes taxes on them. But only if he is an Oriental, if his religion is small, and if he has a powerful political enemy.

Lest one think that statement cruel, it doesn't tell half the story. During the same period of time, the late Cardinal Terence Cooke, Roman Catholic Archbishop of New York, whose residence was about three miles from the courtroom where the Moon action was in progress, held personally, in his own name, assets worth a thousand times the amount Moon was charged with evading. More to the point, the laws of the Catholic Church *require* that the reigning ordinary own its property in his own name. This is known in law as *corporation sole*, a well-established principle.

One will not see the IRS indict any Catholic Bishops for tax evasion. There are two good reasons for that. First, they are too big to fool with *at the moment*. Second, it is well-known that they hold the assets of their dioceses as trustees of their faithful and of the Church.

Behind all the legal niceties, Reverend Moon was tried because the IRS knew that in case of the failure of the evidence, the agency could fall back on public hostility. As a bonus however, if the government should win the appeals from the conviction, it would possess a powerful legal precedent. The IRS can say with a straight face that if it brings Reverend Moon to book for his handling of church funds, what is to stop them from looking into the Catholic, Lutheran and other large church bodies to determine whether they, too, hold personal assets which should be taxable?

Do not be deluded that this has anything to do with a zeal for collecting taxes for the United States Treasury. First, the tax, the fine, the penalties, all together, do not represent a small fraction of what the government has spent in prosecuting the Moon case. The IRS also knows that most of the money over which this issue was raised was generated outside this country.

Given its worldwide scope, the Unification Church assuredly could restrict any assets which might be subject to the arbitrary and hostile jurisdiction of the IRS. In sum, the net economic effect on the United States can only be negative.

What is much more frightening about the Moon matter is what does not appear in Court records. To understand the gravity of the implications of the Moon case, start from the beginning. A religious leader whose every activity is subject to press and probably government scrutiny deposits a large sum of money in an account in one of the largest banks in the world. At the end of the first year, he does not report the interest on that account as income. Beginning here, several things become clear.

First, that amount of interest as a part of the total income of the Church is so small as to be relatively trivial. In any number of cases, the IRS would normally conduct an audit, file an assessment, and demand payment of tax on the income together with penalties and interest. It did none of these. Why, where in similar cases the IRS has negotiated a settlement when the liability was clear, did it decide in this case to proceed criminally where the liability was anything but clear?

Both the IRS and Justice Department take the position that this is just an ordinary, run-of-the-mill handling of an ordinary, run-of-the-mill tax evasion case. That won't wash. If Moon is not a special case, then why was his situation handled so specially by the IRS? They can't have it both ways.

Second, from Reverend Moon's side, very large sums of money, generated by a religious leader running a revivalist campaign, are taken in and expended on the work the Church has undertaken for itself in the United States. On only a miniscule portion of this total, the IRS claims that Reverend Moon is a personal owner and is liable for taxes. Is the IRS thereby admitting that it actually accepts the Unification Church as a religion free from obligation to pay taxes on its assets? No other conclusion is possible.

Does anything that was done with the money suggest surreptitious behavior? Was the money placed in the banks of Switzerland, the Bahamas, Panama? Again the IRS is placed in a dilemma. On one hand, it explains the overt handling of the matter as resulting from the defendant's inexperience. On the other, it argues his sophistication as a successful business man, surrounded by the very best advice that money can buy.

Listen to what the Defense Counsel had to say on this question:

> Ask yourselves as you listen to the evidence in this question: Would a person who had the cash money attributed to Reverend Moon, who wanted to cheat the government, who wanted to defraud the government, put it into a bank account at the Chase Manhattan Bank, and then, if you will, ladies and gentlemen, put right at the top of that account, and you will see it on the charts, Reverend Sun Myung Moon?
>
> . . . the ones that go to the Internal Revenue Service to tell them about interest income, would a person setting out to cheat the United States of America go about putting that bank account into his own name, not hiding his name, say to the government "Here is the money" and say to the government "Come get me"?

Sun Myung Moon appears to remain quite stable as the leader of his religious organization. It is the government which seems unable to take a stable position. Knowledgeable lawyers I have talked with in almost every particular, contend the case against Reverend Moon cannot be made if all the facts are known.

The IRS itself admits that it is prosecuting a religious leader for a minor matter, even if there were an infraction. From my prior knowledge of the IRS and its imperatives, I am not surprised. But now the case is in the hands of the United States Attorney. There could be an abrupt change in the method of handling. Theoretically at least, considerations of fairness and equity should now surface.

On the record, there can be no reasonable doubt that the case against the Reverend Moon was initiated for reasons other than taxes and with goals other than justice in mind. In terse form, the argument is, get Moon, and the Unification Church will fold. In the bargain, the IRS gets a precedent to be used against the larger, more established churches later on. We will let the lawyers argue about the myriad of other problems about the way in which the trial was held. For instance, does a man, who has been maliciously attacked in the press and who is concerned about public fairness because he is an Oriental with little command of the English language, have the right to waive a jury and have the judge alone make the findings of fact? The prosecutor resisted and demanded a jury trial. It was a jury trial.

The choice of court procedure can be critical. Only since the publication of my last edition, have I come into possession of documentation that the government screens juror lists with the tax dossiers of all prospective jurors. What impact does this questionable legal policy have on the impartiality of a jury and how often does it occur? It certainly leaves one to his own conclusions on why the IRS and the Justice Department wanted a jury trial.

It is a difficult question whether a man in Reverend Moon's position could get a fair trial under any circumstances. He is leader of a new sect toward which there is a great deal of overt hostility generated by sensational news coverage and he is a member of a numerically insignificant minority. When one adds to this, the very questionable nature of the charges, is it any wonder that the members of the Unification Church feel that they are being persecuted by the U.S. government?

Perhaps unspoken, but present in the case nonetheless, is the question of the appropriate use of discretion in prosecution. With a marginal case at best, against a member of a minority group and also the leader of a less-than-popular sect, is it not easy then to assume that discretion was not exercised in the Moon case because the goal of the IRS and other powerful forces in this country is to crush the Unification Church? It is clear that any excuse would do, even the pitiful reason used in this case to throw their leader in jail.

But the litany of abuses is not yet complete. No fair analysis of the why and the how of the case could ignore the appalling rationale for attacking the Unification Church through the IRS. If there had been clear complaints within the IRS jurisdiction, so be it. But to use politics and public prejudice to get the IRS into the business of qualifying what constitutes a religion is like throwing gasoline on a hot stove.

There is no question but what the IRS probably received many requests to go after Reverend Moon, but few would have the impact of a prominent senior member of the U.S. Senate Finance Committee. I refer to such a letter sent to the Internal Revenue Service asking that agency to move against the Unification Church. The letter follows in full.

United States Senate
Washington, D.C. 20510

January 9, 1976

Mr. Donald Alexander
Commissioner
Internal Revenue Service
1111 Constitution Avenue
Washington, D.C. 20224

Dear Mr. Alexander:
A large number of my constituents have contacted me about the Unification Church headed by Mr. Sun Myung Moon. Their questions and statements raise doubt in my mind

about the tax exempt status of that organization.

A few constituents writing me have sons or daughters that have been or are members of the Unification Church. Their letters are enclosed for your information. Most of those contacting me have read articles by investigative reporters and copies of those articles are attached.

As I understand, the first test for a tax exemption on religious grounds is that the group must be organized and operated exclusively for religious purposes. The information provided suggests the Unification Church may not meet this test in three ways.

Most of those contacting me question whether the organization is based on a bona fide religion or on mind control techniques. Parents of members and former members state that while initial entry into the group is clearly voluntary, the subsequent actions of members suggest the loss of any ability to make any reasoned or unguided choice but continued participation in the group. This may indicate that the organization is maintained not by religious motivation, but by the calculated eradication or erosion of each member's ability to make an alternate choice. The well-documented process of training and initiation activities appears to substantiate that the organization is based more on mind control and indoctrination than on religious faith.

Many Kansans have advised me that a major purpose of the organization is the accumulation of wealth and power and not the practice or furtherance of a religion. Former members indicate that the primary emphasis of leadership within the organization is the collection of money through the sale of various items. Members of the organization are subjected to great pressure to obtain funds, suggesting that the exclusive prupose of the organization is not a religious one, but that in fact a major goal is the accumulation of wealth.

Some statements by Mr. Moon and activities by some of his followers indicate a substantial political purpose, contrary to the requirement that the group be organized and operated exclusively for religious purposes. As described by the enclosed materials, Mr. Moon has made several statements implying political and governmental objectives. Since many members of the group apparently perceive Mr. Moon to be the embodiment of the Church, the appearance is that his stated intentions are not simply the goals of a private individual but the stated purposes of the organization. The contacts of many followers with members of Congress suggest that the organization is being operated not exclusively for religious purposes but at least to some extent for political purposes.

A second test for tax exempt religious organization, as I understand, is that no part of its net earnings inures to the benefit of any private individual. The attached articles by investigative reporters indicate that the head of the group, Mr. Moon, leads a far more affluent life than could reasonably be expected for any clergyman. This fact, if substantiated, suggests that a substantial portion of the group's net earnings, including the sizeable wealth collected by its members, may accrue to the private holdings and benefit of Mr. Moon. Based on the reports, Mr. Moon may hold properties in this country and others.

Based on the facts reported by my constituents and by articles in the public media, it appears that the tax exempt status of the Unification Church is questionable. It is my feeling, on this basis, that an audit of the organization may be warranted.

Your response would be greatly appreciated.

Sincerely yours,

/s/

BOB DOLE
United States Senator

BD:cav
Enclosures

In fairness, there was a period of time when Congress received heavy mail against Reverend Moon's activities, so a Congressional letter of concern is not unusual. What is unusual, however, is the addressee. If one thinks that his neighbor is guilty of kidnapping, he does not normally report it to the State Department or to the IRS. He properly reports it to the law enforcement authorities.

Asking the IRS to investigate a list of allegations about a church which are clearly hearsay and which are mostly outside their jurisdiction gets into a dangerous area that has traditionally and Constitutionally been off limits.

"Render . . . unto Caesar," the Bible says, "the things which are Caesar's; and unto God the things which are God's."

That division is clear and distinct also in the First Amendment of our Bill of Rights.

Religious freedom and our Constitutional rights depend on the honoring of this distinction. If we allow the expedient application of the three P's—politics, prejudice and public policy—to penetrate the sanctity of the church, the damage to everyone's religious interests could be unending.

Revenue is essential to maintenance of the state and social policies are of great concern to society, but the Internal Revenue Service must not be used in illegal areas in illegal ways to force everyone into a national mold.

The danger of turning the IRS into the "catch-all" enforcement agency for social policy is brought out time and again in the chapters of this book. This agency is developing awesome powers and admits no limits to what it judges to be right or wrong. To achieve its goals, it will lie, cheat, blackmail, and subvert the system of Justice.

Carnage strews the landscape where the IRS has picked the bones of people and institutions illegally and without mercy. Reverend Moon's plight is just one more in a growing list of abuses against citizens and religious institutions.

The IRS tabby cat created to collect taxes in a "voluntary

system" has grown into a full-sized saber-tooth tiger.

For example, there is a section in the Internal Revenue Code which allows disclosure of tax information about "an individual juror" to the prosecutor in a tax-related case. Aside from the exceptions in the section, it remains a felony punishable by fine and imprisonment to reveal any information in the class of tax information by anyone to anyone.

A few years ago, warned by an attorney in South Dakota, I inquired of the Department of Justice whether and how they use this statutory authorization. I was shocked to have the Department admit to me that, using the section as authority, every federal prosecutor obtained routinely the tax situation of every member of every venire panel.

What is important about this is that an entire panel is not an individual juror. Even worse, most of the potential jurors will not be called to sit on a case involving taxes. The *only* case in which a prosecutor is authorized to ask for tax records on a juror is when he is sitting on a tax case.

What this all amounts to is that in every case in which a defendant is tried in a Federal Court, the prosecutor has information about the potential jurors which the defense does not. In any case which involves taxes, the jury is already a target of the IRS and the Justice Department. It would take a brave juror to antagonize the IRS.

As another example, in the matter of the infected jury panels, the government holds true to form. The IRS violates the law. When it is challenged about it, it lies. I wonder what the IRS and the United States Attorney knew about the tax problems of the jurors that the Moon lawyers did not. All of this bending of the rules; torturing out of recognition any canon of legal ethics; subterfuge as to motivation by the government; expenditure of time and money (ours, by the way) to what purpose?

The net result of using government enforcement agencies to press a public policy, produced by the prevailing forces of prejudice and politics, is that everyone is made into the same mold by the same cookie cutter.

Bob Jones University refused religious regimentation by the government and paid the penalty. Others will follow.

Nebraska ministers and church members refused religious regimentation by the government and paid the penalty. Others will follow.

Churches and religious schools have defied the IRS and Title IX regimentation and paid the penalty. Others will follow.

Religious leaders plan to defy the unconstitutional Social Security tax on churches and may well pay severe penalties.

And now with pastors and church members being jailed for practicing their religious beliefs in education, and with ministers like Reverend Moon facing jail over taxes on church funds, the people of America are both afraid and angry.

What do we gain but shame for putting ministers in jail? If Reverend Moon is guilty of some crime, it is the crime of being different, unknown, foreign, and fighting for his beliefs.

If the Nebraska ministers are guilty of some crime, it is the crime of being different and fighting for their beliefs. If the church members in a Nebraska jail are guilty of some crime, it is the crime of being different and standing for their beliefs.

It is time to fight back. We must stop jailing ministers. We must stop jailing church members. And we must stop fining and taxing churches.

Issues like the Moon case, the Nebraska fight and the Social Security tax on churches have rallied the religious forces of the nation as never before. Deep differences between the sects are forgotten as people fight for the right to differ and for freedom from government intrusion into religion.

The Nebraska fight has brought sympathy and support from all sides. The Social Security battle has brought civic and religious forces together in a powerful way. And Reverend Moon has begun to acquire champions from an unusually broad base—religious and political leaders who deeply fear the intrusion of the government into church finances.

The Moon case probably provides the best illustration of how Americans are coming to the defense of religious freedom. A list of their "friend of the court" briefs dramatically shows the kind of army that has come forth to restore our religious independence from the prejudice and politics of government interference.

Amici Curiae Submitting Briefs In The Case of
United States v, Sun Myung Moon

The following are the groups which supported the defense position before the U.S, Court Appeals.

1. *National Council of the Churches of Christ in the U.S.A.*
   The National Council is a cooperative agency of 32 national Protestant and Eastern Orthodox religious bodies in the U.S., having an aggregate membership of over 40,000,000.

2. *American Baptist Churches in the U.S.A.*
   This is a national Baptist denomination of some 6,000 congregations with some 1.5 million members, with national offices in Valley Forge, Pennsylvania.

3. *United Presbyterian Church in the U.S.A.*
   This is a national, Christian denomination with churches in all 50 states. It has more than 2,387,000 active members and more than 8,900 congregations organized into 150 Presbyteries and Synods.

4. *African Methodist Episcopal Church*
   With 6,000 churches with 2,050,000 members, this church operates 5,500 Sunday or Sabbath schools with enroll-

ments of 156,000 and has 6,170 ordained clergy and 13 Bishops for 13 districts.

5.   *Center for Law and Religious Freedom of the Christian Legal Society*
     The Christian Legal Society is a non-profit Illinois Corporation founded in 1961 as a professional association of Christian attorneys, judges, law professors, and law students.

6.   *Unitarian Universalist Association*
     This is a voluntary association of 1,000 societies and fellowships in North America.

7.   *National Black Catholic Clergy Caucus*
     A national association of black priests, brothers, permanent deacons, and seminarians formed in August, 1967, it numbers 700 members.

8.   *American Civil Liberties Union*
     The ACLU is a nationwide, non-partisan membership organization dedicated to defending the principles embodied in the Bill of Rights.

9.   *New York Civil Liberties Union*
     The NYCLU is a state-wide affiliate of the ACLU.

The following additional groups have joined as *amici curiae* in support of Reverend Moon's petition for certiorari to the United States Supreme Court:

1.   *Southern Christian Leadership Conference*
     The SCLC, was founded in 1957 by Reverend Martin Luther King Jr., and other religious leaders to provide Christian guidance and leadership in the struggle for inter-

racial unity, human rights and equality of opportunity. It has over three hundred chapters and affiliates nationwide which include churches, labor unions, and student groups.

2. *Center for Judicial Studies*
   The CJS is a tax-exempt, public policy institution founded for the purpose of promoting judicial and legal reform.

3. *The Church of Jesus Christ of the Latter Day Saints*
   The LDS Church, more commonly known as the Mormon Church, is a worldwide religious movement of more than 5.2 million members which sponsors a 50-state, 100-country missionary effort.

4. *The Freemen Institute*
   The Freeman Institute has a membership of over 250,000 members and contributors and publishes a wide variety of books and periodicals and sponsors many educational programs dedicated to promoting the original principles of freedom and constitutional rights as intended by the Founding Fathers.

Note: Total list available at time of publication.

Subchapter 5

Should Churches Be Tax Collectors?

In the Social Security Reform Act of 1983, the Congress and the President went the final step in making it plain that the United States is at war with the religious community in the United States.

The new law may have been enacted because of the government's desperate search for more money, but the result was alarming—the invasion of the church by the state.

This so-called Reform Act is more like a revolution which disturbs our traditional church-state relationship in two major ways. The more obvious is that employees of churches and religious organizations are now subject to Social Security taxation.

With that new twist comes the obligation of the churches to pay taxes on an equal basis with each employee. They are now, for the first time, and in derogation of their immunity under the First Amendment, required to pay the government a portion of the funds contributed by church givers.

As a result, there is now the unprecedented requirement of paying a tax to the national government to exercise one's religious commitment.

The second and less noted problem caused by the Act is to make churches not merely tax payers, but also tax collectors. All the civil *and criminal* provisions associated with the liability to collect taxes now fall on the head of each church and each pastor. Not only is this another unconstitutional exposure to jail for clergymen, but a long time ago, a valiant Connecticut lady named Vivian Kellums argued successfully in Federal Court that such a role violated the citizen's right under the 13th Amendment not to be subject to involuntary servitude.

It is interesting to note that at the time when many enemies of religion argue that the Churches should not meddle in politics, these same enemies drag the churches directly into involvement in political matters as participants. Many ministers clearly understand the scriptural admonition that no man can serve two masters, and are deeply concerned that they are now required by law to serve the state. This is precisely what the framers sought to avoid by proposing the First Amendment.

To no one's surprise, the driving force behind this new encroachment on religious liberty has been those public officials and special interest groups who are both desirous of bringing churches under the power of the state and those who are willing to take funds from every source possible to finance the money-mulching appetite of government.

Fueled by protests from the religious community, there is now a drive to repeal the offending sections of the Act and many politicians are now nervously claiming that the inclusion of churches was an inadvertence. However, we have seen too often the lack of sensitivity displayed by government toward religion which makes me skeptical of the repeal's chances unless we pull out all the stops. The rule on tax bills usually is, "once in, never out."

Nonetheless, in hopes that something can be done before it is too late, I have introduced legislation to delay the enforcement of the Act for two years to give all those who included the churches by inadvertence a chance to correct their error. My bill in the House is a companion to that of Senator Jepsen's in the Senate.

There is yet a third consequence to the 1983 Act which might not occur even to religious opponents of taxing churches. But surely it has occurred to the Internal Revenue Service. Once you are a taxpayer to the government, and all the more if you are a tax collector, access to your books and records by that government is guaranteed.

In the context of the government's attack on churches through the Internal Revenue Service, the most important information sought by the IRS has been the books and records of the church. Through the back door of Social Security taxes, the IRS now has the absolute right to see all books, records and information on the financial condition of the Church without resort to its traditional use of bluff, threat and bogus administrative orders of various kinds.

Although I have no positive evidence as yet, I will hazard a guess that the original notion for this tax came from the IRS which has had only limited success in forcing churches to open their books to the tax man.

Many pastors are at this time faced with a moral dilemma in dealing with this latest attack on the right to practice one's faith without government interference. The very churches which have preached patriotism and obedience to lawful authority have now been required by the government, which they have so zealously defended, to violate their consciences and the rights of their congregations.

It is not surprising then that many of these ministers have already announced their intention to defy the law and refuse to collect or pay the tax on the Constitutional ground that it is a violation of both the free exercise and establishment clauses of the First Amendment.

Such a refusal could very well meet with wide acceptance in the popular mind. What those, who have launched this attack on religion, might ponder is how far such resistance might lead, if it once gets underway. How many ministers should be punished or go to jail for the government's mistake?

The time to defuse this very explosive situation is now. Government must be removed from its invasion of church domain immediately and quick action by Congress to repeal the Social Security tax against religion would be a welcomed act of good faith.

Subchapter 6

The Invasion of Calvary Temple

The IRS has never seemed to be much concerned with such archaic ideas as truth or justice. In Georgia, it has met a congregation led by a pastor prepared to introduce the tax collector to the truth.

Pastor Robert McCurry of Calvary Temple in East Point, Georgia, publishes a weekly newspaper called the Temple Times. In it he has made many of the same points made in this book. The IRS is either the agent or the principal villain itself in the growing attack by government on religion. The IRS, ever on guard to attack and suppress its critics, sent the pastor and the Church a demand for access to its records. For five years the contest went on. Finally, exasperated by Pastor McCurry's resistance, the IRS sent the Church a letter announcing that it had computed the Church's taxes owed from 1977 through the third quarter of 1983. The liability, without interest or penalties, was claimed to be $213,416.61. Interest and penalties could put the total near a million.

All this money was apparently for income taxes allegedly

withheld by the Church from the salaries of Church employees. Fair enough, you say. Church or no church, if they took money from employees' salaries to be paid to the tax man, the money is owed to the tax man. And you would be right, except for one thing. During that time the church had no employees and consequently had withheld no taxes from salaries which it had not paid.

And here we run into the problem with dealing with the IRS and the United States Tax Court. The normal rules are inverted. When the IRS accuses you, you are guilty until you are proved innocent. So, when you receive an outrageous 30-day letter as Calvary Temple did on October 11, 1983, you either prove you did not owe the IRS any money or you pay the sum demanded, and run the risk of criminal charges of tax evasion.

Back at the beginning of the confrontation, the IRS boasted that it would get the books and records of the church, no matter what law or constitutional considerations stood in the way. The rules now in existence and approved at least tacitly by the Congress allow the IRS to assess any amount it chooses against *anyone*. So it is no trouble at all to pick out a target like Calvary Temple, assess and then get the books it wants, regardless of procedural or constitutional protections which would be available against such activities by any other litigant, including the criminal authorities, federal and state.

I have always contended that the Congress, intentionally or not, set up the IRS to be outside the Constitution. All the lawyers who can dance on the head of a pin will not convince this layman that such maneuvering as is evident in the Calvary Temple case, is not a direct, intended result of the extra-Constitutional powers given to the IRS by the Congress. This has been demonstrated too many times by the increasingly heavy-handed provisions included in each new law passed.

A simple comparison of the extra-legal ways of the IRS with how the Constitution is otherwise used to set murderers, traitors, arsonists and other sociopathic types free or provide unbelievably lenient punishment, makes the point beyond question. A citizen against the IRS has literally no legal protection—and the churches are now facing the same awesome dilemma.

Subchapter 7

Salvation Army
On the Battlefield

There is one organization which is associated in the popular mind with external works of charity and with almost nothing else. It is the Salvation Army . Probably not one person in a thousand knows that the Salvation Army acts out of a totally religious motive to dispense charity in all its works.

Battlefield veterans from four wars have a unique affection for the Salvation Army. Less publicized than other groups, it was everywhere the troops went, distributing food, or a hot drink or a cheering word.

If there is one group which is the farthest from controversy, it is the Salvation Army. But in the new world of Big Brother even the Salvation Army cannot escape the effects of the new overpowering state religion. Recently the City of New York let it be known that it could no longer collaborate with the Salvation Army in distributing charity to residents of the city.

What was the sin which had thrust the Salvation Army into exterior darkness? Had its officials been detected misusing funds or assets? Never! Was its commitment to the poor and unfortunate suspect? Out of the question!

The great City of New York would no longer make use of the services of the Salvation Army to assist the downtrodden unless and until it publicly and officially changed its moral doctrine. The charitable organization must admit that it was in error in calling homosexuality sinful. It is not known whether it must also allege that the gay "life style" is ennobling and virtuous.

This could cause one to wonder whether, under pressure from the American Association of Inebriates, the City might not require the Salvation Army to abandon its time honored work at reforming tipplers as damaging and degrading to the "life style" of a drunk. But there is really nothing to laugh about in this arrogant invasion by the City into the beliefs of a religious group. It should, on the contrary, terrify us.

Led by the most dangerous agency in the country— perhaps in the world—today, the Internal Revenue Service, the national government and local governments under its lead are beginning to harass, suppress and, where possible, destroy religious groups in the United States. We will soon be free to exercise our religion only in the privacy of our homes.

Our freedom of religion will disappear for the most incredible of all reasons. The state will have established its own religion and other religions will be tolerated only so long as they do not interfere with the state religion.

Everything in this chapter points only in one direction, state displacement of religious belief with its own priorities. The Salvation Army case may be the worst case of all because it says that the government may tell you that what you used to believe to be evil is now good.

Summary and Conclusion

A Time for Action

I dearly love America and the great blessings we as free citizens enjoy. And I am proud of the hope the American dream gives to all mankind for a better life, for truth, for justice, for mercy, for fairness.

So, when I first started to notice the rash of religious oppression cases which has appeared in recent years, I experienced a deep concern, especially when the party attacking religious free exercise was usually the government itself.

It is hard to describe the feeling of shame and loss when the sheer number of such cases made it plain that I was looking, not at a single aberration, but at a campaign to suppress religion and bring it under government control.

The first reaction is the feeling of loss. Government forces are consciously working to break free of the limitations imposed on them by the Constitution. Many years ago, I realized that the Internal Revenue Service was working without regard to the Constitution. It had at first appeared that the lust for revenue had blinded these bureaucratic functionaries to the deeper implications of what their attack on religion could cause.

Naturally enough I raised the alarm. Most of my fellow public officials did not see or at least did not respond to the threat. In fact, during all this time, Congress had *increased* its authority to the IRS, giving it even more weapons with which to harass the people. The Tax Equity and Fiscal Responsibility Act (TEFRA) of 1982 and the Social Security Amendments of 1983 make it easier yet to oppress the people.

Now the trickle of cases of IRS abuse of churches has reached a flood stage. In the meantime, other federal and state agencies were beginning the process of stripping away the special status which religion had up to now enjoyed in our society. It became clear, as the fight spread, that the problem we faced was a broad legal difficulty under the section of the First Amendment to the Constitution called the free exercise clause. The entire provision reads as follows: "Congress shall make no law respecting an establishment of religion, or prohibiting the free exercise thereof."

The trend of government was moving rapidly to limit the free exercise of religion. A study of recent history also reveals that the thrust of the bureaucrats in the federal and state governments to constrict the religious rights of the citizens would not be effectively halted by the federal courts. For more than a generation, political considerations had filled federal court appointments at all levels with many men and women whose philosophies and religious faith significantly differed from tradition. Indeed, to many it too often appeared that, as a precondition for admission to the bar, one must be a skeptic and scoffer in matters of religious faith. Thus, in a quite important way the bench and the bar parallel the development of hostility to religion in the federal government.

Then several cases arose in which religious education played a central role. And an entirely different cast was placed on the matter. The ingredients are: 1) a government bureaucracy where many key positions are filled with functional pagans; 2) the power of the government and of the dollar to demand compliance; and 3) an entirely new set of social priorities either initiated by or nurtured by the very same bureaucrats who have been working so assiduously to repress religion. Taken together, they make a potent mix.

I am confident that we are faced, not with a simple free exercise of religion problem, serious as that problem may be, but an issue even more grave which is difficult even to state without it appearing ridiculous. The simplest form of the statement is as follows: In the United States, in the 1980's we are facing the establishment of a state religion.

One has to understand the history of this country to realize how difficult it is to even comprehend such an event. The people who came here from Europe in the 17th Century, came, in the main to escape the heavy hand of state enforced orthodoxy in their own lands. They wanted the right to practice their own religions without interference. The history is not without ironies. Many of these good people were as intolerant of dissent when they acquired power in the new world as those from whom they fled in the old.

To our credit, however, as a people and as a nation, by the close of the Revolutionary War, a century and a half later, religious toleration was the official policy of the new nation and ultimately of all of its states. After a much longer struggle, the official toleration was part of the fabric of the people and the nation. By this century it was unthinkable that any public trust or private right should hinge on a person's faith or lack of it. We had come to accept free exercise as the natural and proper condition of things.

A state religion has not been in our minds for two hundred years. It is, in fact, almost impossible to frame the question in thinkable terms in our century. Nonetheless, difficult to believe or not, we are faced with the emergence of a government religion to which all men must subscribe at the pain of exclusion from the public platform, public employment and perhaps even from public office.

Reflect on some of the issues raised by the cases we have discussed. The outline of a set of essential beliefs emerges. None of them are stated in our Constitution, but some of our judges have found them there. They now have begun to appear in state statutes and ordinances. The creed of this new church has some very sharp features. Some of them are at odds with the faiths professed by the people now bound by this alarming new faith which declares:

1. All sexual activity is good. Homosexuality, lesbianism, man-boy relations, and even incest are now viewed sympathetically.

2. Limitations on the public consumption of sexual products is a violation of freedom of the press. There is no such thing as pornography.

3. Disposition of the byproducts of sex is authorized by the state. Abortion is now a normal, expected activity, without regard to the age or circumstances of the persons seeking such a procedure.

4. The state is the principal parent of the child. His natural parents keep him only at the sufferance of the state.

5. The mental health of the child is impaired by overexposure to religious faith.

Not all of these postulates are imposed with equal vigor by the state, but all of them are part of and are pushed in varying degrees by the government at one level or another.

In the area of negative action, there are varying degrees of prohibitions. Public display of certain celebrations are forbidden. To the public eye, the state is becoming more religiously sterile, more pagan.

The child may not be subjected to exclusively religious education. He must be taught what the state dictates in several areas.

Religion may not allege that the public acts of public officials are good or bad. Churches have lost their tax exemptions for calling elected officials evil.

Acts sanctioned or promoted by the public religion may not be challenged by religion under pain of economic sanctions. Gender mixing in dormitories, for example.

And on and on—sexual and social mores are determined by this new public religion. The raising of children is dictated by this new religion. It goes beyond what any real religion dares to do. It dictates facts and forbids any challenge to those facts.

If you do not believe that, just read recent newspaper accounts of the attacks on the Texas School Book Commission. It had the temerity to refuse to require that biology books in Texas schools mention Darwin. As you know, it is already forbidden to mention God.

The new religion requires that you *believe* in evolution, no matter what the evidence. You are as a consequence required to believe that the opposite of Darwin is wrong.

On the whole, there is more evidence that the modern state makes belief in God an impediment to the advancement in society, than that it is merely neutral. When the state arranges the society in such a way that one set of beliefs, all of them atheistic and pagan, assists the citizen in his dealings within that state; and another set of beliefs, all of them theist and God centered, conspires to the detriment of the citizen, you are very close to saying that the state has established a religion, anti-God though it may be. Such is clearly the case in the United States today.

What is beyond doubt is that the believer is currently under attack in the United States. That attack emanates from the government itself or by the use of government power. The success of that attack depends on the torpor of the believer and his inability to unite with other believers to take back his country. Believers still are numerically greater, have the guarantees of the Constitution and the minds of most people. The time is short, but the prize is eminently worth the fight. If we lose, Diocletian gets the children.

SPECIAL NOTE—*During the last half of 1983, I coordinated the formation of a dynamic group of many of the nation's most prominent religious leaders into a Coalition for Religious Freedom (CRF).*

The mission of this organization is to provide a unified forum for the religious community to effectively deal with the various divisions and levels of government on matters vital to the preservation of religious freedom.

Many other dedicated and prominent citizens are also forming similar groups to fight for the preservation of our First Amendment rights and the impact is beginning to tell on the political scene. However, this is only the beginning of what must be done. The battle for religious freedom can only be won with a great army of alert and united citizens who refuse to yield their civil and religious rights to ambitious government demands.

15

Strategy for Ultimate Victory

I have mentioned earlier the old and accurate maxim that "the power to tax is the power to destroy." Hidden within the welter of statutes and regulations which flesh out the Sixteenth Amendment is a decades-long effort to reshape America—the social goal of the redistribution of wealth. The tool of this effort is the power to tax—"to eat out our substance," as stated in the Declaration of Independence. Using that weapon, the IRS has undertaken to destroy the wealth of the rich, the incentive for the aspiring, and the hopes of the poor in America.

Obviously the attack on the rich has failed, and for a number of reasons. As usual, government underestimated the ingenuity of the taxpayer. No sooner would an expropriation be arranged than someone would find a way around it. Whatever the IRS was able to do about taking the income of the rich, they were less successful in reaching their assets. Even confiscatory estate taxes have failed to disperse the large fortunes in the United States.

Meanwhile, events of recent years have begun to create the suspicion that the principal target of the IRS was not the rich at all. In fact, the heaviest burden of the tax collector has fallen on the smaller taxpayer. There is a cynical old saying that "he who wills the means, wills the end," which is only a fancy way of saying that if the middle class is being crushed out of existence by the IRS, that is what it intends to do.

Inflation has accelerated the effect of "bracket creep" on the working class. More gross income produces less net or spendable income because taxpayers are pushed into higher tax brackets. Continuously rising Social Security taxes add to the problem. Hidden in the system are factors which guarantee that the middle and poorer taxpayers lose ground more rapidly than the rich.

The idea of wealth redistribution has its strength in the old human failing of greed. Who are we to complain if the government is stealing from the rich guy and giving us a piece of what it steals? What is pernicious is that we are now beginning to realize that it is not the rich but the average person who is being fleeced.

Taken in the abstract, wealth redistribution by government action is contrary to the basic concepts of private ownership of property which everyone assumes the government agrees to—the constitutional tradition of "life, liberty, and property." The idea of redistribution only gradually became acceptable to the American people as a limited case involving just the super-rich. The facts, however, reveal that this perception is a distortion of what has really developed.

When the total of IRS-administered taxes is tallied, it is the middle class which is the victim of the so-called wealth redistribution. Over 13 percent of everyone's gross wages is collected as FICA (Social Security) taxes before the income tax is even computed. Add the base rate of 14 percent (rising immediately and sharply to 20 and then 30 percent) and the IRS Robin Hood, stealing from the rich and giving to the poor, disappears and the true picture of Attila the Hun appears.

Much of this is done while the IRS operates like the traditional con man. It spends money taken from us to advertise what a nice agency it is and to sell the idea that we tax ourselves and that voluntary compliance is an American tradition. True enough, when the taxes are fair and equitable. But the question is, why should the tax collector have to sell us on the matter at all?

When the states agreed to allow the federal government to tax the incomes of their citizens, no one conceived of the ornate network of rules and regulations which would go beyond raising funds and reach into controlling the form of society and the degree of freedom to be enjoyed by the citizens of this country.

At the time of the proposal of the Sixteenth Amendment, there appeared to be not the slightest hint of any purpose other than raising revenue. It was left to the future to reveal new ideas in the use of taxes for purposes far removed from simply raising revenues. The use of the income tax as a tool to take from the rich and give to the poor was still twenty years into the future. It would be sixty years before the Brookings Institution would begin to insinuate the idea that all revenue in the nation belonged of right to the government, and that anything left to the citizens was a "tax burden."

Whether redistribution of wealth or tax burden, we have seen the transformation of a revenue amendment and the statute which implements it into the principal instrument for molding a new kind of society in America. In the 1930s, members of the Roosevelt administration stated clearly that the social utility of the Internal Revenue Code was *more important* than its role as a source of revenue.

It is not the voluntary will of the people of the United States that the tax system be used to expropriate property. The original architects of the social aims of the tax laws correctly perceived, however, that as long as only the well-to-do were affected by outrageous revenue measures, the middle class and the poor would presume that it was only another case of the rich trying to protect their preferred status in the society.

Time has now taught us that the use of the Internal Revenue Code as a means of divesting the rich of their wealth, even if such a goal were proper, has been an absolute failure. The persons and families who were rich and super-rich when the Sixteenth Amendment passed are generally the same sixty-seven years later.

The same, however, cannot be said about the middle class or even the poor. Citizens' tax groups have made the public aware that the wage earner works until mid-June just to pay his tax bill. The cruel reality is that the rich stay rich. The poor stay poor. And the middle class gradually sinks under the federal tax burden into a kind of genteel poverty.

A substantial case can be made that the ills of American industry can be traced directly to the tax system and the burdens it imposes. Our industrial plant deteriorates under our very noses. Jobs in the automobile industry, in steel, and in a number of other segments of our economy are lost and "exported" to foreign countries. From a nation of mighty industrial strength, which armed the world in the 1940s, we have become the weakening giant of the 1980s with massive debt and balance-of-payments deficits.

If the social goal of taking the accumulated wealth of the very rich were restricted to just that, it would be wrong enough, but there would be some basis to understand it. However, the American taxpayer is faced with a far more oppressive reality. The IRS is now redistributing not accumulated wealth, but income and wages. *It is no longer a matter of taking from the rich to give to the poor, but taking from everyone to support the bureaucracy.*

We will only mention here that the redistribution idea is

so out of hand that, beyond wealth, or income or even wages, the very right to hold private property is under attack in the estate tax provisions of the Internal Revenue Code. The heirs of small landholders, farmers, and householders alike are regularly forced to sell the very bequest to pay the tax on the estate.

Difficult as it is, we must continually remind ourselves that most of this confiscation is not for the purpose of raising revenues. It is for the purpose of effecting a change in the nature of the United States from a free society to a socialist state. If this charge sounds far-fetched, remember that we have outlined in several chapters of this book a pattern of coercion, harassment, and police-state methods which are not compatible with the United States we know. The methods and the goals go hand in hand. If the accounts of IRS misuse of power mean anything, they mean that something is radically wrong, not just with the collection methods, but with the system itself.

There is always a risk that in directing the attention of the people to the excesses of any government agency, the person pointing the finger of accusation will be branded a zealot or worse. "This fellow," goes the chant, "wants to go back to the eighteenth century. A modern nation cannot survive without the huge revenues necessary to its social needs, its defense, and the myriad other expensive operations which make for the safety and comfort of the people." This attack always changes the subject. The problem is not raising revenues. The problem to which we are directing the attention of the people of the United States is one of method and purpose. How are these taxes collected and for what end? You have seen in the preceding chapters a small part of the method. We have suggested that much of the purpose is a transformation of the kind of government we have until now enjoyed in the United States.

Incredibly, the proof of the purpose of this tax system is

easier than the exposure of the coercive practices for its collection. Five years ago, the Brookings Institution laid down
the principle by which much of the modern left-wing tax theory is guided. The principle is simplicity itself:

ALL REVENUE OF INDIVIDUALS AND CORPORA-
TIONS IN THE UNITED STATES BELONGS TO THE
GOVERNMENT—WHATEVER SUMS ARE LEFT IN
PRIVATE HANDS ARE A GIFT OF THE GOVERN-
MENT.

The idea, mad as it is, is quite clear. The government
could set the tax rate at 100 percent of all money. When it
doesn't, it is spending its own money. Brookings calls the
money it leaves in your hands "a tax expenditure." In this
line of thinking there is the full flowering of the socialist state.
The government owns everything. The people may retain
only what the government feels is necessary to their survival
so that they may produce next year's income for the all-
powerful state.

(Lest we think that this is the aberrant thinking of one
isolated fanatic in some lonely attic, the parents of the tax-
expenditure idea include Alice Rivlin, executive director of
the Congressional Budget Office, and Arthur Okun, one of
the most influential economic advisers to the Democratic
Presidents in the last quarter century.)

For many years, both in and out of Congress, I have been
concerned at the direction of the financing of the federal government. There are some simple but essential norms for the
solution of the problem of enactment and enforcement of tax
legislation. First, any tax legislation must guarantee the production of sufficient revenue to run the legitimate functions
of the national government. Both in this book and in other
works I have emphasized that there are many operations of
the federal government which have just randomly grown, like

Topsy, without sufficient reason. In the future, voluntary tax collection will depend on the conviction in the taxpayer's mind that his money is not being wasted.

There is no longer any room for doubt that our tax laws depend not merely on the confidence of the taxpayer in the fairness of the collection system, but even more upon the reasonableness of the total of the tax burden itself. Recent experiences around the country in what is called the "tax revolt" are not passing fads. People are telling those who legislate for them that there is an equitable limit to the tax load. Beyond that limit lies resistance, loss of confidence in the government, and ultimately the disintegration of the free society into the kind of authoritarian operation capable of extracting unconscionable taxes from a hostile taxpayer.

In addition to protests over the tax-burden question and collection practices which are unfair, a substantial part of the tax protest growing around the nation is fueled by the perception that a major part of the money extracted by the government is simply wasted. Log rolling and bureaucratic grants to study absurdities like the sex life of a rock enrage the populace, not so much because of their size, but because they are so revealing of the mentality of the government agencies involved. They reason that only utter contempt for the plight of the taxpayer could produce the incredible waste of many of the federal agencies created by the government.

Recently, HEW, the biggest money burner on the domestic scene, admitted that more than $6 billion *annually* was thrown away in multiple payments, frauds, and bureaucratic errors. If that didn't get the citizens upset, the explanation was guaranteed to enrage them. It was explained in self-defense that $6 billion is really not so significant in view of the fact that it represented less than 4 percent of the more than $160 billion annual budget of HEW prior to its division into two departments.

HUD was empowered a few years ago by Congress to

guarantee construction projects for low-income housing recipients. The estimated budgetary cost to the taxpayer was $4 billion. As of this writing, HUD has committed *$140 billion* to this one project. The same geometric explosion occurred in the Agriculture Department's Food Stamp Program.

In forty-eight years, the national debt has gone from $2 billion to over $1 trillion, an increase of 500 times the original debt. The annual interest on the national debt is now more than $90 billion, forty-five times the total debt of 1932. No amount of idiot logic about owing it to ourselves or it being only a small percentage of the Gross National Product can jolly the beleaguered taxpayer out of his fear and anger that he, personally and individually, is being pauperized by insane spending policies over which he has little or no control.

The taxpayer needs no degree in economics to understand that unless there is a halt to profligate spending, his tax burden cannot stabilize, let alone diminish. He also knows without benefit of graduate degrees that spending-limit and budget-limit constitutional amendments are bottled up in Congress because a runaway Congress has no intention of turning off the spigot of spending or taxing. How he responds to this unprecedented contempt for his welfare will determine the nature of our government in the near future.

Just as important, whatever taxes are enacted must be understood as fairly distributed throughout the population. It is no accident that the IRS is complaining that there is an underground economy so large that it encompasses more than $200 billion annually. Both legislators and tax collectors have no choice but to step back and try to understand the pressures which changed a basically law-abiding people into tax avoiders. No amount of outcry that the tax laws are like the 55-mile-an-hour speed limit and must be obeyed because the government says so will stem the flight of otherwise honest people into secret, off-the-books income arrangements.

The law of diminishing returns has begun to strike down

oppressive tax levies on the taxpayer. It is here that the legislator finds out that he cannot adopt a godlike stance decreeing that the tax burden can be indefinitely increased and will produce corresponding increases in revenue. Even should the Congress and/or the IRS decide to double or triple the enforcement troops assigned to collection, the cost would fast catch up to any additional revenue realized. Of much more significance, such an approach would inevitably turn the entire tax collection system into one based upon coercion, instead of goodwill; with, I suspect, dire results, not only in the area of revenues, but in a much wider area of government-to-citizen relations which require the voluntary cooperation of the governed.

It is not my purpose here even to discuss the already visible casualties of the complex and counterproductive tax system. Our lagging industrial performance is at least partially the product of the notion that the production of revenue has no effect on the capacity of the taxpayer to survive. It is often our own government's greed which results in the destruction of industry and the export of jobs to foreign competitors. More than 40 percent of the price of an American-made automobile is tax load. A loaf of bread would cost only a fraction of the current price if the taxes on it were removed. The point here is not whether these items should be taxed, but that there is a limit to the amount that the government can extract from its citizens. The need for reasonable limits on spending is bound up in the problems of the IRS and its coercive image.

While no one can claim to have the exclusive remedy for the runaway tax burden and enforcement problem, there are several corrective measures which lend themselves to prompt implementation:

1. *Prohibit, by statute and regulation, the use of quota systems in the investigation, audit, and assessment of tax liabilities.* Our present system takes us back to the ancient evil of

the tax collector being paid a percentage from what he was able to extract from his victim. Quotas destroy any basis for a professional approach to equitable tax collection. Their mere existence is a symptom that tax collection is already in a state of decay.

2. *Improvement and reform of the entire review and oversight procedure of the IRS.* Among the many evils of the current system is the distortion of the judicial system itself in aid of pressuring taxpayers. If a civil rights case is decided in Kansas, the impact of that decision, whatever it is, is felt everywhere in the United States. The government feels itself required to obey and enforce it everywhere. The IRS takes a position unique to itself. When the IRS loses a case to a taxpayer, the case is, as a matter of policy, restricted to that case only. Simplified out of legal double-talk, if an identical set of facts came up again the day after the IRS lost in the same tax district, the IRS would persist in its view of the law. The second taxpayer is forced to commence to litigate a like matter again. The IRS has the resources of the federal government with which to wear down any individual taxpayer and uses them lavishly. Any reform should provide for payment to the successful taxpayer litigant of his attorney fees and legitimate expenses.

The Congress must also tighten its supervision of so powerful an agency. Only an aggressive and continuous overview by the appropriate committees of the Congress has the potential to check abuses before they get out of hand. If there is no continuing check, the IRS will keep claiming to be outside the Constitution, and its own self-discipline, as we have shown here throughout this book, is notoriously inadequate.

3. *Executive restraint in general.* If we are to have any hope of restraining the IRS, the entire group of executive agencies must be restrained. Not long ago, the Congress enacted legislation which created a new executive department, splitting the old HEW into the Department of Health and

Human Services and the Department of Education. Incident to that legislation, Congress reaffirmed its right to legislative veto of Department of Education regulations. During that process, neither the National Education Association nor any other party to the creation of the agency raised any objection to such control. The Department of Education was in existence only a few weeks when Congress vetoed two of the flood of new regulations. The Secretary of Education immediately instructed her subordinates to ignore the Congressional veto and to *implement the regulations immediately.* The bizarre reason given was that to accept a Congressional veto would compromise the independence of the executive branch of government.

The list of similar attempts, some of them successful, of these Frankenstein monsters to get out from under the control of the legislative branch which created and funds them is too long to discuss here. It is enough to point out that the problem of rogue agencies is broader than just the IRS. Unfortunately, it is no credit to Congress that it has done little or nothing to stem the growth of these agencies. Nor has our national legislature successfully kept up its supervisory oversight functions. Citizens should not have to plead with Congress to control the creations it has loosed on the people.

When we described (in Chapter 13) the lengthy and vigorous battle to free denominational schools from the IRS attempt to destroy them, the arrogance and dogmatism of the IRS was really only half the story. We need to remember that the agency which was fighting the Congress was one of its own statutory children. If the Commissioner of Internal Revenue has no hesitancy in challenging the Congress, what chance does an ordinary citizen have to resist? The IRS, along with other agencies, has developed this aura of independence in large measure because of the failure of the Congress to keep a tight rein on its own authority over these agencies.

Short of outright repeal of the Internal Revenue Code,

there are measures now available to curb the appetite of the revenue bureaucracy for independence and power. I have sponsored and co-sponsored several key bills to slow down the loss of our liberties to the runaway tax collector.

Among these are legal and constitutional mandates for a balanced budget; for income, estate, gift, and corporate tax relief; for a spending limitation and repayment of the national debt; for restraints on independent IRS rulemaking; and for a prohibition against Presidential and Congressional authority to engage in deficit spending. Also introduced are proposals for "sunset legislation" (laws that terminate after a given number of years), legislative vetoes, and cost-to-benefit evaluations for proposed laws and regulations, as well as paperwork reduction.

It may be that we are either functionally or psychologically beyond the point at which repairs to this tottering, complicated tax system are possible. There is a strong case to be made for the abolition of the graduated income tax and its replacement by a more efficient and more even-handed revenue-raising measure. Once you look beyond the fanatic urge to use taxes to drag everyone down to the same economic level, there are several alternatives available which could raise revenue without expressing a doctrinaire hatred of success.

The Kemp-Roth approach, of which I am a sponsor, is based upon the theory that a reduction in the marginal tax rates will stimulate the economy and actually produce more revenue. Marginal tax rates are those in excess of the base rate. The rate graduates to 70 percent of taxable income with an effective limit of roughly 50 percent of all taxable earnings. The Kemp-Roth idea is rooted in the economic ideas of Professor Arthur Laffer, who has demonstrated that the economic law of diminishing returns applies to taxation. I have no quarrel with the fundamental ideas expressed in the Kemp-Roth-Laffer theory. In fact, it is these and similar ideas which are at the root of my comments on the self-defeating nature of oppressive tax burdens previously discussed. Like everything else in the political arena, the trick is in finding the Aristotelian mean which maximizes the necessary revenue while limiting the individual burden.

But there are problems with Kemp-Roth which require close attention. There seems to be implicit in the approach a view that federal budgets in the $600 billion range are fine, provided that the mechanical rates of collection are adjusted. Budgets which approach 25 percent of the Gross National Product remain, in my view, a major part of the problem.

They produce a cynicism about the government which is not completely answered merely by cutting the maximum rates. Today the people who fall into the economic middle class are keenly aware that government spending and debt work against them and for people on either side of them in the income strata. Government spending reaches both the affluent in forms of contracts, grants, construction, bank transactions, etc., and the poor in the myriad subsidies to which the federal government has become addicted over the past half century. They see the national debt as a continuing drain on their taxes and a major source of their problems with inflation. It is not lost on them that the affluent deal in tax-exempt government debt obligations. There is little reason for the moderate-income citizens not to view the system as a protective device for everyone except themselves.

In summary, while sympathizing with the notion of a more efficient and less burdensome tax structure as contemplated by Kemp-Roth, I consider it incomplete without a device for limiting federal expenditures in some realistic way. Perhaps it is not yet rational to hope for a deficit-free budget, but we must structure as a goal some method to prevent any Congress from yielding to the opiate of spending funds it doesn't have.

The need to limit the ability of the government to stay

out of budget balance indefinitely was seen many years ago by such farsighted legislators as Senator Carl Curtis of Nebraska. The Curtis-Spence proposal for a constitutional amendment, requiring a balanced budget except in very limited and narrowly defined emergencies, never got the Congressional support it deserved. In the 96th Congress, I introduced a proposed constitutional amendment requiring appropriations not to exceed revenues and requiring the systematic repayment of the national debt.

An alternative to income taxation which has periodically received attention is a value-added tax. In a simplified way, this is a device to add a tax to every step in the construction of a product or the creation of a service. It has two major drawbacks. First, it is difficult to position this tax to produce a given volume of revenue. Much more important, however, is the second disadvantage of such a tax. No matter how it is levied, it tends to fall with the greatest impact on those least able to pay. The fancy name for this kind of tax effect is regressive. The plain truth is that it is unfair. The imposition of a progressive rate tax is unfair in one direction. Its replacement with a tax that puts most of the burden on the poorer people is more unfair in the opposite direction.

Another substitute which has been occasionally mentioned for the income tax is a national sales tax. In addition to having the same problems as the value-added tax, the national sales tax treads on the sources of income of the states and municipalities of the nation. Rather than improving and making the collection of taxes less painful, the national sales tax is likely to disrupt not only national tax collection but that of local governments also.

The Single Rate Income Tax

One of the fundamental alternatives in the method of revenue raising available to the nation is the *single rate* income tax. In this approach, the income tax remains the principal means of raising revenue. The social purposes of taxation are, however, totally abandoned. Everyone pays the same *percentage* of his taxable income without regard to the specific amount of taxable income of the individual. The tax is progressive in the most fundamental sense of the word. The person with a $3,000 taxable income (after basic exemptions and deductions) pays half the amount that a person with $6,000 of taxable income does.

The single rate does not present a major problem. Set at 13 percent, a figure supported by prominent economists, it will produce almost the same revenue as the steeply graduated rates in effect now, on the same admitted income. But it carries with it side benefits which make the idea extremely attractive.

First, it stops the government from attempting social reform by means of the revenue collection system. There is currently no way to get the government to stop trying to change the views, life-styles, and philosophy of its citizens through the use of the IRS. The single rate income tax would be a major step in preserving the little individual liberty we have left to compel the government to give up the mask of revenue enforcement for what is really something else.

Taken by itself, the only justification for the steeply graduated income tax is its goal of redistribution, not any sane revenue purpose. The relatively tiny share of revenue produced by the "marginal rates" which the Kemp-Roth idea rightly attacks is a clear signal of the social rather than revenue purpose of such rates. Whenever the single rate idea is put forward, its opponents universally use two arguments against it. The first cannot be supported by the facts, i.e., that this change would cripple the revenue of the government. The second argument is exactly to the point. It is alleged that this would unfairly benefit the well-to-do. Such an argument is only another way of admitting that the goal is social, to penalize success or to soak the rich.

Second, the single rate income tax would destroy the underground economy and increase the tax base. There is little doubt that the certainty of a reasonable and limited tax rate would induce off-the-books wage earners to return to the tax rolls. Very few of our citizens are natural tax avoiders. They would prefer to maintain their otherwise honest life-style. A limited and reliable tax burden would do much to restore the nearly $250 billion of the underground economy to the tax rolls. Tax revenues would, even at the low single rate figure, probably produce an increase of between $30 billion and $40 billion in federal revenues.

Third, the single rate income tax would induce the return to the tax rolls of a substantial amount of income now artificially hidden from confiscatory taxation by loopholes and tax avoidance devices. Many citizens who now pay tax lawyers and accountants more than their single rate tax would, as a matter of simple economy, return to the tax rolls income now buried in the labyrinth of a complex tax code.

Fourth, the single rate income tax would eliminate most of the cost of the Internal Revenue Service. Under a single rate tax, substantially all individual taxpayers could file their returns on a computer card the size of a business envelope. The ornate review, audit, assessment, police, and coercion functions would become unnecessary. The cost savings of eliminating such activities could exceed *$2 billion annually.*

Fifth, and most important of all, the single rate income tax would bring to an end the dreaded national police with its totalitarian methods. If the accounts which I have given here of the excesses committed in the name of tax collection prove nothing else, they show beyond the slightest doubt that we have let in by the back door a heavy-handed national police force. Americans have always been justifiably wary of the European model of the centralized national police under the control of the ministry of the interior which can overthrow political establishments at will. Our attention has been focused upon the FBI and, more recently, the CIA as threats to become the instruments of terror for a shadow dictator, who controls the country as surely as Himmler and Beria controlled theirs.

What we have failed to grasp is that we had little to fear from the Hoovers, Grays, and Websters and even less from the Helms, Colbys, and Turners. While the media were diverting our attention in that direction, other men, with little or no popular awareness, were building a far more formidable *Geheim Staatspolizei* within the Internal Revenue Service.

When we step back from the individual horror stories to look at the overall picture, we begin to understand that the cost of government cannot be measured in dollars alone. What European or Oriental despotic excess has not been inflicted on our own citizens by the IRS? Night raids, arrests without warrants, incarceration without trial, even beatings and physical abuse are all part of the arsenal of IRS weapons. What better evidence of the dangerous direction of our tax enforcement officials than their claim that they are above the Constitution and outside the law? Is this not precisely the claim made by the KGB and the Gestapo? Were they not also above the law in the name of the security of the state?

One might be led to wonder at how the FBI and the CIA have been kept at the center of national concern while such a monster as IRS grew unnoticed in the very entrails of government. Neither of those agencies has ever even been accused of a tiny fraction of the excesses which have been proved against the IRS. Both of those agencies are, as a matter of record, engaged against the worst elements in our domestic and world society, those who would by force or fraud deprive us of our liberties; while the IRS is engaged in a war against America's citizens.

National leaders of the FBI and CIA have been made defendants and forced to justify their actions against plaintiffs whose sole claim to national fame is their intense and continuing hatred of the United States. Some of these government officials have even been subjected to criminal trials. Without commenting on their guilt or innocence, responsibility or lack of same, I am here raising the question that if the subject of national concern is the abuse of the civil rights of our citizens, *where is there a single indictment or prosecution* of an IRS official or employee for proved violations of the civil rights of decent citizens?

The answer is that there have been none and there will be none. When a Commissioner of Internal Revenue can say to the House Committee on Ways and Means that "the truth is that . . . the only way we can keep people in line, the only way we can keep them honest . . . is to keep them afraid," then we know that the IRS is immune from retribution. Every prosecutor, every judge, every legislator, as well as every citizen, is subject to the same fear.

In his "House Divided" speech Abraham Lincoln told us an eternal truth. No nation can exist half slave and half free. We have, almost inadvertently, created an agency within the government at war with our freedoms. If it is not curbed, in our view, if it is not destroyed, it will inevitably control us all.

I have accused the Internal Revenue Service of being above the law. As was pointed out in the chapters concerned with IRS abuse of religious liberty, the service proposed to tax, without statutory authority, religious and private schools for failure to meet arbitrary IRS norms. Congress passed a law forbidding the implementation of the anti-religious regulation for a limited period of time. The bill passed overwhelmingly in the House and comfortably in the Senate. The stay was included again in the Post Office and Treasury Appropriation bill for 1981. Despite the clear determination of the Congress to prevent enforcement of the regulation, the

IRS has had the proposed restriction of its power thrown out of the authorization bill in the Ways and Means Committee— knowing full well that the provision will be reinstated on the floor of the House. But such is the power and tenacity of the IRS that it continues to fight to have its way in suppressing religious education in America.

The IRS, a creature of statute, has taken an even more revealing step. It has sought and announced that it intends to continue to fight to have federal courts strike down the Congressional prohibition as unconstitutional. Will Rogers once told a story about a horse which got one of its hind legs caught in the stirrup of its saddle. Whereupon the cowboy said to the horse, "Wal, now, if you're goin' to get on, I'm goin' to get off." The IRS seems to have one hoof in the stirrup.

The only sure conclusion to the story of the IRS is that there is no conclusion. Some men have always tried to dominate and control their fellow men. Before the Israelites were borne off by the Egyptians into captivity almost 4,000 years ago, slavery was an ancient institution. The gulags and the concentration camps should serve to remind us of the universality of the drive that some men have for power. We should not be surprised by the fact that this evil trait continues to surface among us.

But we dare not give up the struggle to maintain our freedoms. In a fast-moving world, we sometimes forget that the experiment which is America is barely two centuries old. During that time it has had a few detours and some bitter failures and struggles. We need only remind ourselves that not much more than a century ago, the Supreme Court of the United States found slavery *acceptable*. It cost us a bloody war to keep the experiment of freedom going.

A form of slavery of even more recent vintage is the income tax. Our forefathers funded the nation without it until 1913, and we can fund ourselves without its bad side effects in the future. What we cannot do, like very recent examples, is to allow ourselves to slide into totalitarianism by sloth and a lack of vigilance or by a panic response to the government's alleged needs. The Internal Revenue Service was not brought down from Mount Sinai engraved on tablets of stone. It can be controlled or abolished at the clearly expressed will of the people. But as always, the people get the kind of government they deserve.

It has been the purpose of this book to provide the dark side of the tax collection system of the United States. Mere exposure didn't destroy the Gestapo or the KGB, nor will it destroy our native copy. As a nation, we have gambled that the best government comes out of the full facts. It is out of trust in that common sense that this book has been offered to those who are ultimately our only safeguard—*the people.*

SPECIAL UPDATE—*This book,* To Harass Our People, *along with related political, legislative, and legal activities, has produced a taxpayer revolution in less than four years since it was first copyrighted in 1980.*

I pioneered legislation in 1981 for tax reform called the Taxpayer Protection Act (TPA) and the Tax Simplification Act (TSA). Together with an amnesty proposal, they comprise the Fair And Simple Tax (FAST) program.

The FAST plan utilizes a flat, low-rate personal income tax as an incentive along with new taxpayer protection against IRS abuses and the open door of amnesty to create a fair system which can balance the budget while actually decreasing the burden on the average taxpayer.

In 1981, I organized the Association of Concerned Taxpayers (ACT) and supported other similar groups to inform the public and develop grassroots support.

The ACT and FAST impact has been strong—the first meaningful Congressional hearings on IRS abuses in 30 years

(April 26, 1982), CBS 60 Minutes program on IRS abuses (November 15, 1981 and subsequent segments), a Treasury Department task force study on tax simplification (1982-1984), and Presidential statement of support for the Hansen proposal (White House Documents July 6, 1982) with further affirmation of the principle in the 1983 State of the Union Message.

The President Acts

President Ronald Reagan's 1984 State of the Union Message has now called for action on a plan for tax simplification as I advocated in the chapter you have just read on a "Strategy for Ultimate Victory." This commitment before Congress is a big step forward to reducing the deficit and providing citizens with much needed relief from unfair taxes and IRS abuse.

The President, in his January 25 speech, said, "Let us go forward with an historic reform for fairness, simplicity, and incentives for growth," and called for "a plan for action to simplify the entire tax code."

- *"to make the tax system more fair for all taxpayers,"*
- *"to bring the underground economy into the sunlight,"*
- *"to make the tax base broader so personal tax rates could come down, not go up."*

The door to meaningful tax reform is now open, but it can only happen if concerned taxpayers create an immense groundswell to offset the pressure on the politicians brought by special interest groups who profit greatly under the current corrupt and inefficient graduated income tax.

Documents

Years of dogged investigation into the abuses of the IRS have resulted in a collection of thousands of memos and letters that reside in the files of my Washington, D.C., office. I have selected a small number of these to reprint here, as well as excerpts from the *Congressional Record*. The reader will get a glimpse of the activities that prompted this book.

March 1, 1973

Daryl Coons
Chief, Collection And Taxpayer Service

Monte Hobson
Group Supervisor

"How Can We Prevent Delinquency?"

Based on my personal experience and from discussion with Revenue Officers in Group D - 2, I am summarizing methods of preventing delinquency. These methods are listed in three broad groups entitled

         I. Education
       II. Embarrassment
     III. Procedural

with examples applicable to each respective group.

I. EDUCATION

The single most important method of preventing delinquency is through
education. The tax paying public must be aware of the tax law requirements and of the consequences for failure to abide by these laws.

A. Estimated Tax Payments

A large number of IMF delinquencies occur as the result of self-
employed individuals failing to file and pay estimated taxes. It
is important that these self-employed taxpayers be made aware of
the estimate provision by both public news education and by competent IRS personnel. Revenue Officers and Revenue Agents should receive adequate training so that they routinely indoctrinate self-
employed taxpayers of their extimated tax responsibilities whenever
a potential delinquency exists. Delinquent taxpayers often explain
to Revenue Officers that they were not aware of the estimate requirements.

B. Federal Tax Deposits

IRM (5(14)G-30, FTD Alert, provides Revenue Officers with a "golden
opportunity" to educate employers of their deposit requirements.
Frequently employers fail to comply even after they have been personally contacted by a Revenue Officer. In these situations, it is
necessary to invoke the provisions of IRC 7512 and 7215 as provided
by IRM 5(10)31.
Once the L-54 letter has been issued and the Form 2481 subsequently
put into effect resulting in monthly filing of Forms 941 M there
normally appears to be a breakdown in enforcement. Usually, as a
result of some menial technicality and/or a sympathetic judge who
is reluctant to prosecute these tax violators. The penalty provided by IRC 7215 is rarely applied.

Subject: "How Can We Prevent Delinquency?"   March 1, 1973

In my opinion, IRC 7512 and 7215 is a just and good law which should
be routinely enforced. The tax paying public should be educated as
to the severity of failure to turn over trust fund monies. When an
employer fails to comply with Forms L-54 and 2481, the resulting
penalty should be routine and automatic. In other words, the public
should be educated of the seriousness and of the definite penalty
which will be meted out to trust fund violators. Perhaps, legislation could be enacted to make this penalty automatic in such cases.
To my knowledge, the Boise District has never been successful in
obtaining a prosecution under IRC 7512 or 7215,

C. Mister Businessman Kit

In my opinion, the MBK is not a useful tool for preventing delinquency. The time used for delivery of MBK's could be better utilized
in other enforcement and compliance areas.

D. Subcontractors

One of the most flagrant areas of deliquency is in the subcontractor
area. Many employers subcontract all of their employees, thereby
avoiding payment of payroll taxes. These so called subcontractors
readily claim that the employees have been hired on a bid, piece-
work, commission or contract basis to complete a specific job. The
employers also claim that they have little or no control over these
employees. In some instances, contractors are building homes entirely
with subcontractors thereby avoiding payroll taxes. These so called
subcontractors rarely report and pay taxes on all of the income received for their services.

There is no doubt that an employer-employee relationship exists under the common law between the employer and the subcontractors. A
few examples of areas where this subcontractor employement is abused
include: builders, musicians, contract farming, logging, and certain salesmen. Possible solutions to stop this abuse include:

   (a) Train specialists to work exclusively on employment
        tax cases.

   (b) Require the Audit Division to audit more self-employed
        taxpayers who claim a sizable "Schedule C", Line 10,
        deduction for salaries and wages and yet have not
        filed Form 941.

   (c) Encourage IRS personnel to give speeches explaining the
        common law rule applicable to an employer-employee rela-
        tionship. These speeches could be given at union meet-
        ings, building trade conventions, farmers co-op meetings,
        etc.

   (d) Mail Publication 539 (Withholding Taxes From Employees'
        Wages) to all employers who have a tendency to subcon-
        tract.

II. EMBARRASSMENT

A proven method of preventing delinquency has been through embarrassment of certain taxpayers.

A. Federal Tax Liens

Many taxpayers never become aware that a tax lien has been recorded against them. Even though tax liens are open for public inspection, few people actually become aware that a tax lien has been filed against a specific taxpayer.

A method of preventing delinquency is to inform the public of the names of taxpayers against whom a lien has been filed. This could be accomplished by publicizing this information in the Vital Statistics sections of various newspapers. This method was utilized in Twin Falls, Idaho for a short period of time. It was accomplished by the Revenue Officer contacting and convincing the local newspaper reporter to pick up Federal Tax Lien filing information and publicize the names of these taxpayers along with other public information, such as marriages, divorces, suits, judgments, etc. It became immediately evident in the Twin Falls area that the word had gotten around and that certain delinquent taxpayers became embarrassed as a result of their tax liabilities becoming public knowledge. The Twin Falls newspaper discontinued publicizing tax lien information after a short period of time due to the numerous complaints and criticisms received from the delinquent taxpayers.

B. Seizure Action

Delinquency in the St. Maries area has been reduced through the ingenuity of a Revenue Officer. The Revenue Officer seized a car which was owned by a chronic delinquent in the St. Maries area. The Revenue Officer found this car parked on the main street of downtown St. Maries and proceeded to seize the auto by placing warning notices on the car windows. The Revenue Officer secured the car by placing a large log chain around the car's bumper and on adjacent parking meter. The local St. Maries newspaper became aware of this seizure and as a result, placed a picture and story on the front page of the newspaper.

C. Attorneys And Doctors

Six prominent attorneys in the Sandpoint area had repeatedly been delinquent in the payment of their income tax. A Revenue Officer seized the office of the Sandpoint prosecuting attorney. This seizure was consummated by affixing hasps and locks to the doors of the attorney's office. Considerable publicity occurred through radio, television, and newspapers as a result of this seizure. Delinquency has been greatly reduced in the Sandpoint area as a result of this seizure and the embarrassment to the prosecuting attorney.

A similar situation occurred when a doctor's office was seized. The doctor's patients could not keep their appointments, and as a result, considerable publicity was generated.

It has been my experience that seizures which result in "sensationalism" tend to remain fixed in the public's mind, and are a great deterrent of delinquency.

III.   PROCEDURAL

A. Timeliness

It is important to contact a taxpayer as soon as possible after
a delinquency occurs. Often, five or six months elapse before a
taxpayer is personally contacted. A delinquent taxpayer should
have the impression that immediate enforcement will occur.

Input of Q codes (TC 148) and prompt enforcement of accelerated
trust fund cases will help in making timely contacts and thereby
reducing delinquency.

B. IRC 6020 - B

The Revenue Officer's hands are tied when it comes to requiring
a taxpayer to furnish information and/or prepare a return. If
the taxpayer refuses to comply, a long drawn out process evolves
(summons, referral to Audit) before an assessment is finally made.
Delinquency could be reduced if the Revenue Officer had the authority to make an immediate arbitrary assessment and proceed to
enforce collection. Under current manual procedure, such cases
must be referred to the Audit Division for completion. This procedure may take several weeks before an assessment is made. An
example of how an RO could utilize IRC 6020-B is as follows:

> Revenue Officer contacts taxpayer who refuses, stalls,
> delays, or procrastinates to file 941 or furnish infor-
> mation. The Revenue Officer could "size up situation",
> number of employees, etc., and advise the taxpayer that
> an arbitrary assessment will be made in an amount in ex-
> cess of what is probably actually owed. The Revenue Of-
> ficer's supervisor could phone in a prompt assessment
> resulting in immediate enforcement of the delinquency.

C. Firm Collection Policy

Too much emphasis is placed on statistics. Certain cases must be
closed (by survey, 53, not liable, etc.) in order to meet predetermined goals and to compete with other Districts. When the percentage of cases 53'd increases substantially, the word tends to
get around to the public that IRS is not uniformly enforcing collection. The same holds true for part-payment agreements. Everyone knows of someone else who is on the "easy pay plan".

In order to prevent delinquency, the IRS must take a firm stand
towards collecting all delinquent taxes and requiring taxpayers
to file all returns which are required by law. This goal can be
obtained by increasing the number of Revenue Officers. An RO
should have ample time to do extensive returns compliance work,
rather than devoting the majority of time to enforcing collection
and obtaining delinquent returns.

M. Hobson

March 2, 1973

Daryl Coons
Chief, Collection And Taxpayer Service

Ralph Hutchinson
Group Supervisor

"How Can We Prevent Delinquency?"

Marginal taxpayers in inefficient, non-profitable businesses are probably responsible for a larger percentage of delinquencies than any
other segment of the tax paying public. The most apparent characteristic of these enterprises is the ability to start business with an
absolute minimum in capital equipment, cash reserves and other assets, e.g. service stations, restaurants, and construction trades.

The Collection Division has been faced with a two-pronged problem
for many years:

    (1)   Prevent delinquencies by stern, prompt enforcement action
          which forces the taxpayer to discontinue business.

    (2)   Accomplish the above without undue pressure from the pub-
          lic and the elected officials.

In my opinion, this cannot be done and we must realize that complaints
will be an integral part and result of such measures. We must not be
oversensitive to these complaints and requests for leniency.

Law addition and other approvals that would help in other areas:

    (1)   Require known prior delinquents to pose a cash bond before
          commencing business (as does the State).

    (2)   Require farmers to withhold income taxes.

    (3)   In collaboration with the State, require license applicants
          to prove filing and paying of HUT and liquor and beer stamps
          before a license is issued.

    (4)   Provide more man hours for cold canvass operation.

    (5)   A more religious and systematic use of P.L. 85-321.

                        R. Hutchinson

July 23, 1973

Chief, Collection and Taxpayer Service Division

Ralph Hutchinson
Group Manager, D-1

Internal Audit Report - Seizures and Sales

Ten seizure cases have been reviewed in an effort to gather information to adequately respond to your request.

Finding 1: Comparison of Estimated Costs to Net Proceeds From Seizures and Sales

As an afterthought, it is impractical to attempt to determine the
seizure costs as compared with the gross proceeds of sale. The Internal Audit Report says, in part: "There are questionable benefits
from seizing low value property as a means of encouraging compliance
with tax laws." I disagree with the conclusion for the following
reasons:

(1) As an enforcement agency, we cannot measure compliance on a
profit and loss case basis.

(2) Each seizure and/or sale and the attendant publicity result
in compliance which cannot be measured.

(3) Seizures of low value property often result in the taxpayer
having an increased awareness of his problem and taking concrete
measures to resolve it.

Four of the seizures studied in which the property was redeemed resulted in the collection of approximately $21,000 in delinquent tax-
es. Prior investigation disclosed that there was no other approach
available which would result in immediate collection.

One unresolved seizure resulted in the conviction of a known tax
protestor for the forcible rescue of seized property.

Two seizures on the same taxpayer (cash register and liquor stock)
resulted in securing only $300 but effectively precluded a habitual
delinquent from incurring additional taxes.

I feel that the above examples prove that in many instances, seizures are one of our most effective collection and compliance tools.

Dec. 31, 1975

District Director, Boise

Regional Inspector, Western Region

Taxpayers Who May Advocate Violence Toward Western Region Personnel

We are transmitting a list of individuals in your District who
may advocate violence toward government officials including Revenue
employees.

The list was compiled from a system of records dealing with
criminal law enforcement and was exempted from disclosure under 5 U.S.C.
522a(j)(2) by the Commissioner. You are not to make this list a part
of your system of records or associate it with any individual's record
which you have. Any requests for access to the list under the Freedom
of Information Act or Privacy Act should be directed to the Inspection
Service.

We are currently in the process of identifying other individuals
in your District who may have a propensity toward violence. Additional
information will be forwarded periodically. Specific inquiries should
be forwarded to this office as the need arises for additional information
concerning any of the individuals listed above.

(SIGNED) F. R. ROWE

F. R. Rowe
Regional Inspector

July 1, 1975

Sam Pedin, Field Branch Chief
Seattle, Washington

Monte Hobson, Group Manager 11-00
Boise, Idaho

Caroline Smith, Revenue Officer

    Caroline Smith was under my supervision from the beginning of her
Revenue Officer career through January 6, 1975.

    I considered Caroline as being one of the most effective Revenue
Officers in the group. She independently initiated appropriate
enforcement action on her accounts. As an example, she seized three
snow mobiles, a camper, and miscellaneous equipment from a taxpayer
who has a long history of procrastination with other Revenue Officers.
In another case, she immediately recognized the potential for a
prosecution under IRC 7512, and subsequently referred the case to
Intelligence.

    Caroline has developed excellent work habits. She documents all
pertinent history and she records committments on her desk calendar.
She is punctual in keeping appointments and in initiating enforcement
action (levy, seizure, summons, etc.) where appropriate.

    Other employees frequently consult Caroline for her opinion and
assistance in resolving difficult problems. Through her affiliation with
Office Branch and her knowledge of I.R.M. Part 5, she has gained
expertise in handling varied and complicated issues. The employees
respect Caroline for her mature judgement in weighing all the facts
and alternatives before making a decision.

    Caroline was one of the most enthusiastic Revenue Officers in the
District. I have complete confidence that she will continue to be
an outstanding Revenue Officer in the Seattle District.

_____

Monte Hobson

Internal Revenue Service
memorandum

date: June 16, 1976

to: Bob Burkett
Special Procedures Officer
Boise District

from: Chief, Intelligence Division
Boise District

subject: Tax Resisters

Attached is a list identifying tax resisters in Idaho. This list
is provided to you for tax administration purposes. This list has
a control number and should not be duplicated. It should also be
maintained under lock security. The list will be periodically
changed with names either added or deleted as the situation requires.
Upon the receipt of a new list, forward the old list to the Intelligence Division for destruction.

If you identify any individuals who are not listed, please forward
this information to me with an explanation as to why you believe the
individual is a tax resister.

I would also like to know if any of the individuals identified on the
attached list are currently the subject of an audit examination or a
collection assignment. If there is any question regarding the list
or tax resisters, do not hesitate to call me.

Ryan T. Corrigan

December 15, 1977

CONGRESSIONAL RECORD — *Extensions of Remarks*   E 7389

EXTENSIONS OF REMARKS

IRS ABUSES—A CHILLING EFFECT

HON. GEORGE HANSEN
OF IDAHO
IN THE HOUSE OF REPRESENTATIVES
Thursday, December 15, 1977

Mr. HANSEN. Mr. Speaker, the tax collector can be a worthy servant of the people who provides the funds for operation of the necessary services of government or he can be a feared and despised creature of costly and burdensome bureaucracy and tyranny.

This is particularly so at the Federal level in the case of the Internal Revenue Service. Reprisal and intimidation by this agency can have a chilling effect on our first amendment guarantee of "freedom of speech" and "the right * * * peaceably to assemble, and to petition the Government for a redress of grievances."

My letter of December 13, 1977, to Mr. Jerome Kurtz, Commissioner of Internal Revenue, spells out a very real problem in this regard which no Member of Congress or any American citizen can afford to ignore.

The letter follows:

DEAR MR. KURTZ: As a Member of Congress representing Southern and Eastern Idaho, I am deeply concerned for the welfare of the citizens of my district who were victims of the 1976 collapse of the Teton Dam.

Thousands of people in the Upper Snake River Valley were violently thrown out of their homes causing death and injury to many and hundreds of millions of dollars worth of damage to homes, farms, businesses, and other property. Total communities were destroyed.

These people were driven from their homes, farms, and businesses by government irresponsibility, the failure of the Bureau of Reclamation to perform to its usual high standards. The Congress and the President rose to the occasion by assuming necessary responsibility and quickly allocating federal resources and a four hundred million dollar fund to help rehabilitate and fully reimburse the victims.

The victims themselves assisted by an amazing display of effectively organized volunteers drawing heavily from surrounding counties and states, and even coming from distant areas, created a miracle in terms of recovery time and reduced losses for government reimbursement. Millions of hours of volunteer assistance organized by churches and other private sources coupled with local, state and federal government resources have in some eighteen months restored the area to near normalcy.

But it isn't the same. People died. Family treasures, priceless and irreplaceable, are gone forever. Lives and living patterns were disrupted and can never really be restored. Glittering new stores, homes and equipment often replaced the old which seems more than fair on the surface, but does it really compensate for months of despair and disruption and for loss of income and the efficiency of normal conditions? Many people cannot even return to pre-flood businesses and circumstances because the shortages of housing and labor cause disproportionate rent, salaries and other cost factors.

The point I make is that the communities affected by the Teton flood and all the surrounding area are unique, especially so for tax purposes. It will take special handling to assure fairness and prevent the subversion of the will of Congress in fully restoring the people to pre-flood circumstances.

Since I was given early reason to believe by Internal Revenue Service action that the flood victims were going to have difficulty with IRS tax policies, I introduced legislation to provide necessary relief. This was done in the year of the flood, 1976, and again at the beginning of this term of Congress in January, 1977. The Bill, HR 382, has been referred to the House Ways and Means Committee and is looked on as a probable necessity depending on ongoing practices by IRS in handling the returns of those economically affected directly and indirectly by the flood.

To establish whether the IRS can accommodate by attitude and by regulation to the circumstances of the people in the Upper Snake River Valley of Idaho without additional or special legislation, I have conducted a year-long investigation and study which I feel have established rather conclusive results pending only your input which I now invite.

To be perfectly candid, I am shocked at my findings and believe you could not react much differently based on the evidence. I realize you are relatively new to your position so I present the following for your information as well as in hopes that corrective action will be taken where necessary to end abuses and give assurances that IRS will confine itself to its role as a tax collecting agency.

I am deeply concerned that we have no sooner gotten people back on the farm and in their homes and businesses after the failure of a Bureau of Reclamation project only to face having many of them pushed out again by the Internal Revenue Service. Only this time it may be intentional and a subversion of Congressional intent if there is wholesale assessment of such things as capital gains taxes against reimbursements paid by the Bureau of Reclamation.

What makes me believe this will happen? First, the IRS attitude about household furnishings reimbursements which was only resolved after considerable pressure; second, the latitude of IRS auditors to allow and disallow particularly in such unusual circumstances; and third, the recent history of IRS activity in the Western Region of the United States and Eastern Idaho in particular.

It is the third area I especially view with alarm, an area which also profoundly affects points one and two.

I find the IRS has an abominable record over the past four or five years of assault against the people living in the Teton Dam Flood area and seething turmoil within its own ranks over policies, procedures, and personnel.

Provable policies of gross discrimination against IRS employees are rampant and ongoing, and a scandalous violation of taxpayers' civil rights continues on broad scale.

1. Why is the IRS making such a strong effort to purge Mormon agents from key Eastern Idaho audit positions particularly in the Idaho Falls area?

2. Why is the IRS so concerned about getting tough with Mormon Church officials that they would send in a roving office auditor from another state for special target audits in contravention of general IRS procedures?

3. Why would an IRS "violence list" be periodically circulated containing the names of Idaho citizens having no record of violence?

4. Why would IRS agents go to conservative meetings to make lists of license plate numbers which were then expanded to watch lists of names, addresses, business addresses and positions in the Mormon Church—and why were no liberal groups similarly monitored, if extremists were the target?

5. Why would IRS agents anonymously contact individuals who politically complained of high taxes in letters to the Editor and place them under automatic investigation? The right of free speech seems to have its liabilities.

6. Why would IRS agents maintain a full-scale clipping file from the newspapers on taxpayers regarding vacation trips and other activities? I'm not sure the taxpayers realize the extent to which individual privacy has been invaded by big government.

7. Why should IRS prosecute waitresses so diligently in Eastern Idaho with allegations of big income from tips when it is well-known that the payscale in the area is much below the national norm?

8. Why should IRS have planned an armed door-to-door search by some 30-40 agents in communities north of Idaho Falls to demand the showing of tax returns, an operation finally halted at the Washington level when collection officers complained that someone might be hurt or killed?

The story, as I understand it, is partially one of near paranoia and over-reaction to a handful of so-called tax protestors in the Upper Snake River Valley which coincidentally has a large percentage of Mormons. IRS management at the local, State, and Regional levels have given continual indication that they don't trust Mormon agents to audit Mormon Church officials despite frequent pronouncements by the Church that people should be law abiding and pay their taxes.

This suspicion by IRS officials has apparently prompted a policy of obvious discrimination in promotion and assignment of agents in numerous places throughout the West and especially in East Idaho. This can be readily documented in a number of cases where complaints of discrimination were filed and IRS was forced to clean up its act.

Since this employee juggling program ran into difficulty and IRS couldn't get locally oriented agents out of East Idaho and the Upper Snake River area fast enough, they resorted to compensating measures such as the roving auditor program, the pavlovian reactions to political gatherings and letters to the editor, and the planned armed search.

There was hope that a recent change of State IRS Directors might alter the situation, but the harassment and shuffling of employees goes on with indications of reprisal action and unusually high numbers of transfers. The only change appears to be in the objective, but this is very significant. The tax protestors, who were never more than small potatoes, are now taking a back seat to the fertile possibilities of auditing for Capital gains among thousands of flood victims with a four-hundred million dollar reimbursement. For this, it appears IRS is still trying to move out those agents who know the most about the people and their situations and who could and would do the fairest job, and bring in non-local auditors. The continued instances of discrimination, harassment and reprisal against employees would suggest that the taxpayers are in for a rough time.

This I hope is not the case and nothing could please me more than to receive your assurance of this. The flood victims are being paid very carefully for their losses, and for IRS to collect taxes from these reimbursements subverts the intent of the relief legislation and could work a real hardship on many people.

I will not stand by and allow the Teton area people to be further victimized. If IRS plans any kind of tax auditing action to reduce the reimbursements granted by the Bureau of Reclamation, I will seek immediate passage of my bill and any other appropriate legislation to obtain the necessary relief and fair treatment.

Certainly there can be no more social and political monitoring of news releases on citizens, no more discriminations against employees to get at certain taxpayers, no more unusual procedures such as roving office auditors to target certain taxpayers, no more license plate games and religious watch lists, no more "violence lists" containing non-violent people whose greatest sin might be an unkind word for IRS, no more possibilities of a random armed search of taxpayers' homes.

Such projects and programs do not enhance people's confidence in government and can only be harmful to the effectiveness of IRS. In fact, the special harassment of some 40 waitresses in the Idaho Falls area has put you in a position where there is no faith in IRS and citizens are being forced into tax protest roles. I'd hate to think that IRS would deliberately set out to create problems to frustrate taxpayers to harsh action so that some bureaucrat can ride to glory by putting down an uprising.

If this indeed can happen, then a massive mishandling of thousands of cases in the Teton flood reimbursement situation by IRS could result in a terrible confrontation.

I don't want a confrontation, and neither do the people in Eastern Idaho, but their independent nature will not tolerate oppressive government and this must be understood right now as we go into the first full tax year after the flood occurred.

It is important for IRS to assure the people of Idaho and the nation that there will be an immediate end to employee discrimination and civil rights abuses against the tax-payer. It is important also that a declaration of IRS intent be had regarding the unique situation involving the Teton Disaster reimbursements.

The power of the arbitrary audit, the possibilities of intimidation over filing details and judgment factors, and the required waiver of Fifth Amendment Rights make IRS, if used wrongfully, the most dangerous threat of destructive cancer to our system of self-government and our individual rights and freedom. IRS must be totally objective, color-blind, non-political, and religiously and philosophically neutral. The virtual impossibility of your task makes your challenge great and the consequences of your failure a "hell" for the victims.

I am alarmed that too many have already been irreparably harmed by IRS abuses, both employees and taxpayers. I am concerned that confidence in government has eroded to such dangerous proportions. I am hopeful that you can give assurances that strong corrective steps are being taken and that you will make proper recommendations to me and my colleagues in Congress as to what legislation is necessary to get the nation's tax collection system out of the gutter and on to the high road.

Sincerely,

GEORGE HANSEN,
Member of Congress.

COMMISSIONER OF INTERNAL REVENUE

Washington, DC 20224

FEB 2 4 1978

The Honorable George V. Hansen
House of Representatives
Washington, DC 20515

Dear Mr. Hansen:

I have delayed answering your letter of December 13,
1977 awaiting the results of investigations of your charges.
While we have not completed all of our various inquiries,
I can provide answers to most of the points you raise and
will furnish further information as indicated below.

You raised several distinct points about the administration of the tax law as it applies to the victims of the Teton
Dam disaster.

The first point concerns the substantive tax law applicable to payments made by the Bureau of Reclamation to
victims of the disaster for losses which they sustained.
That law is set forth in the Internal Revenue Code and is
more fully described in a letter from Mario Lombardo, Chief
of our Individual Income Tax Branch, to Gilbert Stamm, Commissioner of the Bureau of Reclamation, dated October 13, 1976.
A copy of Mr. Lombardo's letter is attached and designated
Attachment 1. The Internal Revenue Service has no authority
to change the law nor to excuse taxpayers from complying with
it. Further special relief for victims of the Teton Dam
disaster would have to be legislated by Congress. In view
of your interest in such relief, a copy of your letter has
been forwarded to Donald Lubick, the Acting Assistant
Secretary for Tax Policy.

We are, however, mindful of the complexities of existing
law and the need for affected taxpayers to understand clearly
the tax consequences of the various courses of action available to them. Service personnel in our Boise District began
an "outreach" program to assist taxpayers in understanding
the tax consequences of their actions and complying with the
requirements of law. On June 9, 1976, twelve trained IRS
tax assistors were added to the staffs of Disaster Assistance
Centers. At the same time, our telephone operators completed
special training to aid the disaster victims and a special
District Technical Committee was established to handle
inquiries. These efforts are more thoroughly discussed in
the "Teton Report" appearing as Attachment 2 to this letter.

Department of the Treasury   Internal Revenue Service

-2-

The Honorable George V. Hansen

In July, 1976, the District Director of our Boise
District sent a letter to taxpayers informing them of the
type of records needed to support their treatment of compen-
sation payments on their 1976 returns. In February, 1977,
during the filing season, the District Director sent another
letter to taxpayers, enclosing worksheets and summary schedules
to aid in return preparation and specifically informing
taxpayers of the nonrecognition of gain election available
under Section 1033 in the event of the acquisition of "like
kind" replacement property within two years. These letters
and their enclosures appear as Attachments 3 and 4 to this
letter.

On October 27, 28 and 29, 1976, seminars were held by
our employees for disaster victims in Rexburg, Idaho, under
the auspices of the University of Idaho. These seminars
were attended by over 500 taxpayers and practitioners. The
reaction of taxpayers to these seminars is described in a
letter dated November 5, 1976 from the Center for Business
Development and Research of the University of Idaho, which
appears as Attachment 5 to this letter.

Thereafter, the District Director issued a "Teton Dam
Disaster Income Tax Update" setting forth in question and
answer form the questions asked and the answers given at a
meeting held in the Idaho Falls City Counsel Chambers on
November 28, 1977. This update appears as Attachment 6 to
this letter.

These efforts were augmented by weekly visits by Service
personnel to facilities provided by the Inter-Faith Council
in Rexburg, Idaho, by the ongoing programs of two Service
offices in the disaster area and through our Statewide toll
free telephone assistance.

On the whole we believe the record reflects that Service
personnel have provided extraordinary assistance to a group
of taxpayers with extraordinary needs. We are proud of the
efforts of our Boise personnel. Nevertheless, we recognize
that in particular instances our personnel may have provided
misleading, unclear or inaccurate advice to taxpayers on these
complex issues despite their best efforts not to do so. I
have been informed that you recently conducted hearings in
your District and may be aware of such instances. I ask that
you bring specific examples to my attention, or to the
attention of the Boise District Director, Philip Sansotta, so
that we can initiate a review of these specific cases and make
any appropriate adjustments to those returns.

In your letter you ask "Why is the IRS making such a
strong effort to purge Mormon agents from key Eastern Idaho
audit positions particularly in the Idaho Falls area"?

The Honorable George V. Hansen

Any such effort would be a violation of Federal law, established IRS policies and my personal convictions. Our investigation to date does not provide any basis for your allegation. Mr. Sansotta has advised me that of eight technical selections (tax auditors and revenue agents) made in the Boise and Idaho Falls offices within the last 18 months, 6 have been Mormons. Moreover, the Group Manager of the Idaho Falls office, appointed more than two years ago, is a Mormon. Nevertheless, I have asked Warren Bates, our Assistant Commissioner (Inspection), to have our Internal Audit Division conduct a thorough investigation of these charges. Mr. Bates is coordinating this investigation with our National Office Equal Employment Opportunity staff and our National Office Equal Opportunity Officer, Barbara Thompson. If you are aware of any specific instances of discrimination in our employment practices based on religion or on any other such factor, I urge you to bring them to the attention of Mr. Bates, Mrs. Thompson or me so that they may be investigated and, if true, appropriate action taken. I will provide you with the results of our investigation when it is completed to the extent we are permitted to do so under the law. I feel very strongly, however, that specifics concerning this charge, if any, be made known to us so that appropriate actions may be taken.

You asked "Why is the IRS so concerned about getting tough with Mormon Church officials that they would send in a roving office auditor from another state for special target audits in contravention of general IRS procedures"?

We are aware of no facts which would substantiate your allegation and again if you know of any I urge you to communicate them to us.

I might mention that of the 58 Internal Revenue Service districts, 19 are so-called "key districts" which provide centralized field expertise in two specialized and complex areas of our enforcement responsibility -- employee plans and exempt organizations. The Boise District is not such a "key district" and relies on Seattle, Washington to provide experts necessary to conduct examinations in these two areas. This is a nationwide procedure and not unique to Boise or Seattle. Perhaps this procedure has caused confusion among some of your constituents.

With the exception of our general key district examination program in these areas, we are aware of only one auditor who was not permanently assigned to an Idaho office who audited returns in that area. That individual was a new audit trainee who worked in the Boise District (and specifically in the Idaho Falls office) for approximately six months prior to his first permanent assignment in Portland, Oregon. That individual received no special assignment while in Idaho Falls;

-4-

The Honorable George V. Hansen

to the contrary, he was restricted to the less complicated type of examinations normally reserved for new trainees undergoing on-the-job training.

Underlying these two statements is the broader allegation that the Service discriminates in its personnel and examination policies based on religion. I consider this an extremely serious charge which should not be made unless supported by specific facts. I assure you that any such cases will be thoroughly investigated and if proven true severe actions will be taken. However, I know of no such case.

Your letter questions why the Internal Revenue Service maintained a so-called violence list and kept lists of license plate numbers of those attending certain meetings which you characterize as "conservative meetings". You also stated that the Internal Revenue Service had planned "armed searches" of taxpayers' homes in the Snake River area.

Based on the information then available, each of these questions seems to relate to certain actions undertaken to protect our personnel against tax protestors advocating violence. High level Internal Revenue Service managers were seriously concerned that certain tax protestors belonging to organizations which advocated the violent disruption of tax administration posed a threat to the physical safety of our enforcement personnel. This concern was shared by the Federal Bureau of Investigation (FBI). The principal group advocating violent interference with the administration of the tax laws was the Sheriff's Posse Comitatus (SPC). This group's activity initiated in the western part of the United States within the boundaries of our Western Region. Accordingly, most actions undertaken by the Service in response to those threats also occurred in the Western Region.

On December 5, 1975 the Deputy Commissioner issued guidelines to the Regional Commissioners and Regional Inspectors. The guidelines included: (1) the maintaining of liaison with other law enforcement agencies including the FBI by our Intelligence Division and Inspection Service; (2) authorization to solicit information concerning the SPC and similar organizations restricting that authorization to information that concerned individuals involved in efforts to disrupt tax administration, or to information directly tax related, or involving potential assaults or threats against Service employees. On July 26, 1976, the Deputy Commissioner issued a Manual Supplement (93G-171, renumbered 9G-35) on the same subject. Copies of the December 5, 1975 memorandum and the July 26, 1976 Manual Supplement, respectively, appear as Attachments 7 and 8 to this letter.

Pursuant to these directives, our Inspection Service began to gather information on various tax protestor groups which, in their organizational documents or other pronouncements, advocated violent interference with the administration of the tax laws. During December, 1975, our Inspection Service in

The Honorable George V. Hansen

the Western Region furnished a list of names of 25 individuals
who were reportedly members of groups advocating violence to
the District Director, Boise, Idaho. The agencies which
furnished the information to Inspection were the FBI,
Idaho State Police and our own Intelligence Division.
The Idaho State Police named two individuals as known
members of the SPC. Of the other 23 names (all furnished
to us by the FBI), all but two were listed on charter
petitions of the SPC on file in various counties in Idaho.
Of the remaining two, one individual was a reported member
of the SPC who had been arrested on an assault charge by
local police. ⋇/   The other individual was reported to
be a member of the Vigilant Committee of 10,000 by a local
Idaho newspaper. According to local police sources in the
Rexburg, Idaho, area, the Vigilant Committee of 10,000
also advocated the violent disruption of tax administration.

        Some of the information obtained by Inspection from
the sources described above did include license plate
numbers of individuals who were attending or were parked
in the vicinity of SPC meetings. However, the license plate
information was never used as the sole basis for placing
an individual's name on the list furnished to the District
Director. Generally, no name was included on the list unless
the person was also identified from some other source as being
a member of the SPC or another organization advocating violence.

        The purpose of the list was to provide management with
some indication of those individuals who presented some
threat to our personnel, so that our personnel, forwarned
of the possibility of violence, could take appropriate
precautions in carrying out their duties. This list was
to be used for no other purpose, and we would appreciate
being informed of any allegations of its use for other than
its intended purpose. We have an obligation to protect the
safety of our own personnel and I believe we would have been
negligent to do less than we did in the face of the express
goals of these groups.

        The planned activities to which you refer in your
letter as an "armed search" were also a reaction to concerns
for the safety of our personnel in view of the activities
of SPC and similar organizations. Among the compliance
techniques occasionally used by the Service are canvassings
of areas by revenue officers who knock on doors and ask occupants
to produce a copy of their tax return as evidence of their
compliance with the tax laws. Such canvassing techniques
are usually performed in areas where comparisons with

---

        *Known members of the SPC attempted to serve a summons
on the county Sheriff to have the charge against that
individual dismissed.

-6-

The Honorable George V. Hansen

other publicly available information shows an abnormally low percentage of return filings. The revenue officer conducting the canvassing does not search the houses in question; rather, he or she asks the occupant to produce a return and, if no return is produced, simply note this fact. These revenue officers are not armed.

Such a canvassing was planned for a community in the Snake River Valley. In view of the high number of identified SPC members in the area, however, local personnel considered having our unarmed revenue officers accompanied by special agents or by our Inspection personnel, who were to act as escorts, available to assist only in the event of violence against our unarmed personnel. In view of the possible confrontations which might have resulted, this proposed canvassing program was cancelled after review by appropriate management officials at the district, regional and national levels.

In your letter, you allege that Internal Revenue Service personnel have placed under automatic investigation individuals complaining about higher taxes. We have no knowledge of any such activities, nor do we approve of or condone such activities. If you are aware of specific instances in which taxpayers claim that they have been selected for audit or other investigation under such circumstances, please provide that information to Mr. Bates or to me and we will initiate appropriate inquiries.

You ask why IRS agents maintain a clipping file on taxpayers regarding vacation trips and other activities.

In keeping with our established procedures, the Internal Revenue Service gathers directly tax related information from a variety of sources, including newspapers, concerning possible failures to comply with the tax laws. Our experience indicates that taxpayers frequently fail to report the value of prizes such as vacation trips as income on their returns. We follow up on this information to determine whether the prize income has been reported on the taxpayer's return.

In your letter, you allege that the Internal Revenue Service has prosecuted waitresses in eastern Idaho for failure to report tip income. No waitresses have in fact been prosecuted. In Idaho, as elsewhere, where we find indications that tip income is not being reported, we assess deficiencies with respect to that unreported income. Accordingly, the waitresses in eastern Idaho have not been subjected to special scrutiny with respect to tip income.

I have tried to be responsive to your concerns and assure you that the Service will not tolerate discrimination in either its personnel policies or in its examination policies based on

The Honorable George V. Hansen

religion. Any facts at all to support your allegations in this
regard should be made known to me. Generalized allegations of
this sort without specific factual support do a disservice to
the thousands of dedicated people who make up the Internal
Revenue Service.

Sincerely yours,

Enclosures
Attachment 1 - Letter from Mario Lombardo
               to Gilbert Stamm, dated 10/13/76
Attachment 2 - "Teton Report"
Attachment 3 - Letter from District Director
               of the Boise District to Taxpayers,
               dated July, 1976
Attachment 4 - Letter from District Director
               of the Boise District to Taxpayers,
               dated February, 1977
Attachment 5 - Letter from the Center for Business
               Development and Research of the
               University of Idaho to the District
               Director of the Boise District
Attachment 6 - "Teton Dam Disaster Income Tax Update"
Attachment 7 - Memorandum from the Deputy Commissioner
               of Internal Revenue to Regional Commissioners
               and Regional Inspectors issuing guidelines,
               dated December 5, 1975
Attachment 8 - Manual Supplement 9G-35

GEORGE HANSEN
Second District, Idaho
1125 Longworth Building
Washington, D.C. 20515
Tel. (202) 225-5531

COMMITTEES-SUBCOMMITTEES
BANKING, FINANCE AND
URBAN AFFAIRS
General Oversight and
Renegotiation
Domestic Monetary Policy
(Ranking Member)

VETERANS' AFFAIRS
Cemeteries and Burial Benefits
Medical Facilities and Benefits

Congress of the United States
House of Representatives
Washington, D. C.

Idaho District Offices:
UPPER SNAKE RIVER VALLEY
211 Federal Building
Box 740, Idaho Falls 83401
Tel.: 523-5341

SOUTHEASTERN IDAHO
305 Federal Building
Box 1330, Pocatello 83201
Tel.: 232-0900

MAGIC VALLEY
1061 Blue Lakes Blvd. N.
Twin Falls 83301
Tel.: 734-6466

WESTERN IDAHO
442 Old Federal Building
Boise 83701
Tel.: 384-1876

March 9, 1978

Mr. Jerome Kurtz
Commissioner, Internal Revenue Service
1111 Constitution Avenue, NW
Washington, D. C. 20224

Dear Mr. Kurtz:

I have received your February 24, 1978 response to my inquiry of
December 13, 1977 and appreciate the information you provided.
However, I must say that I am amazed at some of your answers to my
questions.

The naivete you expressed in certain areas which are matters of
extensive record with your agency is incredible, as was your apparent
lack of comprehension of the impact certain IRS practices admitted by
you could have when revealed to the public.

Plain and simple, what I see in your letter is severe administrative
overkill in tax collection practices and a stonewalling or coverup
of IRS harassment activities and abuses of civil rights of employees
and taxpayers. Since you are relatively new to your task as
administrator, I can assume you still rely heavily upon others for
your facts and advice so my complaint about the response you signed
is not intended to be personal. However, I assume I can take seriously
your offer to correct IRS abuses when they are pointed out to you,
which I am prepared to do extensively.

This letter will serve to briefly advise you of glaring examples
where your letter is in serious error on situations well-known to your
agency. Extensive material is being prepared to support my concern
for IRS attitudes and procedures which will appear daily in the
Congressional Record beginning on the date of this letter. I hope
you will have someone alerted to making this material available to
you and that corrective action will be taken to prevent further abuse
of taxpayers and employees.

Regarding error number one, you state on page 3 paragraph 4: "Our
investigation to date does not provide any basis for your allegation"
of employee discrimination on a basis of religion. You further state,
"If you are aware of any specific instances of discrimination in our
employment practices based on religion or on any other such factor, I

Mr. Jerome Kurtz
March 9, 1978

urge you to bring them to the attention of Mr. Bates [Warren Bates,
Assistant Commissioner (Inspection)], Mrs. Thompson [Barbara Thompson,
National Office Equal Opportunity Officer], or me..."

Mr. Kurtz, I have been talking to Mr. Bates about this matter since
last November and his inspection files are full of just this situation
I describe. Not only this but the National Treasury Employees Union
newspaper called The Bulletin for December 31, 1975, features a story
entitled "NTEU Secures Promotions for Two Denied Jobs Due to Religious
Discrimination."

In addition to this I have a letter addressed to me from Equal Employment Opportunity Officer Barbara R. Thompson dated August 6, 1976
concerning the request from the President of the Idaho NTEU with
reference to two IRS employees confirming complaints of religious
discrimination, findings of an investigation into the charges and
IRS efforts at adjustment in accord with the Civil Service Commission
regulations.

Unfortunately the situation continues to this day with additional
complaints of discrimination and retaliation before various arbitrating
authorities. Other cases are also in evidence which will be made
public to refresh IRS memories.

Error number two is your statement in the last paragraph of page 4
that you "know of no such case" regarding "the broader allegation
that the Service discriminates in its personnel and examination
policies based on religion." The personnel aspect has already been
dealt with under the topic of Error Number One, above. However, the
discrimination is no less true in the IRS procedures regarding taxpayers.

I will outline and document in the Congressional Record series instances
of apparent discrimination and special treatment by IRS involving
donations to religious educational institutions, missionary support
programs, church contributions, auditing practices and general attitudes
toward certain taxpayers based on religious affiliation.

Error number three concerns your cloak and dagger operation involving
the compilation and distribution of violence lists and lurking at
meetings to secure license plate numbers of people meeting in free
assembly under the First Amendment of the Constitution, and armed
searches where taxpayers are bluffed by a random door-to-door shakedown into producing tax returns which they are forced by no law to do.

You can protest all you want that your efforts are only designed to
protect your employees and that there is no pressure on the taxpayers
confronted, but your methods betray you.

The Nixon White House long ago demonstrated the folly of keeping
ridiculous lists with absurd titles. If you wanted to alert your
employees to questionable or dangerous practices of people or groups
such as you ascribe to the posse comitatus, then why don't you properly
entitle the list and stipulate the exact problems which may be encountered? Instead, by your own admission, you lumped everybody
together in a most fearsome and damning description of their potential

Mr. Jerome Kurtz
March 9, 1978

for violence despite the fact that virtually all of them had no
personal law enforcement record whatsoever of criminal or violent
acts.

What an overkill and disservice to the right of free speech and free
assembly for you to categorically label citizens never accused or
proven guilty by any court as if they were criminals prone to violence.
The list is not titled "Posse Comitatus" or some other appropriate terms,
but "Taxpayers Who May Advocate Violence Toward Western Region
Personnel." It was further qualified that "the list was compiled from
a system of records dealing with criminal law enforcement..."

This doesn't minimize the danger to your employees, it encourages
confrontation. You further engage in confrontation activities by
the door to door compliance checks which could be done much more
simply by a cross checking of city directory or other lists with your
tax return files. And the fact that armed agents would accompany the
collection agents in the encounter with taxpayers along with the
license plate snooping is further indication that your total effort
is geared towards confrontation. This, of course, is only part of an
ongoing program of harassment and embarrassment practiced by IRS
which I will document in the Congressional Record. Such means of
inducing compliance of the nation's tax laws is repugnant to any
thinking citizens and dangerously akin to dictatorship.

Error number four concerns your statement on page 7 paragraph 3 that
"we have no knowledge of...nor do we approve of or condone..."
"automatic investigation of individuals complaining about higher taxes."
I have documentation to the contrary, at least one case of which you are
familiar from your reports on my January hearings in Idaho Falls.
This instance regarding Larry Fullmer of Pocatello and others will be
documented in the Congressional Record.

For you to be checking on every person who writes a letter to the editor
and clipping papers regarding possible vacation trips and prizes taxpayers
may receive certainly shows you have a high overhead operation with
more employees than you can professionally and constructively keep busy
not to mention a serious abridgement to basic rights of free speech
and privacy. Certainly the outcry against lists and files on citizens
raised in recent months against the FBI and CIA is no less applicable
to the IRS and the public stands to be rightfully indignant.

Error number five is where you draw a fine line between the IRS's
ability to arbitrarily "assess deficiencies" with respect to alleged
unreported income as opposed to being prosecuted. You have the power
to reverse the traditional American system of justice and adjudge
guilt and assess deficiencies and fines before a court can act. The
taxpayer is then placed in a position of proving himself at his own
expense against government attorneys paid by his own tax money. The
waitresses have been harassed and I intend to document the circumstances.

Finally the main reason for my concern remains the Teton Flood victims
and the attitude they are destined to face in the Administration of tax
policies particularly in areas of capital gains.

It has been previously proven by earlier compromise by IRS under latitude allowed by law that reasonable adjustments can be made in regulations. I had hoped for some willingness on your part to look into this but it appears the Congress will have to deal with this as well as overall need for adjustment legislation. It is unfortunate that in priding yourself at service to the flood victims you couldn't offer more than lots of employees and facilities to make the extraction of taxes more easy.

I am taking this matter to the Ways and Means Committee and will keep you advised of further developments.

Sincerely,

GEORGE HANSEN
Member of Congress

September 20, 1978

CONGRESSIONAL RECORD — *Extensions of Remarks* E-5149

STOPPING AN IRS THREAT TO PRIVATE SCHOOLS

HON. GEORGE HANSEN

OF IDAHO

IN THE HOUSE OF REPRESENTATIVES

Wednesday, September 20, 1978

● Mr. HANSEN. Mr. Speaker, in the last several years, the progressive deterioration of public schools in many parts of the country have led to the establishment of private schools. When I speak of deterioration, I have reference not only to a lower level of learning achievement, but also to spectacular increases in crime at schools, and the progressive establishment of an atheistic and secularist religion to impart alien values to our young children. It is also true, and cannot be denied, that some schools were established for the sake of avoiding desegregation.

Comes now the Internal Revenue Service, which on August 22, 1978, proposed that all schools—I repeat, all schools formed or expanded at or about or after the implementation of desegregation plans in the respective communities will be presumed guilty of systematic racial discrimination and their tax-exempt status revoked retroactively.

Mr. Speaker, we have become inured to the routine contempt the IRS has chronically demonstrated for accepted civilized standards of fairness, something which has its roots in the regrettable presumption that in tax matters the citizen is guilty until proven innocent, an innocence that has to be proven at the expense of the taxpayer, no matter how groundless or frivolous the charges. The proposed regulation I have mentioned to you is a fresh example of this attitude. It proposes to make a blanket finding of racial discrimination and automatically harass all private schools, putting on its victims the onerous burden of proving their innocence. At the same time, it says that it will be practically impossible to refute the charge unless there is an affirmative action program operating.

I have objections to all of this, which forms the substance of the proposed regulation. But what shows truly brazen boldness on the part of the Internal Revenue Service, what puts all their previous efforts at trickery in the shade, is the fact that they have the astonishing gall

to say that this is an insignificant regulation, a mere procedural change which does not merit public hearing.

If you will consult section 556 of title 5 of the United States Code, you will find that Congress insisted that rulemaking be done in the open. Only strictly internal and procedural matters—such things as meeting times and personnel matters—should be exempt. The regulation I have referred to was published August 22, 1978, in the "notices" section of the Federal Register, sandwiched between a docket notice and a notice about a certain-pension plan's exemption from a particular rule. Despite its substantive nature, the proposed regulation was not published in the proposed rules and regulation section, but was buried in the back. Moreover, in the proposal itself, the IRS makes the absurd assertion that the proposed regulation is not significant, and thus that it does not come within the scope of 5 U.S.C. 556.

The position of the IRS is silly. There is no merely procedural matter, but a substantive proposition that calls into question the tax liabilities, supposedly long past settled, of hundreds of thousands of citizens for many years past. It obviously has the gravest conceivable implications for the survival of private schools, and certainly gives the IRS wide scope for abuse and harassment. It is nonsense to claim that the regulation, whatever its merits, is not significant.

What is involved here is not actually a matter of racial discrimination, nor is it really a tax matter. Since the regulation explicitly includes church-related schools, and since there is nothing in the regulation that could not later be applied to churches themselves, what is involved is a very deep first amendment question. It is a patent evasion to label this regulation "procedural" and claim that it is of no significance.

In this transparent maneuver, Mr. Speaker, the Internal Revenue Service is in violation of at least the spirit, if not the letter, of the law and Executive orders governing the making of administrative rules and regulations. To stop this outrageous flouting of congressional intent, I have today introduced legislation which takes no issue with the substance of the proposed regulation, but prohibits the so-called procedure from coming into effect until the IRS has complied with all the requirements of Treasury regulations for public notice and hearing. It states, in short, that this is indeed a significant regulation and must be treated as such.

If, after an open hearing in accord with the law and elementary canons of ordinary fairness, the IRS goes ahead with this proposed regulation, there will be nothing in my bill to prevent it. But that open hearing is the least that IRS can do to avoid disgracing itself and giving further impetus to the tax revolt.●

February 21, 1979

CONGRESSIONAL RECORD — *Extensions of Remarks*   **E 605**

PRIVATE SCHOOLS AND THE IRS

SPEECH OF

HON. GEORGE HANSEN

OF IDAHO

IN THE HOUSE OF REPRESENTATIVES

Monday, February 19, 1979

Mr. HANSEN. Mr. Speaker, I appreciate very much the opportunity to testify before you and this subcommittee regarding the planned assault on the Nation's private schools by the Internal Revenue Service (IRS).

Mr. Speaker, I am the congressional "whistle blower" who exposed the presumptuous and secretive move by the IRS to broaden its control over, as well as "discriminate" against, private schools which has become a national outrage.

Hidden among the "Notices" section of the August 22, 1978, Federal Register—sandwiched between routine announcements instead of appearing in the section on Proposed Rules and Regulations—was an IRS proposal that all private schools formed or expanded at or after the implementation of desegregation plans in the respective communities, will be presumed guilty of systematic racial discrimination and their tax-exempt status will be revoked retroactively.

The IRS long ago seems to have lost its sense of mission as a tax-collection agency and with all the grace of the hobnailed gestapo has embarked on a course of implementing and enforcing social reform with the view that Americans are basically dishonest, uncharitable, bigoted, criminal-minded and even violent to deal with.

These may seem like strong words, Mr. Speaker, but the shocking story on IRS behavior that I will reveal to you today will prove my point.

For years we have become progressively inured to the routine contempt the IRS has chronically demonstrated for accepted civilized standards of fairness, something which has its roots in the regrettable presumption that in tax matters the citizen is guilty until proven innocent, an innocence that has to be proven at the expense of the taxpayer, no matter how groundless or frivolous the charge.

To demonstrate that this is not taxpayer paranoia. I submit for the record a shocking paragraph from a recently acquired IRS memo dated November 19, 1976, which clearly states that taxpayers should be intimidated with expensive unwarranted lawsuits. The communication addressed to the Regional Counsel, Salt Lake City office, from Group Manager, 1004, Boise District Office, declares:

> It is stated you do not wish to litigate a case you may lose. However, failure to attempt litigation will foster their program far more than a loss in court. At least by litigating, the Taxpayer is forced to produce the necessary substantiation. In addition, the Taxpayer is committed to spend time and money defending his position. Perhaps the inconvenience alone will inspire future compliance.

Now Mr. Speaker, with this attitude the IRS has been creeping into the social reform enforcement business for many years and began in 1975 requiring schools to state that they are nondiscriminatory in order to keep their tax-exempt status. The Washington Post of October 14, 1978, confirms this reality in reporting that Virginia's "Prince Edward School Tax-Exempt Status is Revoked by IRS."

The regulation proposed in August for IRS to become a big-time civil rights enforcer was a further extension of a malignant spread that has taken them from the confinement of simple tax collection to impact on many sensitive areas of the body politic.

In its usual sweeping manner the IRS proposed to make a blanket finding of racial discrimination and automatically harass all private schools, putting on its victims the onerous burden of proving their innocence. At the same time the IRS pointed out how it would be practically impossible to refute the charge unless there is an affirmative action program operating.

This serious constitutionally questionable IRS action was brazenly taken without congressional authorization in circumstances that dwarf all their previous efforts at trickery. To cover up their attempt to "hide" the Federal Register notice, the IRS had the astonishing gall to say that this is an insignificant regulation, a mere procedural change which does not merit public hearing.

Frankly, the position of the IRS is not only absurd and dishonest, but it is dangerous. This is not merely a procedural matter, but a substantive proposition that calls into question the tax liabilities, supposedly long past settled, of hundreds of thousands of citizens for many years past. IRS auditors will have a field day. It obviously has the gravest conceivable implications for the survival of private schools, and certainly gives the IRS wide scope for abuse and harassment.

Having watched the IRS swoop down on the hapless victims of the Teton Dam disaster of 1976 and scoop up capital gains taxes arbitrarily imposed on flood claims reimbursements, I am not surprised to see them again gleefully anticipating the financial squeeze they can put on those private schools identified as discriminatory and the taxpayers who have supported them.

And lest we believe the IRS has any conscience about forcing private schools or anyone else out of business by taking their last farthing, let me cite to you an alarming memo dated March 2, 1973, to the chief, Collection and Taxpayer Service, from a group supervisor in Boise entitled, "How Can We Prevent Delinquency?"

Marginal taxpayers in inefficient, non-profitable businesses are probably responsible for a larger percentage of delinquencies than any other segment of the tax paying public. The most apparent characteristic of these enterprises is the ability to start business with an absolute minimum in capital equipment, cash reserves and other assets, e.g. service stations, restaurants, and construction trades.

The Collection Division has been faced with a two-pronged problem for many years:

First. Prevent delinquencies by stern, prompt enforcement action which forces the taxpayer to discontinue business.

Second. Accomplish the above without undue pressure from the public and the elected officials.

In my opinion, this cannot be done and we must realize that complaints will be an integral part and result of such measures. We must not be oversensitive to these complaints and requests for leniency.

Law addition and other approvals that would help in other areas:

1. Require known prior delinquents to post a cash bond before commencing business (as does the State).

2. Require farmers to withhold income taxes.

3. In collaboration with the State, require license applicants to prove filing and paying HUT and liquor and beer stamps before a license is issued.

4. Provide more man hours for cold canvass operation.

5. A more religious and systemic use of Public Law 85–321.

What is involved in the proposed IRS regulation regarding private schools is not actually a matter of racial discrimination, nor is it really a tax matter. Since the regulation explicitly includes church-related schools, and since there is nothing in the regulation that could not later be applied to churches themselves, what is involved is a very deep first amendment question.

It is a patent evasion to label this regulation "procedural" and claim that it is of no significance and this remains true despite the recent softening of the IRS under public and congressional pressure to get out of the business of enforcing social reform where private schools are concerned.

The fact that the new proposal still retains the questionable percentage requirements subject to arbitrary interpretation by IRS leaves the "tiger in the tank" with broad latitude and virtually unlimited areas to prowl as regulations are adjusted and expanded in the future.

Mr. Speaker, I must warn you. The IRS is the last agency which should be entrusted with any responsibility for legal judgment regarding civil and religious rights.

If the two IRS memos quoted earlier have not sufficiently disturbed you, let me now inform you of an attempt by IRS officials in the highest positions to literally terrorize a small community in my congressional district by staging a massive armed door-to-door search and then cover up not only this particular incident but other equally shocking atrocities being committed against citizens of this Nation.

In November 1975 some 25 specially selected IRS personnel were directed to participate in a project calling for a confrontation and armed shakedown of 167 citizens in Fremont County, Idaho—citizens who, beyond belief, found themselves on an IRS "hit list" largely because of the size of their church donations, because of time devoted to church service, because of extended serious illness or death, and because of assorted other similar reasons.

A neurotic IRS, suffering apparent paranoia over the tax resistors movement in the Nation, decided the percentage of returns in the St. Anthony area was too low and initiated the "Fremont County Returns Compliance Program (RCP)" to educate the public about tax laws.

The word "educate" has very ominous meaning when civic and business leaders, clergymen, elderly female church organists, young men just back from serving 2-year missions for their church with no income, and people in extended hospital confinement or on social security disability pensions are included on IRS lists of citizens considered dangerous to contact or who may advocate violence— citizens slated for contact by armed Federal agents who would be asking them to produce their tax returns.

The project, which was to last a week, was canceled only 4 days before it was scheduled to begin because certain less militant IRS employees balked and complained to their union which finally forced a decision in the Washington office of the IRS Assistant Commissioner for Inspections.

It has taken over 2 years to get to the bottom of this story and in the process I find that the tactics used in dealing with the citizens of Fremont County, Idaho, are not unusual in IRS operations across the Nation, and this can now be documented.

The Nixon enemy list is tame compared to the IRS violence lists and the identified abuses and coverups of the CIA and FBI in recent years also exist in the IRS, perhaps to an even greater degree.

Commissioner Jerome Kurtz and other officials have repeatedly provided false and misleading information apparently designed to obscure or justify the heavy-handed mtehods of the IRS, information which is readily refuted by IRS documents.

I was told the armed confrontation was planned to deal with a list of tax resisters provided by the FBI but can prove that such a list (which itself can be challenged) was not prepared until nearly 2 months after the Fremont project was canceled and that list had no residents of Fremont County included.

In other words, Mr. Kurtz justified the planning and approval of an armed search with a list that was not applicable to the area involved and did not even exist during the period of the operation. This is an intolerable abuse of facts.

Furthermore, I was told the Fremont project was to protect IRS personnel and that the hit list was to include only men over age 20. However, I find that the IRS included women on their list contrary to instructions and violated their own rules in creating a confrontation which could have caused violence rather than prevent it.

Although there is documentation to prove that the search was only canceled because of employee complaints, a letter from Mr. Kurtz would have us believe that the canvass was canceled because, of all things, it might provoke the very confrontations the mission was originally set up to create.

A long list of examples of such duplicity could be provided, and is evident in the attached narrative of the Fremont County project which I submit for the RECORD at the end of my remarks. However, if there is any question as to the acceptability of this type of operation among IRS officials, let it now be laid to rest.

Just 7 days after the project was scrubbed on November 14, 1975, the coordinator of this project was given a memorandum of appreciation by an IRS group manager who stated:

I was very impressed with the Plan of Action which you originated.

And on January 30, 1979 the Idaho district director announced the selection of this same IRS employee for a GS-12 position as disclosure officer.

In the meantime, the Idaho district director, who supervised the planning of the Fremont project, has now been promoted to national director of the Disclosure Division of IRS, where ironically he is responsible for administration of the Freedom of Information Act, the Privacy Act and the new disclosure laws.

Mr. Speaker, the Fremont project was planned, canceled and covered up at State, regional, and national levels so there is no way this activity can be discounted as an isolated incident. The blundering, bullish manner in which IRS handled civil and religious rights in the Fremont project can be rehearsed many times over in other situations in Idaho and across the Nation with substantial documentation.

I have cited many valid constitutional objections to the IRS having any role in the interpretation and enforcement of social reform programs.

These objections are bolstered with a practical concern for allowing an agency with such a poor track record to have broad license in sensitive decisions regarding matters of religious and civil rights.

IRS has demonstrated that it is

neither mentally nor mechanically flexible enough to deal with religious and personal differences and this is true even down to the very decision we currently face. Even in backing off from the original August pronouncement IRS has, in reality, reserved the right to make selective judgment regarding private schools which gives them broad latitude for arbitrariness and harassment.

For instance, in singling out certain denominational academies as possible exceptions, IRS is opening a pandora's box where other exceptions are demanded and where those rejected can be expected to pose costly time-consuming challenges to the Government.

It is absolutely absurd to continue to allow the IRS to run like a rampant bull in a shop stocked with the fragile porcelain of human rights. It is time to confine IRS to the tax-collection mission for which it was instituted.

I urge this Congress to take all necessary action to stop the implementation of the proposed IRS rules regarding private schools. I further strongly urge appropriate congressional committees to hold oversight hearings on the abuse of taxpayers by the IRS such as I have outlined today.

And finally, I urge Congress to consider legislation I have introduced, and any other of like nature, which will reform or restrict the mission of the Internal Revenue Service before it does significantly more damage.

Mr. Speaker, in closing I submit for the record House Joint Memorial No. 2 from the Idaho State Legislature transmitted to me on February 6, 1979, "which urges the U.S. Congress to prevent proposed Internal Revenue Service regulations from becoming effective that eliminate the tax exempt status of private schools that do not conform to certain rules and regulations regarding minority membership."

A JOINT MEMORIAL

We, Your Memorialists, the House of Representatives and Senate of the State of Idaho assembled in the First Regular Session of the Forty-fifth Idaho Legislature, do hereby respectfully represent that:

Whereas, the Internal Revenue Service, Department of the Treasury, has announced a proposed revenue procedure relating to private school tax exemptions; and

Whereas, the proposed revenue procedure will, in effect, establish quotas for minority participation in tax exempt private schools; and

Whereas, such quotas have been held discriminatory in a recent United States Supreme Court opinion; and

Whereas, the use of private schools should be encouraged in order to help take the burden from public schools.

Now, Therefore, Be It Resolved by the members of the First Regular Session of the Forty-fifth Idaho Legislature, the House of Representatives and the Senate concurring therein, that we are deeply concerned with such a proposed procedure and strongly urge that the Congress take such immediate action as necessary to prevent such proposed procedure from becoming effective.

Be It Further Resolved that the Chief Clerk of the House of Representatives be, and he is hereby authorized and directed to forward copies of this Memorial to the President of the Senate and the Speaker of the House of Representatives of Congress, and the honorable congressional delegation representing the State of Idaho in the Congress of the United States.

AN ARMED IRS SHAKEDOWN

I have recently discovered official Internal Revenue Service documents which show, in some detail, an attempt by the IRS to literally terrorize a small community in my congressional district by staging a massive armed door-to-door search. These same documents have also helped me prove that there has been and still is an extensive and ongoing attempt by IRS officials in the highest positions to coverup not only this particular incident but other equally shocking atrocities being committed against the citizens of this Nation.

What I am about to present is a real-life horror story, one chapter in a whole book of outrageous IRS violations of the basic rights of American citizens, which I will continue to expose.

On October 2, 1975 a meeting of IRS division chiefs and the Idaho district director was held in Boise, Idaho, apparently with the knowledge and approval of national headquarters, to discuss coordination of what was later termed a "planned armed, door-to-door search" in St. Anthony, Fremont County, Idaho.

Howard Martin, then district director of the IRS, authorized what was to be known as the Fremont County returns compliance program (RCP) on October 16, 1975. The purpose of the program was ostensibly "to determine the degree of voluntary compliance, to secure any delinquent returns and to educate the public about tax laws."

The IRS, under the direction of Revenue Officer Sherrill Ohman, began immediately to gather data on the citizens of St. Anthony and to cross reference driver's license receipts with existing IRS files. From this effort, the IRS developed a list of 167 taxpayers to be confronted.

The criteria for being placed on the list was simple enough—a male licensed driver from Fremont County between the ages of 21 and 65 with any irregularities in his tax history for any of the years 1972, 1973, and 1974 appeared to automatically qualify, even if there was obviously no illegality involved.

These tax irregularities or aberrations, which would likely be picked out on the microscreening of taxpayer returns used for the selecting process, seemed to include such things as, first, reporting unusually high church contributions; second, not filing because of physical or mental handicap; third, not filing because of no income such as students and missionaries; fourth, not appearing to file because of change of name or address; fifth, not filing because of death; sixth, being previously audited whether for good cause or because of clerical error or IRS error, or substantiable large deductions; seventh, filing an improper return; eighth, not filing a return; ninth, delinquency in tax payments, and so forth. Given this large number of determining factors, the final list grew to 167 names, a number approximately equal to one-fourth of the heads of households in the small city of St. Anthony, the Fremont county seat.

The people involved, though not necessarily, and probably not, illegal or improper in their tax filings, still were listed on forms entitled "Delinquent Return Information and Returns Compliance Records" and handled under a covering letter or memorandum which suggested ominously that these randomly selected people may be dangerous to contact.

Not only was the list wrongly suggestive of taxpayer status and temperament, but it was so sloppily and erroneously assembled as to present further complications to an already inflammable project. It will be noted on the list I hereby submit that women were included when only men were intended to be and the spelling of many of the names is so inaccurate as to make the list almost useless. I have supplied what I believe to be the proper spelling of names in parentheses where possible:

Brent Powell, Charles Wesley Rash, Ronald G. Remington, Clayton Reum, Brent Crofts Rhodehcuse, Theril B. Ricks, James Jean Rumsey, T. J. Ryan, William Renton Siddoway, Robert Smith, Terry Lynn Hobles, Harry K. Horrell, Grant I. Howard, Mark Hale Howard, and Gean Jackson.

Jerri Lee Jenkins, Jack Douglas Kapor, Robert E. Kohlenger, Eugene LeCheminer (Le Cheminant) Lillis Burbank Michelsen, ... ward Garvis (?), Gary Hobbs, Mont Carlos

Howard, Glen Lyman Jackson, Gerald Vernon J . . ., and Richard F. Jergensen.

Russell Kay Johnson, . . . Dee Angell, Kenny Leo Beddes, Randall Bergeson, Jim Birch, Richard Reynolds Blake, Robert Lynn Carraway, Roy Graude (Grende), Bruce Kay Crapo, Clyde Raymond Garrett, Montie Jo Jackson, and Lillis Birch Johnson.

James Kim Kirkham, Ossie D. Mason, Dennis D. Maynard, Charles D. McMinn, Morris Gordon Nielsen, Douglas C. Peck, Jimmie Remington, Hal Andrew Rumsey, Lance Stoddard, Roger Willete, and William Edward Wocelka.

Dale Larson, Don Coy Larson, Thomas Steven Robison, Monte E. Rydalch, Lynn Wesley Schulties (Schuldies), Brian D. Schuldies, John R. Seely, Cecil E. Shitmore (Whitmore), Torger J. Skalet, Thomas R. Stilley, Charles Alonzo Stoddard, George Kino Sutterfield, Randall K. Abbegern, Solomon E. Angell, Solomon E. Angell, Jr., and William Arndt.

Paulo Brassanini, Kenny L. Beddes, Rodney G. Chandler, Damaris L. Clark, Randell D. Cogburn, Douglas L. Curr, Lester Ricardo Daniel, George E. Davis, Marvin Duane Thompson, Frederick Leo Wahl, Edward H. Weaver, Jean Chandler Worrell, Louis R. Bergesen (Bergeson), and Alton Birch.

Johnathan Blain, Ramiro Cadena, David Barry Cazier, David Dean Clark, Samuel Richard Davis, Steven Hawkes, Otis W. Jefferson, Curtis M. Kary, Edwin L. Larson, Willis Clark Mason, William Rody McAndrews, Michael Lee Nielsen, Curtis Alex Orgill, Steve Bacon Packer, and Rial Palmer.

Floyd R. Parker, Edward Horace Weaver, Don Winegar, Russell Arthur Severyn, Dale Lamar Swensen, Merrill J. Walker, Van Ranav Weaker (Weaver), Charl Lee Worrell Winters (Charles), Evan Arthur Blanchard, Richard Dee Burbank, William Craig Cashing, and Burke Clark.

J. Howard Clark, Carrie Thomas Cox, David Alan Dennis, Samule Rodney Fife (Samuel), Merrill Jean Grunbalgh (Greenhalgh), Franklin Albert Miller, Michael R. Miller, Terry R. Miller, Robert Alan Murdoch, and Wallace Pierce Murdoch.

Merle Parker, Afton Owens Toone, Joel T. Young, Wayne E. Welker, Dennis Allen, Randall Bergeson, Dennis Sinclair Birch, Lowell Edgar Birch, Rhea Mecham Blake, . . . J. Collette, Grant Arthur Hathaway, Alvin Gayle Hathory (Hathaway), Dan R. Hill, John Ho, Morris Lincoln Nielson, Alex D. Orgill, Lionel Ray Parker, Jerry Raymond Parkett, and Donald Andrew Peck.

My findings show that this list contains several local clergymen, L.D.S. (Mormon) missionaries (away from home for 2-year periods without an income), people incapacitated in hospitals, people on disability pensions, prominent businessmen and farmers and even a 61-year-old lady church organist.

However, to the best of my knowledge, none of the people listed, with the possible exception of one known to have been involved in a tavern scuffle, I have every reason to believe that most, if not all of them, were properly filing and paying their taxes.

The list was sent, on October 30, 1975, to inspector in charge, Don DeBoer, "to enable screening by the Inspection Division: Identification of those individual taxpayers which may be dangerous to contact." Mr. DeBoer was and is chief of inspection for the Ogden region and his immediate supervisors are the Assistant Commissioner and the Commissioner of the Internal Revenue Service.

On November 3, 1975, Howard Martin approved staffpower for this project of approximately 25 IRS agents, more than one-third of which were to be armed. The following IRS personnel, none stationed in the project area, were involved:

Don DeBoer, Bob Higgins, Gerd Hattwig, Sherrill Ohman, Monte Hobson, Diane Medina, Gene Bryan, Jim Quam, Hugh Pierce, Rick Owens, Ray Boone, Gary Hellekson, Keith Farrar, Stan Leake, Shirley Sterling, Shirley Sisson, Bob Hanmer, Kathy Corrigan, Jim Welty, Peggy Newcomb, John Eastham, Warren Packard, and Larry Kimbrell.

The Freemont County RCP program "plan of action," written in October 1975, reads like a military invasion strategy. It includes terms such as "protecting personnel."; "report of threat or assault."; "summons preparation."; and calls for the installation of telephone lines to "first, headquarters; second, inspection; third, intelligence; fourth, St. Anthony Police; fifth, sheriff's office, and sixth, operations base. The technical procedure descriptions of the program included: First, extensive discussion of anticipated situations and how to react; second, briefing on intelligence; third, briefing on assaults or threats; fourth, briefing on protection.

Some local IRS agents, when informed of this strategy, questioned the advisability of this operation which was contrary to basic procedure and vigorously pointed out that this type of unusually aggressive action on the part of the IRS could result in serious misunderstandings and even intimidation of innocent citizens into hostile and perhaps violent confrontation with IRS personnel.

One IRS employee described the operation as a naked attempt to grab power:

They can bring in enough agents to have an army of their own. The important thing is * * * their policies are creating a situation here that is harming not only the citizens, but it is harming the IRS.

Because of pressure from concerned agents within the IRS, the project was

cancelled only 4 days before its proposed inception. The memorandum, dated November 7, 1975, which canceled the program states:

To: All participating personnel, Fremont County RCP.
From: Acting Chief, CTS, Boise district.
Subject: Total cancellation of entire project.
The decision has been made to cancel all plans for this RCP program. Those individuals previously notified to attend an orientation meeting on November 11, 1975, and to be present in Idaho Falls during the week of November 17, 1975 should cancel their plans and resume normal activities. All reservations and transportation plans are also being cancelled as of this date.
RALPH HUTCHINSON.

This cancellation in no way indicated that the upper levels of the IRS objected to the project. As a matter of fact, the project coordinator received a group manager's "memorandum of appreciation" dated November 14, 1975 just 1 week after the project was terminated. Note the sentences stating, "I was very impressed with the plan of action which you originated" and "I sincerely appreciate your enthusiasm and dedication in this project." The memo follows:

SHERRILL OHAMN,
Revenue Officer,
MONTE HOBSON,
Group Manager.

MEMORANDUM OF APPRECIATION

I would like to compliment you on your performance in coordinating the proposed Returns Compliance Program in Southeastern Idaho. I was very impressed with the Plan of Action which you originated.

You have demonstrated that you are fully capable of organizing and implementing a complex assignment. I have complete confidence in your ability to handle any project assigned to you, and I look forward to working with you on future projects.

I sincerely appreciate your enthusiasm and dedication in this project.
MONTE HOBSON.

Furthermore, shortly after this incident, Howard Martin, the Idaho State Director of IRS who approved these projects, was promoted to National Director of the Disclosure Division of IRS—the agency responsible for administering the Freedom of Information Act, the Privacy Act, and the new disclosure laws.

The fact that a small town full of innocent people nearly suffered a full scale armed invasion is certainly in itself a terrifying story—but the tale does not end here.

A few months after the above abortive attempt to "educate" the citizens of St. Anthony, the waters from the faulty

Teton Dam swept through this same area turning many of the small towns into so many piles of rubble and mud.

My office, along with other members of Idaho's congressional delegation and departments of the Federal Government, moved quickly to assist in rehabilitation efforts and to insure that the victims were properly reimbursed by the Federal Government for their losses. And just as quickly the IRS moved in and attempted to retrieve as much money as possible for the U.S. Treasury in the form of capital gains taxes.

Beginning during this period of the summer of 1976, I came to really see a mentality and driving force behind the IRS, that caused me grave concern. Not only was I appalled at the callous attempted application of capital gains taxes, but I began to see a similar pattern of overkill in other matters concerning taxpayers. Only through congressional pressure did IRS give some ground on an item-for-item application of capital gains procedure regarding replacement of household goods of flood victims, and it was during this hassle that I discovered that the IRS had recently composed a "violence list" on citizens in the Teton disaster area—names of a number of Idahoans considered prone to "advocate violence toward Western region (IRS) personnel."

The list consisting of 25 people and dated December 31, 1975, is as follows:

District Director, Boise.
Regional Inspector, Western Region.
Taxpayers Who May Advocate Violence Toward Western Region Personnel.

We are transmitting a list of individuals in your District who may advocate violence toward government officials including Revenue employees.

The list was compiled from a system of records dealing with criminal law enforcement was exempted from disclosure under 5 U.S.C. 522a(j)(2) by the Commissioner. You are not to make this list a part of your system of records or associate it with any individual's record which you have. Any requests for access to the list under the Freedom of Information Act or Privacy Act should be directed to the Inspection Service.

Kenneth A. Anderson, Rexburg, Ivan Barney, Rathdrum, Wayne Beck, Thorton, Leonard Brasham, Kootenai County, Roy E. Cliff, Priest River, Robert W. Dixon, Sandpoint, Ron K. Fairchild, Rupert, Del Ray Holm, Bonneville County, Charles H. Miller, Coeur d'Alene, Joseph E. Nielsen, Sugar City, Herman L. Shyping, Hayden Lake, and Jack A. William, Priest River.

Richard W. Bevan, Rexburg, Henry Joseph Blake, Jr., Sandpoint, Clair E. Blaser, Rexburg, Richard G. Butler, Hayden Lake, L. D.

Harold Crawford, Priest River, Robert Eddy, Sandpoint, Glenn P. Glissner, Coeur d'Alene, William Matt Junttila, Priest River, S. M. Nelson, Hayden Lake, Detsel A. Parkinson, Rexburg, John D. Strode, Sandpoint, Jack H. Wright, Rexburg, and Roy G. Harn, Rathdrum.

We are currently in the process of identifying other individuals in your District who may have a propensity toward violence. Additional information will be forwarded periodically. Specific inquires should be forwarded to this office as the need arises for additional information concerning any of the individuals listed above.

F. R. Rowe.
Regional Inspector.

Recognizing that some of the 25 persons on this second so-called violence list were responsible civic, political and religious leaders, I checked with local law enforcement officers to determine if any of these men had criminal records—particularly a record which would lead the IRS to consider them as being dangerous to contact. I found that, regardless of their individual attitudes toward filing and paying taxes or how their tax money was spent, there was no real evidence to justify the inclusion of their names by the IRS on a list of persons prone to violence other than the fact that they may belong to an organized tax-protest group.

Certainly, the IRS should be able to distinguish between a nonviolent tax-complainer and an aggressive activist tax-resister. No one can condone the nonpayment of taxes due by an individual, but the first amendment of the U.S. Constitution guarantees a person's right to complain as long as he does not violate the law. I suspect the only violence some of the people listed might have is the feeling they experience in being arbitrarily and even haphazardly placed on a roster of protestors prone to violence when they have properly filed and paid their taxes. It is a crime for some IRS bureaucrat, who is too lazy to do his homework, to prepare a list which can place the lives and honor of people in jeopardy.

When I learned that the IRS had intended to use a "violence list" in conjunction with an armed door to door search in eastern Idaho, I submitted the approximate date and general location of the project to IRS Assistant Commissioner Warren Bates with serious questions regarding IRS operations in my congressional district. In December 1977, under the Freedom of Information Act, Mr. Bates was requested to provide my office with specific documents related to my concerns, and I specifically asked for copies of inspection reports of an investigation of the armed search which I learned had been conducted. After considerable double-talk, vacillation and delay, I was to finally receive nothing of substance.

In ·the meantime, on December 13, 1977, I sent a detailed letter to IRS Commissioner Jerome Kurtz which stated in part:

Why would an IRS "violence list" be periodically circulated containing the names of Idaho citizens having no record of violence?

Why would IRS agents go to conservative meetings to make lists of license plate numbers which were then expanded to watch lists of names, addresses, business addresses and poitions in the Mormon Church—and why were no liberal group similarly monitored, if extremists were the target?

Why would IRS agents anonymously contact individuals who politically complained of high taxes in letters to the Editor and place them under automatic investigation. The right of speech seems to have its liabilities.

Why should IRS have planned an armed door-to-door search by some 30 to 40 agents in communities north of Idaho Falls to demand the showing of tax returns, an operation finally halted at the Washington level when collection officers complained that someone might be hurt or killed?

Why would IRS agents maintain a full-scale clipping file from the newspapers on taxpayers regarding vacation trips and other activities? I'm not sure the taxpayers realize the extent to which individual privacy has been invaded by big government.

Over 2 months later on February 24, 1978, a reply was received from Mr. Kurtz, which included the following statements:

Your letter questions why the Internal Revenue Service maintained a so-called violence list and kept lists of license plate numbers of those attending certain meetings which you characterize as "conservative meetings". You also stated that the Internal Revenue Service had planned "armed searches" of taxpayers' homes in the Snake River area.

Based on the information then available, each of these questions seems to relate to certain actions undertaken to protect our personnel against tax protesters advocating violence. High level Internal Revenue Service managers were seriously concerned that certain tax protestors belonging to organizations which advocated the violent disruption of tax administration posed a threat to the physical safety of our enforcement personnel. This concern was shared by the Federal Bureau of Investigation (FBI). The

principal group advocating violent interference with the administration of the tax laws was the Sheriff's Posse Comitatus (SPC) This group's activity initiated in the western part of the United States within the boundaries of our Western Region. Accordingly, most actions undertaken by the Service in response to those threats also occurred in the Western Region.

On December 5, 1975, the Deputy Commissioner issued guidelines to the Regional Commissioners and Regional Inspectors. The guidelines included: (1) the maintaining of liaison with other law enforcement agencies including the FBI by our Intelligence Division and Inspection Service; (2) authorization to solicit information concerning the SPC and similar organizations restricting that authorization to information that concerned individuals involved in efforts to disrupt tax administration, or to information directly tax related, or involving potential assaults or threats against Service employees. On July 26, 1976, the Deputy Commissioner issued a Manual Supplement (93G-171, renumbered 9G-35) on the same subject. Copies of the December 5, 1975 memorandum and the July 26, 1976 Manual Supplement, respectively, appear as Attachments 7 and 8 to this letter.

Pursuant to these directives, our Inspection Service began to gather information on various tax protester groups which, in their organizational documents or other pronouncements, advocated violent interference with the administration of the tax laws. During December, 1975, our Inspection Service in the Western-Region furnished a list of names of 25 individuals who were reportedly members of groups advocating violence to the District Director, Boise, Idaho. The agencies which furnished the information to Inspection were the FBI. Idaho State Police and our own Intelligence Division. The Idaho State Police named two individuals as known members of the SPC. Of the other 23 names (all furnished to us by the FBI), all but two were listed on charter petitions of the SPC on file in various counties in Idaho. Of the remaining two, one individual was a reported member of the SPC who had been arrested on an assault charge by local police.* The other individual was reported to be a member of the Vigilant Committee of 10,000 by a local Idaho newspaper. According to local police sources in the Rexburg, Idaho, area, the Vigilant Committee of 10,000 also advocated the violent disruption of tax administration.

Some of the information obtained by Inspection from the sources described above did include license plate numbers of individuals who were attending or were parked in the vicinity of SPC meetings. However, the

---

* Known members of the SPC attempted to serve a summons on the county Sheriff to have the charge against that individual dismissed.

220 DOCUMENTS

license plate information was never used as
the sole basis for placing an individual's
name on the list furnished to the District
Director. Generally, no name was included
on the list unless the person was also
identified from some other source as being a
member of the SPC or another organization
advocating violence.

The purpose of the list was to provide management with some indication of those individuals who presented some threat to our
personnel, so that our personnel, forewarned
of the possibility of violence, could take appropriate precautions in carrying out their
duties. This list was to be used for no other
purpose, and we would appreciate being informed of any allegations of its use for other
than its intended purpose. We have an obligation to protect the safety of our own personnel and I believe we would have been
negligent to do less than we did in the face of
the express goals of these groups.

The planned activities to which you refer
in your letter as an "armed search" were also
a reaction to concerns for the safety of our
personnel in view of the activities of SPC
and similar organizations. Among the compliance techniques occasionally used by the
Service are canvassings of areas by revenue
officers who knock on doors and ask occupants to produce a copy of their tax return
as evidence of their compliance with the
tax laws. Such canvassing techniques are
usually performed in areas where comparisons with other publicly available information shows an abnormally low percentage
of return filings. The revenue officer conducting the canvassing does not search the
houses in question; rather, he or she asks
the occupant to produce a return and, if no
return is produced, simply notes this fact.
These revenue officers are not armed.

Such a canvassing was planned for a community in the Snake River Valley. In view
of the high number of identified SPC members in the area, however, local personnel
considered having our unarmed revenue
officers accompanied by special agents or
by our Inspection personnel, who were to
act as escorts, available to assist only in the
event of violence against our unarmed personnel. In view of the possible confrontations which might have resulted, this proposed canvassing program was cancelled
after review by appropriate management
officials at the district, regional and national levels.

The response I received from Mr. Kurtz
was both disturbing and puzzling—disturbing because his description and justification of the so-called planned activities—that is the armed search—did
not square with IRS information in my
possession and did not comply even to
established IRS guidelines for employee
safety which I herewith submit from an
IRS memorandum dated April 25, 1977:

Protestors accounts (TDAs, TDIs, OIs,
RCPs) are currently assigned directly to the

Revenue Officer having responsibility for
a particular area. Unless the assignment is
preidentified as a protestor case (3949 TDI,
correspondence, etc.) the Revenue Officer
generally has no advance knowledge of a
potential protestor problem.

Once the assignment has been identified
as a "Protestor": the following precautions
and instructions prevail:

1. Do not make an appointment with a
known protestor outside of IRS facilities.
This instruction is to promote an impromtu
meeting with the protestor, so that he cannot gather his accomplices for any confrontations.

2. Whenever possible, two Revenue Service employees should be present when dealing with protestors.

3. Secure as much information as possible on first contact (e.i. books, records,
bank accounts, history, financial statements, etc.)

4. Revenue Officers should not engage in a
verbal exchange on constitutionality of
the Revenue laws or valuation of currency
philosophy.

5. If protestor or situation appears to be
out of hand, withdraw immediately.

The puzzling part of the Kurtz reply
was in how much he was willing to say
about the proposed armed operation on
one hand while on the other his assistant, Mr. Bates, was telling me that he
could not provide any information regarding that project and, in fact, specifically denying the existence of any report on the operation described by Mr.
Kurtz.

Shortly after I received these conflict-
ing denials and descriptions from top
IRS officials, I was able to obtain from
other sources key portions of the so-
called "nonexistent material" which, I
have since learned, was apparently in
the possession of Mr. Bates all the time
he was making denials. The total picture
of the armed confrontation is now available despite the Bates denials and considerable misinformation in the Kurtz
letter.

The disjointed and unresponsive nature of the workings of the leadership of
the Internal Revenue Service has demonstrated well the same weaknesses that
cause the agency to continue to be hated
and feared by a vast number of Americans who daily feel its unnecessarily arbitrary and heavy hand and too often
receive only deceit and coverup instead
of fair redress for grievances.

Mr. Kurtz states that the December
1975 list identified a high number of SPC
members in the area in which the "canvassing activity" was to have taken place.
This is patently untrue. First, the December list is plainly after the fact, since

the IRS armed "canvassing activity" had already been planned, approved and then aborted over a month before the December list came into existence. Second, the December list does not even contain one name of a resident of Fremont County, where the armed Government agents planned to invade the homes of unwary taxpayers.

In other words, Mr. Kurtz justifies the planning and approval of an armed search with a list that was not applicable to the area involved and did not exist during the period of the operation. This is an intolerable abuse of the truth.

Mr. Kurtz claims that "the actions taken by the IRS were necessary to protect our personnel against tax protestors advocating violence." If Mr. Kurtz believes this—he lives in a pipedream. The IRS action as described by its own employees was geared to expose IRS agents to danger in an attempt to intimidate and terrorize people into tax compliance (even though most, if not all, of them were already in compliance).

Mr. Kurtz further states that the purpose of the list was to "provide management with some indication of those individuals who presented some threat to our personnel, so that our personnel forewarned of the possibility of violence, could take appropriate precautions in carrying out their duties. This list was to be used for no other purpose . . .". This is absolutely untrue. Mr. Kurtz obviously knew of the Fremont County RCP program since he describes it in his letter. This being the case; it is outrageous for him to claim that the list was not abused since it was to be used to precipitate a confrontation. In fact, the very idea of such a list is abusive, despotic and poses a serious threat to the lives, honor and constitutional rights of any citizen whose name appears thereon.

These illegal and immoral practices of the IRS have not ceased; instead they are spreading and becoming more flagrant. I have proof that the production and promulgation of these lists continues. The harassment, embarrassment, and legal and financial pressures applied by the IRS relentlessly even though some corrections are made from time to time. The civil and constitutional rights of taxpayer and employee are not in safe hands when an agency creates so-called violence lists to protect its agents from senior citizens, invalids and clergymen, and then goes to extravagant lengths to obscure the very existence of such lists.

An IRS employee recently expressed such concern when he stated:

My reason for asking to see someone outside the IRS system is that I do not trust IRS management because of prior scandals that have been covered up.

To finally drive home the fact that the IRS seems to view American taxpayers as basically dishonest, uncharitable, bigoted, criminal-minded and even violent to deal with, one only has to point out the fact that they recently (1978) changed the name of the division handling possible tax fraud cases from the Intelligence Division to Criminal Investigations Division. Considering the small fraction of those investigated who are indicted or convicted, this is an ugly choice of names; especially when one considers the onus it puts on that poor innocent taxpayer whose friends and business associates are contacted by the IRS criminal investigator.

A canvass was planned to solicit evidence from an area which was suspected of having a high percentage of violence-prone people who did not pay their taxes. The reason for the canvass was precisely that the IRS had already decided that its target group was hostile, in other words that confrontations were to be expected; in anticipation of these expected confrontations the service determined to provide armed escorts for its men.

Mr. Kuntz then turns 180 degrees and would have us believe that the canvass was canceled because, of all things, it might provoke confrontations. This means we are expected to believe that the reason for planning the raid was the reason for calling it off. The difficult job of the tax collector demands more responsible direction from its leaders.

In addition, Mr. Kuntz tells us that such canvasses are common and only the presence of armed agents makes this one different that IRS agents regularly go door to door asking people to produce their own copies of their tax returns as evidence of filing.

Any first year law student could tell Mr. Kurtz that production of a copy of a tax return is not evidence of anything, and particularly not evidence of having filed the original. On the other hand, failure to produce the tax report copy is not evidence of failure to file.

In addition to all this, that same first year law student could tell Mr. Kurtz that failure to file is not necessarily a crime and that a mere failure to file without much more information about the situation would tell his canvassing agent absolutely nothing. But remember who was to be canvassed in this situation, 167 people whom Mr. Kurtz erroneously passed off as a list of tax resisters. What did he expect such people to do?

Beyond even this comic opera aspect of collection enforcement, there is a much more serious question. Do IRS agents, at the direction of the Service, go about entrapping citizens on tax laws? Do they warn these citizens of their basic rights, that they have no duty to provide the agent anything? Do the canvassers tell their victims that consequences could follow from discussing their taxes with the Service without legal assistance?

They are, after all, seeking evidence of crime; that is, failure to file a tax return properly. Taken at it's face value, Mr. Kurtz' explanation for an armed foray upon citizens against whom no charges had been filed, gives the picture of incompetent Government administration, armed with computers, legal proc-

ess, and all awesome array of IRS fact-gathering, collection expertise and coercive brilliance, deciding instead, with or without guns, to send agents door to door to gather facts and enforce collection.

Knowing the background and experience of Mr. Kurtz, it is difficult, if not impossible, to take his explanation seriously. Rather it would seem obvious that the IRS had decided deliberately to create a confrontation in hopes of forcing an incident from which the IRS could massively react with public acceptance to be rid of those who protest and resist taxes. The IRS, after a shooting incident, could assert their need for even more guns, for even greater authority and to be exempt from respecting the "Bill of Rights."

All totalitarian governments have at least one agency which, in the name of protecting the regime, claims the right of total control of the citizens. We can do without an American Gestapo or KGB.

ABOUT THE AUTHOR

George Hansen is a leading Congressional troubleshooter who:
—Led efforts to get Christians out of Nebraska jail, and founded national Coalition for Religious Freedom.
—Led efforts to open doors to the American hostages in Iran, and prevent war or Soviet takeover of area.
—Led the fights to stop Panama Canal giveaway, and prevent Castro-Soviet takeover of Nicaragua and Central America.
—Led the first U.S. Friendship Delegation to repair relations with Taiwan, and save vital trade and defense partner.
—Led efforts to secure release of Americans jailed in Bolivia and paved way for return of U.S. citizens jailed in other countries.
—Led the effort to defeat OSHA warrantless inspections with U.S. Supreme Court victory, and get America on road to deregulation.

Mr. Hansen, who represents Idaho's 2nd Congressional District, is a senior member of the House Banking Committee and the Ranking Republican on the Domestic Monetary Affairs Subcommittee. The Hansens have five adult children and Mrs. Hansen (Connie), a former elected member of the Pocatello City Council, serves unpaid as the Congressman's Administrative Assistant.